The
Medical Marijuana
Maze

Health & Learning Resource Center at RMC Health
7525 W. 10th Ave.
Lakewood, CO 80214
Courier Code: C976

The
Medical Marijuana
Maze

Policy and Politics

Nancy E. Marion
University of Akron

CAROLINA ACADEMIC PRESS

Durham, North Carolina

Library of Congress Cataloging-in-Publication Data

Marion, Nancy E.
  The medical marijuana maze : policy and politics / Nancy Marion.
    pages cm
  Includes bibliographical references and index.
  ISBN 978-1-61163-283-5 (alk. paper)
  1. Marijuana--Therapeutic use--Political aspects. 2. Marijuana--Therapeutic use--United States. I. Title.

RM666.C266M376 2013
362.29'5--dc23   2013030665

CAROLINA ACADEMIC PRESS
700 Kent Street
Durham, North Carolina 27701
Telephone (919) 489-7486
Fax (919) 493-5668
www.cap-press.com

Printed in the United States of America

Contents

The
Medical Marijuana
Maze

Chapter 1

Introduction

Overview: This chapter provides an introduction to the text, and introduces the concept of medical marijuana, including the conditions for which it is used and the legal status.

Introduction

The marijuana plant is one of the oldest psychoactive plants known to man. It is cultivated in a variety of climates and soils around the planet and is used for both recreation and medicine. According to the United Nations, marijuana is "the most widely used illicit substance in the world."[1] Despite evidence that marijuana use can provide relief for those suffering from debilitating medical conditions, the use, possession, cultivation, and distribution of marijuana, even if it is for medical reasons, remains illegal in many U.S. states and by the federal government. The legal status of medical cannabis is a hotly disputed issue that affects patients, health care providers, lawyers, and law enforcement officials on the state and federal levels. Throughout the past several decades, the debate over medical marijuana has become more public and has received more attention. This book is an examination of the issues surrounding medical marijuana and its use, legally or illegally, in the U.S. today.

Terms

It is important to define some key terms related to the medical marijuana dispute before moving forward. One of those terms is "cannabis." This is the scientific name for the plant that provides marijuana. The cannabis plant has been used for both medicinal and industrial purposes for hundreds of years.

The fibers of the cannabis plant are extremely strong and durable, providing excellent raw materials for cord and rope. The word "marijuana" comes from Mexican Spanish, but the reason for this name, or the origin of the name, is not clear.[2] Generally, when people refer to "marijuana" they are referring to the dried leaves and tops of the cannabis plant that are used for recreation or pleasure (to achieve the feeling of being "high" or in an altered state). In the end, the word "marijuana" refers to same plant as the word "cannabis." Most people use the two terms interchangeably to refer to the same plant material.[3]

When cannabis plants are used for fiber, ropes or clothing, the plant is referred to as hemp. The Chinese used hemp fibers for fabric and ropes starting as far back as 1000 BC. Fishing nets were also made of hemp. The world's oldest piece of paper dates back to around 500 BC and was made of hemp fibers.

The term "medical marijuana" or "medical cannabis" refers to the use, possession, and/or cultivation of the cannabis plant (marijuana plant) for medical purposes.[4] It includes the ingestion of parts of the plant in one form or another, but it also refers to ingesting synthesized versions of the active chemical compounds found in the cannabis plant, known as cannabinoids. Legally, the difference between medical marijuana and recreational marijuana use is whether it has been recommended by a licensed physician as a way to medically treat a diagnosed medical concern. The plant used for medical marijuana, or medicinal cannabis, is no different than standard marijuana used for recreational purposes.

Types of Marijuana

There are two primary types, or species, of marijuana (or cannabis). One of those is the species *Cannabis sativa*. This plant commonly grows to a height of twelve to sixteen feet and has long stalks, sparse foliage, and slender leaves. These plants are usually grown for industrial purposes, particularly for fiber and textile use, because of its strong fiber and seeds. This plant contains only small amounts of the psychoactive elements for which marijuana is known.[5]

The second type of marijuana is the *Cannabis indica*. A native to India, this plant usually only grows to a height of four to five feet and is more densely foliated with bushy, broad leaves. The fibers of this plant are not strong enough nor long enough for industrial fiber production, but the plant contains more psychoactive components (cannabinoids) than the other species and is therefore cultivated for the medicinal and psychoactive properties of the flowers.[6]

In addition to these two primary species, there are hundreds of subspecies of marijuana, and experts often debate their scientific classifications.[7] Some marijuana growers have been able to combine the best traits of both for a more potent, yet strong, strain of marijuana that can be used for both recreation and medicine. *Cannabis sativa* can be cultivated in such a way as to produce a higher level of the therapeutic compounds more likely to be found in *Cannabis indica*.

Marijuana has around 400 chemical components, or cannabinoids. Cannabinoids can serve as appetite stimulants, antiemetics, antispasmodics, and have some analgesic effects.[8] The major psychoactive chemical component in marijuana is delta-9-tetrahydrocannabinol, more commonly known as THC.[9] When a user smokes marijuana, THC passes from the lungs to cannabinoid receptors on the surfaces of nerve cells in the part of the brain that influences memory, concentration and coordination. THC is believed to interact with parts of the brain that play a role in pain sensation, memory, and sleep.[10] The effect that marijuana has on these parts of the user's brain is referred to as "being high."

The other cannabinoids in cannabis have different properties. Cannabidiol (CBD) may relieve convulsions, inflammation, high blood pressure, anxiety, cough, pain, congestion and nausea, and inhibit cancer cell growth. Recent studies have shown that cannabidiol is effective in treating schizophrenia. The types of marijuana that have high amounts of CBD may be helpful to patients suffering with multiple sclerosis, frequent anxiety attacks and Tourette syndrome. CBD is a major component of medical cannabis because it does not have psychoactive properties and therefore does not cause a feeling of being "high."

The compound β-caryophyllene reduces inflammation. It also does not have psychoactive properties. It has been demonstrated to provide relief of interocular pressure and therefore effective for treating glaucoma.[11]

Pharmaceutical companies have tried to mimic the compounds in naturally-occurring THC and create synthetic forms of the drug as a way to help patients relieve their symptoms. These companies have been able to extract the cannabinoids from marijuana and synthesize them to create drugs that act as marijuana in the body. One of the first cannabis-based prescription medicine was Sativex. Created by GW Pharmaceuticals, Sativex was first launched in the United Kingdom in June, 2010. It is a mouth spray that is approved as a treatment for spasticity (muscle tightness) in patients with multiple sclerosis.[12] It has since been authorized in Spain, Canada, the Czech Republic, Denmark, Germany, Sweden, and Austria. In the U.S., a patent was granted for Sativex in 2001, to be used for pain associated with cancer.[13]

In the 1970s, Pfizer Pharmaceutical Company created a drug called levonantradol that was based on the makeup of THC. It was hoped that the pain-killing, or analgesic, effects of THC would be mirrored in this drug. Unfortunately, the side effects were too intense to make the drug useful. The side effects included sleepiness, red eyes, dry mouth, dizziness and dysphoria.[14]

Another synthetic form of THC is found in dronabinol, a pill given to patients. However, a pill can sometimes be difficult for some patients to swallow, particularly those suffering from nausea and vomiting. If the pill is ingested, it sometimes can take hours before it provides any relief. Additionally, the drug is very expensive. Since the drug contains only one active ingredient found in marijuana, which naturally contains a variety of active components, many patients report that the drug does not work.[15]

Dronabinol is sometimes sold under the brand name Marinol (Marinol is the brand name for the generic drug dranabinol). Marinol is available by prescription from a licensed physician.[16] The drug, manufactured by Unimen Pharmaceuticals, is sold to patients as a pill in the U.S. and Canada but as a mouth spray in other countries. Some patients claim that Marinol does not have the same effects as smoked marijuana, or may take longer to work. Other patients claim that Marinol gets them "high" and is therefore not effective as a treatment. In Denmark the drug is used for treating multiple sclerosis, and in Canada it is used for AIDS-related anorexia and for nausea and vomiting that is sometimes associated with cancer chemotherapy. Marinol was approved by the FDA in 1985 in the U.S. as an appetite stimulant and for nausea.[17]

Another synthetic cannabinoid, Cesamet (Nabilone), is available in Canada, Mexico, the United Kingdom, and the U.S. This drug, manufactured by Valeant Pharmaceuticals International, was approved for use in the U.S. in 1985. It is used for treatment of chemotherapy-related nausea and vomiting.

Canasol is a cannabis-based medication used to treat patients suffering from glaucoma because it relieves intraocular pressure that is caused by late-stage glaucoma. It was created by ophthalmologists Dr. Albert Lockhart and Dr. Manley E. West, and distribution began in 1987 in the United Kingdom, several U.S. states, and several Caribbean nations. It is notable for being one of the first cannabis-containing pharmaceuticals to be developed for the market and being one of the few such pharmaceuticals to have ever been legally marketed in the U.S.[18]

Medical Marijuana

Whether the compounds are natural or synthetic, some doctors and their patients point to the possible medical benefits of marijuana or cannabis for treating many physical ailments. Advocates of medical marijuana argue that some seriously ill patients can benefit from using the plant as a drug and that they should be able to access it after consultation with a licensed physician. Further, supporters point out that some patients may get better results from smoking marijuana than from using marijuana in other forms, including prescription synthetic drugs.

Overall, the studies on effectiveness and safety of medical marijuana are not conclusive. On one hand, many studies present evidence that patients who use cannabis are not harmed by its use. These studies show that the drug is not toxic for users and that there has never been a documented death from marijuana use. Moreover, many studies in recent years have demonstrated the possible therapeutic value of cannabis to treat multiple illnesses and conditions.

The safety of using medical marijuana when compared to other FDA approved drugs to treat ailments is becoming more clear. The FDA investigated the number of deaths caused by marijuana as compared to the number of deaths caused by seventeen FDA approved drugs (the Adverse Events Report). The document revealed that there were at least some deaths where marijuana had been used near the time of the patient's death. Although they note that "that information … has not been scientifically or otherwise verified,"[19] the report shows that marijuana was not the primary suspect in the death in any case.[20] Moreover, a study by UCLA found no association between marijuana use and lung cancer. The finding of this study also suggests that marijuana may even have some protective effect on lung cancer.[21]

Other studies have shown that the cardiovascular effects related to marijuana use do not pose serious health problems for users who are otherwise young and healthy. The American Medical Association reported that, based on previously completed studies on smoked marijuana, the drug use can be beneficial to certain patients. It is particularly helpful for those patients who need to manage pain, increase appetite, and treat nausea.[22]

However, in that same report it was noted that the evidence regarding the effects of smoked marijuana for patients who have been diagnosed with epilepsy and immune diseases such as lupus was less positive. They point out that for some patients, marijuana use has resulted in side effects such as a increased heart beat and short-term memory loss.[23] Moreover, the British Lung Foundation reported in November 2002 that 3–4 marijuana cigarettes a day are as dangerous to the lungs as 20 or more tobacco cigarettes a day.[24]

Other research shows that the long-terms effects of smoking marijuana are less than those caused by smoking tobacco. A report published in the Journal of the American Medical Association (JAMA) indicated that exposure to moderate amounts of marijuana smoke is not associated with the negative effects on pulmonary function. The study was completed by investigators at the University of California San Francisco who looked at data from 5,115 men and women who used marijuana over a twenty year period in four cities.[25]

In 1999, the Institute of Medicine (IOM), part of the National Academy of Sciences, concluded that the scientific data on medical marijuana indicates that there could be benefits from using medical marijuana for certain patients.[26] There could be therapeutic value of marijuana use to relieve some symptoms including pain, nausea and vomiting, and lack of appetite. In particular, the IOM found that marijuana gave some medicinal benefits for patients suffering from MS, AIDS and cancer, and gave some medicinal benefits to patients that they do not get from traditional medications.[27] However, they cautioned that smoked marijuana can deliver harmful substances to the user. They concluded that additional clinical trials could develop more effective methods to deliver the drug to patients. They also recommended that smoked marijuana be used only for short periods (less than six months) by those patients who suffer from debilitating symptoms and only after all other medications have been tried, if it is expected that the symptoms will be relieved by the drug, and that any treatment be administered under medical supervision.[28]

A study in 2009 by Keele University Medical School found that use of cannabis use is not associated with psychotic disorders. Another study by an international team from the University of Maryland's school of medicine reported that the use of cannabis by patients suffering from schizophrenia and other psychotic disorders is associated with a lower risk of mortality.[29]

At the same time, other studies seem to show another story concerning the use of medical marijuana. They cite the potentially negative side effects of using cannabis as a medication, including those that conclude that the use of cannabis causes psychotic and violent behaviors and caused those who used the drug to go insane. Recent studies show that people who smoke cannabis can harm their lungs not only from the smoke but because some plants may contain dangerous microorganisms. The American Society of Addiction Medicine points to the high potential for abuse. Opponents of medical marijuana also argue that these laws may entice people without medical conditions to grow and use of the drug more widely.

Ingesting Marijuana

Regardless of the results of these studies, thousands of patients have turned to using cannabis as a way to achieve relief from symptoms of illnesses. In some cases, the effectiveness of the drug is determined by the mode of ingestion. There are multiple ways to ingest marijuana, and different methods of ingestion results in different effects on the body. Marijuana can be smoked, eaten, or made into a tea.[30] Most patients using medical marijuana ingest the drug by smoking it. Inhaling cannabis allows the active components to be absorbed into the blood stream more quickly and with greater effectiveness, and the effects reportedly last longer.[31] However, some people feel that smoking marijuana can cause harm to the body. They claim that when marijuana is smoked, harmful gases such as carbon monoxide, carbon dioxide, tar and ash are released, which has been identified with an increase chance of cancer.

Another common way to ingest cannabis is through cooking or baking with it. Edibles include cookies, brownies, chocolate bars, cakes and ice cream. Marijuana infused butter allows patients to use the drug without making others aware of it. The same holds true with olive oil infused with marijuana.[32] This method also allows for a slower release of compounds into the body rather than an immediate release into the blood stream, leading to a different impact on the body.

Users can also get the drug through other methods such as capsules, lotions and salves for skin or surface ailments. These do not make a patient feel "high" but instead remove the sensation of pain. Others choose to use a vaporizer. These are devices that heat the marijuana so that the vapors can be inhaled. Vaporizing is a much healthier way to ingest marijuana. Some patients choose to use the drug by making it into tea. Those who make their tea with milk or cream find that it helps to extract the medicinal properties more efficiently. Research has also shown that spraying a cannabis extract under the tongue can provide an almost immediate relief from pain.

Two companies, CanChew Biotechnologies and Medical Marijuana Inc., have plans to release a CBD enriched chewing gum.[33] The gum will be called CanChew and will contain CBD oil. The gum will not contain THC so users will not feel "high" (see chapter 11).

Medical Uses of Marijuana

Regardless of how the marijuana is ingested, patients suffering from multiple diseases and ailments have used the drug for many purposes.[34] Some of those are described below.

AIDS Wasting Syndrome (Cachexia)

For many years, AIDS wasting syndrome was a common complication of HIV infection. The syndrome is caused extreme weight loss and/or cachexia (loss of weight, decreased appetite, fatigue, nausea, and muscle atrophy). Because one common side effects of marijuana use is an increased appetite, it is often used by patients with AIDS and/or cachexia. Clinical trials in the 1970s showed that for HIV-positive patients, cannabis stimulated the appetite and triggered both food intake and weight gain.[35] The results of the trials also showed that patients' moods improved.

Alcohol Dependence/Withdrawals

Several studies have been conducted to provide a better understanding of the possible use of marijuana as a treatment for patients with alcohol dependence/withdrawals. This research shows that in most cases, cannabis use helps with both acute alcohol withdrawal and alcohol dependence, even after the withdrawals. Moreover, marijuana use can reverse and help prevent against alcohol poisoning.[36]

Alzheimer's Disease

Alzheimer's disease is an incurable, progressive disease of the nervous system that is characterized by memory loss. There are presently no drugs to stop the progression of the disease. Research shows that cannabinoids can inhibit the progress of Alzheimer's disease and may be a therapeutic approach to treating the symptoms associated with this ailment.[37]

Anorexia

Anorexia, or the loss of the desire to eat (the loss of appetite), sometimes occurs when people have a distorted sense of obesity and their own body size. These patients are sometimes unable to maintain a healthy body weight.[38] Decreased hunger is also a common symptom for cancer patients and AIDS patients. In these patients, marijuana (specifically THC) helps improve their appetite and results in weight gain.[39]

Cancer

For about twenty years, researchers at California Pacific Medical Center have been investigating the compounds found in marijuana and have concluded that Cannabidiol (CBD) has the property to "turn off" the DNA that might cause cancer.[40] Other research found, similarly, that cannabinoids are a "broad range inhibitor of cancer."[41] Specifically, Delta-9 THC has antitumor effects on certain cancer cells and inhibits cancer cell growth,[42] particularly breast cancer[43] and certain lung cancers.[44] This research seems to indicate that marijuana seems to treat not only the cancer itself (the growth of cancer cells and tumors) but also the side effects of the treatment. Because cannabis has anti-emetic (anti-nausea) properties, it's useful for treating nausea that often results from treatment. The American Medical Association (AMA) reported that in three controlled studies with 43 total participants, there was a reported "modest" anti-nausea effect of smoked marijuana in cancer patients undergoing chemotherapy. It is especially useful for those patients who are unable to eat because the drug can be administered in many ways (smoked, vaporized, or given under the tongue).[45]

Crohn's Disease

Patients with Crohn's disease have a defect in their intestines that allows bacteria to leak into the intestinal tissue, causing inflammation and pain. Some patients also suffer from a secondary condition called Ulcerative Colitis, in which the tissue can rupture and bleed. It appears that the CBD and THC found in marijuana are an effective treatment for these patients. Marijuana helps to reduce the inflammation, regenerates bowel tissue, helps to ease the cramps associated with intestinal irritation, and boosts the patient's appetite.[46]

Depression

Clinical depression can be caused by many factors, including biological (i.e. a chemical imbalance in the brain or a hormonal disorder) or genetics. Many times, people diagnosed as depressed are treated with prescription medication. Recent studies have indicated that marijuana may be an effective treatment because it is a relaxant and can help patients sleep and reduce anxiety that is often associated with depression. Marijuana can serve to "lift" the patient's mood. Moreover, there is no evidence that long-term use of marijuana causes depression.[47]

Diabetes

There is some evidence that the use of cannabis might help stabilize blood sugar in diabetic patients. It is neuroprotective, meaning that it helps to protect the nerve covering (myelin sheath) from inflammation and reduces the pain associated with this condition, called neuropathy. Some believe that the anti-spasmodic effects of marijuana help to relieve the muscle cramps from which many diabetics suffer.[48]

Fibromyalgia

Research from Spain has shown marijuana provides relief for those patients with fibromyalgia, a chronic ailment that causes stiff muscles, pain and severe exhaustion in patients. The study results indicate that marijuana use reduced the symptoms of fibromyalgia, as well as improved the overall mental health of the patient.

Glaucoma

Glaucoma is an eye disease that results in increased intraocular pressure (IOP) that can lead to cataracts and eventual blindness in patients. Marijuana has been shown to reduce the IOP in patients. However, some researchers, including the National Eye Institute (NEI) and the Institute of Medicine (IOM), believe that marijuana does not provide a better treatment for glaucoma than prescription drugs. Instead, the method of treatment may influence the effectiveness of the drug. Study results indicate that patients who used a synthetic form of marijuana had lower IOP when taken orally, intravenously, or through inhalation, but not when applied topically to the eye. The drug reduced the eye pressure for about three to four hours. So far, there have not been any long-term studies of the effect of marijuana on glaucoma patients.[49]

High Blood Pressure (Hypertension)

The long-term effects of high blood pressure may include damage to artery walls, blood vessels, and organs such as the heart, liver and kidney. Heart attacks are common in those who suffer from hypertension. Other dangers of high blood pressure include strokes, brain aneurysms, constricted blood vessels in the kidneys and torn or damaged blood vessels in the eyes, sometimes leading to permanent blindness. Long-term hypertension can also cause brain damage and memory loss. Studies indicate patients with high blood pressure who use marijuana have fewer symptoms. It is thought that the marijuana may work by opening the blood vessels, thus lowering the hypertension.[50]

Insomnia

Patients with insomnia, or the inability to fall asleep or remain asleep, do not feel refreshed when they wake up. Insomnia can be caused by many conditions. Patients are often prescribed sedative pills, which can cause some patients to wake up groggy or in a "fog." Those who use marijuana report that they sleep more soundly and do not wake up dazed.

Migraines

Migraines can be seriously disabling to those who suffer from them. They are caused by spasms and narrowing of the blood vessels leading to the brain. The reduced blood flow results in lower oxygen levels, which then triggers the blood vessels outside the brain to dilate. Some patients experience an aura, an over-sensitivity to sound, vomiting, difficulties with driving, walking, or talking. Cannabis has been prescribed for those with migraines in both England and America for many years. The cannabinoids in marijuana help to reducing swelling, pain and nausea. Cannabis can also help to alleviate muscle cramps of the neck and shoulders that sometimes accompany migraines.[51]

Multiple Sclerosis

Multiple sclerosis is a chronic degenerative disease of the central nervous system. The symptoms of MS include muscular weakness, a loss of motor control, and inflammation. Many patients become permanently disabled, or even die from the disease. Research shows that marijuana can help to reduce the symptoms associated with MS, including depression, fatigue, incontinence, pain, and spasticity.[52]

Nausea/Vomiting

Nausea is often a common symptom of other ailments such as cancer, epilepsy, or multiple sclerosis. Marijuana increases the appetite in patients suffering from the diseases. Cancer patients undergoing chemotherapy are also given cannabis to reduce nausea.[53]

Pain

It is reported that currently 86 million Americans suffer from some sort of chronic pain, including 11 million people that claim their pain to be a significant disability.[54] There are many causes for chronic, severe pain, including disease (AIDS, cancer), injuries, or degenerative disorders. It can be a primary condition or the symptom of another disease and can vary in duration and severity. Marijuana is considered to have an analgesic quality, and therefore can be used to treat pain of all kinds. Other drugs exist to alleviate pain, such as morphine (oxycodone or Demerol), but these drugs only work temporarily and may make some patients unable to function normally. It may be said that marijuana may not take away pain, but rather the awareness of pain by relaxing tense muscles.[55]

Research supports the use of marijuana to relieve pain. In one 2007 study, a trial of 50 AIDS patients found that 52 percent of those who smoked marijuana reported a 30 percent or greater reduction in pain. Only 24 percent of those who got placebo cigarettes reported the same lessening of pain.[56] Another study published in 2004 showed that roughly a quarter of all AIDS patients were using cannabis as a means of reducing pain, among other symptoms.

Seizures/Epilepsy

Epilepsy is a neurological condition that can cause seizures in patients with the disease. Seizures can range from brief (almost unnoticeable) episodes to full body convulsions, called "grand mal" seizures. Some kinds of epilepsy can be controlled with anticonvulsant drugs, but some do not respond well to drugs. Some drugs also cause side effects including emotional disorders, swollen gums, a decreased production of red blood cells, and softening of the bones. In rare situations, side effects may include loss of motor control, coma, or death. Anticonvulsant drugs only completely stop seizures in about 60 percent of patients. More recently, there has been some interest in the use of CBD to treat patients with epilepsy. It seems to show that CBD helps to reduce the number and severity of seizures in patients.[57]

Other Diseases/Symptoms

Marijuana has been used to treat many other diseases and symptoms. Some of these are described in Table 1.1.

Legal Status

Presently, the laws regarding the use of medical marijuana/cannabis vary. Internationally, many countries are recognizing the potential medicinal value of marijuana. The United Nations' Single Convention on Narcotic Drugs classifies the plant as a Schedule IV drug, meaning that member countries can choose whether to allow its use for medicine or research. Many countries have legalized medical marijuana and others have decriminalized it, including Israel, Belgium, Austria, Spain, Finland, the Netherlands and the Czech Republic. Although medical marijuana is illegal in most countries, some countries allow it for treatment under a physician's care.

In Canada, medical marijuana was made legal by Health Canada in 2000. It is allowed for those patients who have been diagnosed by a doctor with cer-

Table 1.1: Medical Conditions Reportedly Improved with Medical Marijuana Use

Addiction	Dry Mouth
Anxiety	Epilepsy
AIDS	Diarrhea
Arthritis	Gastritis
Asthma	Hepatitis
Attention Deficit Disorder	Huntington's Chorea
Autism	Insomnia
Bipolar	Irritable Bowel Syndrome
Breast Cancer	Mesothelioma
Constipation	Neurodermitis
Delirium	Rheumatoid Arthritis
Depression	Spasticity
Diabetes	

Sources: Roger A. Rofman, Marijuana as Medicine Seattle: Madrona Publishers, 1982; Martin Martinez, The New Prescription: Marijuana as Medicine, Oakland: Quick American Archives, 2000; "Can Medical Marijuana be used to treat Bipolar" http://www.medical-marijuanablog.com/benefits/bipolar.html; Alison Mack and Janet Joy, Marijuana as Medicine? The Science Beyond the Controversy, Washington, D.C.: National Academy Press, 2001.

tain conditions, or as a way to provide compassionate end-of-life care for some patients. In Canada, the government provides marijuana to patients through the brand CannaMed. Many patients complained about the lack of selection and low potency. Illegal "compassion clubs" popped up that make many strains of marijuana and other products available to patients. Patients can grow their own cannabis, if approved by Health Canada.

In the United Kingdom, the patients can legally use the cannabinoid-derived drug Sativex instead of marijuana. The use of medical marijuana is accepted as a mitigating factor in the courts. However, possession of small quantities of marijuana does not usually warrant an arrest or court appearance. Certain cannabinoids are permitted for medical use, but these are strictly controlled.

In 2008, the Austrian Parliament approved the cultivation of marijuana for scientific and medical uses. Cultivation of the drug is controlled by the Austrian Agency for Health and Food Safety. And in Israel, medical marijuana has been allowed since the early 1990s for patients suffering with cancer or pain-related illnesses such as Parkinson's, multiple sclerosis, or Crohn's Disease.

Pharmacies began distributing medicinal cannabis by prescription in the Netherlands, as well as other drugs containing cannabinoids (Dronabinol, Sativex), in 2003. The Office of Medicinal Cannabis, found within the Ministry of Health and Sports of the Netherlands, oversees the distribution of the medicine. In Spain, medical marijuana was legalized in the late 1990s and early 2000s by local governments. The parliament of the Catalonia region was the first to vote for medical marijuana in 2001, followed by the parliaments of Aragon and the Balearic Islands. Spanish law prohibits the sale of cannabis but not consumption, although a person consuming the drug on the street can be fined. Cannabis consumption clubs have been established throughout the country, beginning in 1991. These clubs are non-profit associations that grow cannabis and then sell it to members at cost.[58]

In the U.S., marijuana remains classified as a Schedule I substance under U.S. federal law through The Controlled Substances Act of 1970, alongside LSD, PCP, ecstasy, methamphetamines, heroin, and other dangerous drugs. This means that, according to the U.S. government, cannabis has no accepted medical use and a high potential for abuse.[59] Despite calls by many medical organizations, including the American College of Physicians, to reclassify the drug to allow for more research, cannabis possession, use and growth remains illegal.

Despite this, many states have recognized the possible medicinal value of marijuana and have made it legal under certain circumstances. Today, eighteen U.S. states have passed laws to legalize or decriminalize the use of medical marijuana when recommended by a physician as a way to relieve symptoms of certain diseases or disorders. Most of these laws require patients to meet specific requirements, such as having a physician's written recommendation or registration with state officials. Because of these new state laws, thousands of ill people in the U.S. have chosen to use marijuana for its medical properties (see chapter 3).

The first state to legalize cannabis and allow patients to use the drug for medical reasons was California, which passed the Compassionate Use Act in November 1996 through a ballot initiative. The proposal received 55 percent of the vote. Not long after, voters in Colorado passed a proposal to legalize medical marijuana, followed by other states, including Alaska, Montana and Nevada.

If medical marijuana is legalized in a state, cannabis dispensaries may be established as a way to provide the drug to patients. These can range from small storefronts to bigger operations that operate more like pharmacies. In New Jersey, after voters passed a new law, the Greenleaf Compassion Center was opened as a small, family-run organization that would provide medical marijuana to around 300 patients living in that area. However, they found the need to be much higher, and they now provide the drug to around 600 patients.[60] At one legal dispensary in Denver, the price for one ounce of marijuana is $350. Since June 2001, over 17,000 patients have registered with dispensaries in the state. Currently, patients must pay a $90 registration fee, and are permitted to purchase no more than two ounces of marijuana at a time.[61] Typically, dispensaries have security procedures to limit walk-in visitors.

Dispensaries characteristically provide patients a selection of different strains of marijuana, each having different effects. The people who work in dispensaries and clubs, sometimes called "bud tenders," are normally very knowledgeable about the use of cannabis for medicinal purposes and assist patients in choosing the correct strain of marijuana for their symptoms. Most require that patients become members of the club prior to purchasing marijuana. In order to become a member, the patient must show written verification of a diagnosis from a doctor, fill out an application form and pay a fee.

Because marijuana use, possession, and distribution is illegal, the Food and Drug Administration does not regulate the marijuana that is available in dispensaries. Therefore, the quality and potency of the product can vary.[62]

There are also currently no uniform standards for operating a dispensary or club, forcing them to self-regulate. Most centers are highly regulated. In California, there were around 500 dispensaries, some of which were shut down for providing marijuana to those without prescriptions from a doctor. Some dispensary officials say they inspect their suppliers and use labs to check the potency of their product, though states do not generally require such measures.

Every time a dispensary employee provides cannabis to a patient, or when that patient uses the drug, they are violating federal law, even though the state may have legalized medical marijuana. In cases where federal laws and state laws are contrary to the other, the federal law is the Supreme Law in the land and takes precedence over state laws. This means that marijuana users (and distributors) in those states that have legalized medical marijuana can be arrested and/or prosecuted for their actions by the federal authorities. Patients who are arrested on drug charges may be able to use their medical status as a legal defense as a way to reduce any charges or penalties, but not always. A patient who is arrested may show a doctor's recommendation for marijuana, or they could claim the defense of medical necessity based on the nature of his or her health condition, but this does not guarantee that they will not be charged with crimes and/or prosecuted for them. The penalties for federal medical marijuana violations may include prison time, fines, or both, depending on the nature of the offense.

The same holds true for those who dispense or provide the drug to patients. Even if dispensary owners and growers are licensed by a state that has legalized marijuana, they remain in violation and federal laws and can be arrested for possession, sale of an illegal drug, cultivation, possession of marijuana paraphernalia, drug trafficking and intent to distribute marijuana, depending on the amount of marijuana or number of plants they possess. In reality, every dispensary in the U.S. is in violation of federal law. Users and distributors can both be arrested and imprisoned, so long as marijuana is classified as a Schedule I narcotic by the federal government. If marijuana would be moved to Schedule II, it would change the enforcement of it. Marijuana advocacy groups have attempted to reverse the federal laws, claiming that since so many people use the drug, the law should be changed to reflect that the drug is so widely accepted.

In 2009, growers, dispensary owners, users and caretakers were hopeful when officials in the Obama Administration's Justice Department announced that it would not enforce federal marijuana laws on authorized users of medical marijuana or their caregivers. However, the Department resumed raids on dispensaries in 2011 and put pressure on publishers who run ads for medical marijuana dispensaries.

Current Book

The current book provides an overview of the issues surrounding medical marijuana and its status as a legal drug. The book begins by providing a history of medical marijuana in Chapter 2, with an examination of current state laws in Chapter 3 and the states were medical cannabis laws were considered in Chapter 4. The political actions taken regarding medical marijuana and the influence of these political actors are the topics of the next chapters. Chapter 5 will show how executives on the federal, state and local levels have reacted to medical marijuana, and Congressional reaction is the focus of Chapter 6. Both federal and state courts have made decisions regarding medical marijuana, which is the discussion presented in Chapter 7. There are many interest groups that are concerned with either passing or blocking both federal and state legislation, and these groups are described in Chapter 8. Chapter 9 focuses Federal and state bureaucracies that deal with medical marijuana in some way. The tenth chapter describes how medical marijuana has impacted campaigns, and Chapter 11 presents the businesses that have emerged since the issue has expanded. In the end, the book will discuss the maze of medical marijuana as it exists in the U.S. today.

Review/Discussion Questions

1. What are some medical conditions for which medical marijuana has been used?
2. Discuss the different methods of ingesting medical marijuana. What are the pros and cons of each?
3. Describe the legal status of medical marijuana in other countries.
4. How should medical cannabis be provided to patients?
5. What are some health effects of using medical marijuana?

Key Terms

Cannabis
Cannabis Indica
Cannabis Sativa
Hemp
Marijuana
Medical Marijuana
Synthetic Marijuana

Chapter 2

History

Overview: Marijuana has been part of world cultures for many years, being used for both medicine and recreation. The history of marijuana use, and medical marijuana in particular, is described in this chapter.

Introduction

Marijuana has been used for both recreation and medication since ancient times. In every part of the world, people have used cannabis to treat many types of health problems. At the same time, governments have tried to regulate its availability and use. The following provides a history of medical marijuana uses and policies over time.

Early Medical Marijuana Use

Marijuana use probably originated in China and from there spread to many other civilizations around the world. In the Chinese culture, marijuana seeds were used for both food and medicine as they are a renewable food source rich in B vitamins, protein, and amino acids. As such, it was China's second or third most important agricultural food source for thousands of years.[1] Not only did cannabis provide a food source for the Chinese, it was also a durable textile fiber that provided strong rope and fabric. When the Chinese invented hemp paper around 200 BC, it revolutionized record-keeping processes that became essential to an orderly, functioning government.[2]

Marijuana was mentioned in a Chinese medical reference from 2737 B.C., appearing in the writings of Chinese emperor Shen Nung.[3] A Chinese medical text from 1578 AD describes that the Chinese used marijuana to treat hundreds of problems,[4] such as vomiting, parasitic infections, and hemorrhage. It may also have been used to treat diarrhea, dysentery and to stimulate the appetite.[5] The powers of marijuana as a medication for rheumatism, gout, malaria, and absent-mindedness were described. Mention was made of the intoxicating properties, but the medicinal value was considered more important. Early writings describe Chinese surgeon Hua T'o as performing surgeries such as "organ grafts, resectioning of intestines, laparotomies (incisions into the loin), and thoracotomies (incisions into the chest) ... rendered painless by means of an anaesthetic made from cannabis resin and wine." [6]

While marijuana use was mentioned in early China, it was also used in other regions of the world. Other cultures known to have used cannabis include the Hindus and Nihang Sikhs from ancient India and Nepal. More than likely, the ancient Assyrians used marijuana in their religious ceremonies because of its psychoactive properties.[7] The drug moved into Greece where it was used to relieve inflammation, earaches, and edema.[8] Some Greeks used it to get rid of tapeworms, stop nosebleeds and reduce pain in the ear; others used it to dress wounds and sores on their horses.

Ancient Jews and early Christians may have used the drug, as did the early Sufi Muslims.[9] Muslims used marijuana recreationally because drinking alcohol was banned in the Koran. In ancient Egypt, evidence from ruins indicates that cannabis was used to treat gout, rheumatism, foot pain, eye problems, and hemorrhoids. Cannabis has been used in Africa since the 15th century. There it was used to treat snake bites, facilitate in childbirth, and as a treatment for malaria, fever, blood poisoning, anthrax, asthma, and dysentery.[10] In Rome, a doctor in the army of emperor Nero, Discorides, recommended marijuana as a treatment for many ailments, including earaches.[11]

Medical Marijuana in America

In 1492, Christopher Columbus brought cannabis to America. The ships that Columbus and his crew sailed to America were well stocked with marijuana. They reportedly had enough marijuana to last them until they arrived in the new world and could plant and harvest more.[12] In 1611 in Jamestown, marijuana was a major commercial crop alongside tobacco and was grown as a source of fiber. The settlers relied on hemp fiber as an important export. In 1619, the colony of Virginia declared that all people were required to grow hemp, and actually imposed penalties on those who did not produce it.[13] Those colonists who complied were rewarded with colonial coins.

In 1765, George Washington began growing cannabis as hemp at his plantation home in Mount Vernon and did so for about thirty years. There is some evidence in his journals that provides evidence that he also grew cannabis for medicinal reasons and for its intoxicating value.[14] The second and third presidents of the U.S., John Adams and Thomas Jefferson, also grew marijuana for hemp. Jefferson reportedly had part of his private garden reserved for cannabis. However, there is no evidence that he smoked hemp, tobacco, or any other substance.[15]

In the 19th century, an Irish physician and surgeon for the British East India Company, William Brooke O'Shoughnessy, studied the Indian medical literature and their use of cannabis. Also a professor of Chemistry at the Medical College of Calcutta, he began experimenting with marijuana on animals and patients (including himself), to help treat muscle spasms, stomach cramps and pain. O'Shoughnessy then introduced the drug to Europe and America as a new treatment for many ailments such as rheumatism, convulsions and muscle spasms related to tetanus and rabies. In 1839 he wrote a paper entitled *On the Preparation of the Indian Hemp or Gunja* in which he reported about the medical success of marijuana and called for more scrutiny of the drug.[16]

Based on O'Shaughnessy's experiments, the use of cannabis rose through the late 1800s. At that time in the U.S., medicines with a cannabis base were readily available in pharmacies.[17] Early Americans used it to treat skin inflammation, rabies, and tetanus.[18] In 1854, the United States Dispensatory listed many uses for cannabis extracts, and recommended that cannabis be used for neuralgia, gout, tetanus, hydrophobia, cholera, convulsions, spasticity, hysteria, depression, insanity, and uterine hemorrhage, and for promoting relaxed contractions during delivery. Marijuana was listed in the United States Pharmacopeia from 1850 until 1942 as an effective way to treat labor pains, nausea, and rheumatism.[19]

In 1890, Sir John Russell Reynolds, personal physician to Queen Victoria, reported that cannabis use was useful for treatment of dysmenorrhea (painful menstruation), migraine, neuralgia, convulsions, and insomnia. Reynolds called cannabis "by far the most useful of drugs" in treating "painful maladies." By that time, hemp production was replaced by cotton as the major cash crop in southern states.

Cannabis was a common medicine throughout the 19th Century. It was used primarily as a pain reliever until the invention of aspirin. Some patent medicines during this era contained marijuana, but it was a small percentage compared to the number containing opium or cocaine. There were at least 2000 cannabis medicines prior to 1937 with over 280 manufacturers. The first restrictions on the sale of the plant in America came in 1906.

1906 Pure Food and Drug Act

The Pure Food and Drug Act was passed in 1906 by Congress and then signed by President Roosevelt. The intent of the new law was to form a new agency called the Food and Drug Administration (FDA) to oversee the safety of all foods and drugs that were meant for human consumption. The law also limited the sale of certain drugs without a prescription. Another key provision of the new law required that some drugs that were identified as being habit-forming be labeled as such.[20] Thus, if the product contained any alcohol, morphine, opium, cocaine, heroin, marijuana or other addictive substances, it had to be labeled. When this law was passed, it was the first time that drugs had any federal oversight to protect users. However, there was still no pre-market approval for drugs.[21] The 1906 law restricted cannabis use to FDA-approved research studies only. It also denied importation of the drug into the U.S. from Mexico if it was not intended for medical purposes.[22]

In the meantime, many states were outlawing marijuana. In 1911, Massachusetts became the first state to outlaw cannabis. Maine, Wyoming and Indiana followed suit and passed laws in 1913. The following year, similar laws were passed in New York City, and in 1915, cannabis was outlawed in Utah and Vermont. Colorado and Nevada passed laws in 1917 to ban marijuana use.[23]

1914 Harrison Tax Act

In 1913, Democratic Representative Francis Burton Harrison of New York proposed a new law to regulate narcotics. Signed into law by President Woodrow Wilson in January of 1915, the Harrison Tax Act was the first federal law to control narcotics in the U.S. by making it illegal to import, export, or use opium for non-medical reasons. While the law regulated the use of opium, morphine (and its derivatives), and cocaine for medical use, it did not focus on amphetamines, barbiturates, marijuana, hashish, or hallucinogenic drugs.

Under the law, anyone who produced, imported, manufactured, compounded, dealt in, dispensed, sold, distributed or gave away opium or coca leaves or their derivatives would have to register with the government and pay a special tax. This meant that doctors would have to register and receive a stamp from the Government in order to prescribe the drug to patients. No doctor wanted to pay this high tax, so the use of these drugs for treatment reasons was impacted. Moreover, pharmacists could only sell opium or cocaine to those who had a prescription from a physician, dentist or surgeon. There was also an extremely high tax placed on every non-medical exchange of these drugs.[24] Because of these changes, if someone was found to be in possession of a drug, they would be punished for tax evasion instead of drug possession. It thus became the role of the Treasury Department to enforce the law.[25]

Further, under the law, all people who imported, manufactured, produced, compounded, sold, dispensed, or distributed cocaine and opiate drugs also had to keep records of all transactions.[26] Anyone who purchased narcotics was required to keep records for two years, and the records had to be kept on file at the local revenue offices.

Although the Harrison Act outlawed the buying or selling of marijuana for non-medicinal uses, it did not prohibit medicinal marijuana at this point and it was still being used as such.[27]

By the 1920s, marijuana was becoming more widely used for recreation, possibly because of Prohibition that made alcohol unavailable for enjoyment. In particular, marijuana became popular with jazz musicians and others in show business.[28] Marijuana clubs, otherwise known as tea pads, were opened in every major city. Since marijuana use was not illegal at that time, these clubs and the use of marijuana in the clubs, were largely ignored by authorities. These users were not much of a nuisance to themselves or the communities, and their marijuana use was not considered to be a significant threat. During this time, the use of marijuana became more commonplace.[29]

Additional federal regulations were passed in 1922, when Congress approved the Narcotic Drug Import and Export Act, also called the Jones-Miller Act, after its sponsors, Wesley Jones (R-WA) and John Miller (R-WA). By passing this law, Congress attempted to eliminate the use of narcotics except for legitimate medical use. They established the Federal Narcotics Board to regulate the import and export of opiate drugs and other psychoactive drugs. This way, they could control the quality of drugs being used for medical reasons. The law also placed a ban on all recreational consumption of opiates.

By 1930, Harry Anslinger had been appointed as the commissioner of the Federal Bureau of Narcotics. He opposed marijuana use for any reason,[30] and made sure the public learned about how powerfully addictive and harmful the drug was. He said, "Marihuana is an addictive drug which produces in its users insanity, criminality, and death."[31] He called it a "gateway" drug that would encourage users to try other drugs and become addicted to them. He also successfully linked cannabis to Mexican immigrants, which is how the drug became known as marijuana. In 1936, the film "Reefer Madness" showed how marijuana use could ruin the lives of those who use it. It was intended to scare American teenagers from using cannabis for fun.[32]

By this time, all states had enacted laws to regulate marijuana. New drugs were developed that were used as a treatment for pain such as aspirin, morphine, and then other opium-derived drugs so the need for marijuana as a medicine was decreasing. However, until the 1940s, the American Medical Association (AMA) was still promoting cannabis use for medical reasons.

The Marijuana Tax Act of 1937

Cannabis was made illegal by the federal government in 1937 when the Marijuana Transfer Tax Act was passed, more commonly known as the Marijuana Tax Act. President Roosevelt signed the law on October 2, despite a lack of debate and some controversy over the bill's content. The American Medical Association (AMA) objected to the legislation. Dr. William C. Woodward, testifying on behalf of the AMA, told Congress that the organization had no evidence that marijuana was a dangerous drug and warned that a prohibition would lose sight of the fact that future investigation may show that there could be substantial medical uses for cannabis.[33]

The Marijuana Tax Act was modeled after the Harrison Tax Act and placed a tax on cocaine and opium products, but technically did not ban marijuana outright. Anyone who bought, sold, or grew marijuana had to register with the federal government and purchase a stamp from the Treasury Department. The exact price of the stamp varied. Producers and medical professional had to pay $1 per year; individuals who were not medical professional had to pay $5; and importers and manufacturers would have to pay $24. It was illegal to grow or possess marijuana without the stamp, and anyone found to have marijuana without the tax stamp was subject to a fine of up to $2,000 and up to five years in prison.[34]

However, the Treasury Department did not issue any tax stamps for marijuana, essentially making growing, selling and possessing marijuana illegal. Moreover, the tax made it difficult for physicians to prescribe marijuana. After the passage of the Act, prescriptions of marijuana declined because doctors generally decided it was easier not to prescribe marijuana than to deal with the extra work imposed by the new law.[35] Most doctors found it easier to prescribe other drugs to their patients.[36] Fundamentally, this new law ended its medical use.[37]

When the new Tax Act was implemented, those who grew marijuana found that it was too expensive to do it legally. If a grower did not pay the tax, they could be arrested on federal charges. This meant that any products that included marijuana were taken off the legal market and forced onto the black market, basically changing marijuana from a legal substance into a criminal one. [38] In 1969, the Marijuana Tax Act was ruled unconstitutional by the Supreme Court in the case of *Leary v. United States*.

1938 U.S. Food, Drug and Cosmetic Act

In 1938, the Congress passed the U.S. Food, Drug and Cosmetic Act (FDCA) that required the FDA to regulate the safety of food and drugs and the labeling of them. New drugs had to receive the FDA's approval before being sold to the public. Any drug that was on the market prior to the passage of new law could still be purchased by patients as long as they were marketed for the same ailment and it had the same chemical makeup.

Just a few years later, in 1942, marijuana was officially removed from the U.S. Pharmacopoeia, which is a source that establishes standards for medicines and foods in the U.S. When this happened, all medical uses of the drug were also erased.[39]

Boggs Act of 1951

In the early 1950s, Senator Hale Boggs (D-LA) introduced an amendment to the Harrison Narcotic Act. The bill, supported by Harry Anslinger and signed by President Truman, increased mandatory minimum sentences for drug offenses. Any person who imported or brought opiates, cocaine, or marijuana into the U.S., or anyone who received, concealed, bought, sold transported or trafficked in the drug could potentially be fined up to $2,000 and be sent to prison for 2–5 years. If it was a second offense, there would be a possible sentence of five to ten years; and for a third offense it could be ten to twenty years. Under the Boggs Act, marijuana was treated the same as other narcotic drugs and was no longer considered medication. It was made clear that marijuana had no therapeutic value, so its use would be considered abuse.[40]

That same year, two members of the House of Representatives, Hubert Humphrey, Jr. (South Dakota) and Carl Durham (North Carolina), proposed an amendment to the Food, Drugs and Cosmetics Act. The amendment, called the Durham-Humphrey Amendment, defined the drugs that could not be used safely without a medical prescription, and required that their sale be limited. Specifically, the amendment created two categories of drugs: prescription and over-the-counter. More dangerous drugs (i.e. any that could be habit forming) would be considered a prescription drug and would therefore require a prescription for purchase.[41]

Narcotic Control Act of 1956

Anslinger continued to support tougher drug laws and he was able to convince President Eisenhower to do the same. Four years after the Boggs Act was passed, Congress passed, with the support of Anslinger and Eisenhower, the Narcotics Control Act that categorized marijuana in the same class as heroin. It established higher penalties for the production, distribution and use of opiates and marijuana. A person convicted of a first offense of marijuana possession would be sentenced to a mandatory 2–10 years in prison. For more serious offenses, an offender could be sentenced to death. Punishments were also increased by many states as well. The Act included provisions for surveillance and apprehension of those who used or trafficked in drugs.[42]

1960s

Throughout the 1960s, marijuana continued to be used by college students and "hippies" as a symbol of rebellion against authority.[43] Veterans returning from the Vietnam War were also using the drug as a way to deal with injuries and post-traumatic stress disorder (PTSD). Public concern about the use of marijuana was high, and the government continued to place it high on their agenda.

One change that was made occurred In April of 1968, when President Johnson established the Bureau of Narcotics and Dangerous Drugs as a response to a dramatic increase in the use of marijuana and other drugs during that time period. The reorganization eliminated the Federal Bureau of Narcotics, found in the Department of the Treasury, and the Bureau of Drug Abuse Control, found in the FDA to the Department of Justice.

More attention was given to marijuana when the United Nations put it in the spotlight in 1961. The members passed Treaty 406, the Single Convention on Narcotic Drugs. This was a plan to eradicate cannabis cultivation and use across the world by modernizing and coordinating international approaches to controlling narcotics. The treaty describes measures that each participating state or nation could adopt as a way to prevent the misuse and trafficking of cannabis. In particular, Article 49 of the treaty states, "The use of cannabis for other than medical and scientific purposes must be discontinued as soon as possible but in any case within twenty-five years...."[44] The U.S. agreed to be part of the Convention in 1967, which then formed the basis of a new legislation passed in 1970.

1970 Comprehensive Drug Abuse Prevention and Control Act

Public support continued for reforming marijuana laws. In October 1970, President Richard Nixon signed the Comprehensive Drug Abuse and Prevention and Control Act of 1970, more commonly known as the Controlled Substances Act (CSA). The intention of this legislation was to regulate the legal drug industry and at the same time, curtail importation and distribution of illegal drugs throughout the United States.

The law classified drugs based on the potential for medical use and the potential for abuse. There were five schedules (or categories) of drugs established, depending upon how dangerous they were, their potential for abuse and addiction, and whether they had any recognized medical value.[45] All substances were categorized and placed into one of the schedules. A drug placed in Schedule I meant it had no medical value along with a substantial, or high, potential for abuse. Schedule II drugs were those that have some limited or accepted medical purpose, but a high potential for abuse. These included barbiturates and amphetamines (morphine and cocaine). Schedule III includes those drugs with high medical use and high potential for abuse, including morphine and codeine. Those drugs placed in Schedule V have a low potential for abuse and an accepted medical use. Mandatory minimum sentences for drug offenses were also established for possession, possession with intent to sell, sale, and sale to a minor for each drug category. More information on the drug schedules is presented in Table 2.1.

Marijuana was place in Schedule I of the CSA, along with heroin, LSD, hashish and other hallucinogens. However, the language of the act separated out marijuana from other drugs and lowered the maximum criminal penalty for possession of an ounce of marijuana to one year in jail and a $5,000 fine, with judicial discretion to use probation or a conditional discharge.[46] As a Schedule I drug, it was now illegal for physicians to prescribe the drug to their patients.

While this law was being debated, the Congress established the National Commission on Marijuana and Drug Abuse, otherwise known as the Shafer Commission, after its chairman, former Pennsylvania Governor Raymond P. Shafer. The committee was given the task to study the current federal policy regarding marijuana and make recommendations for change. The Commission's report, entitled "Marijuana, a Signal of Misunderstanding," was made public in March of 1972. In it, the Committee members acknowledged that the drug had not been tested completely and there was not a good understanding of the effects of the drug. While previous studies indicated that marijuana users were physically aggressive, lacked self-control, and were

Table 2.1: Criteria for Scheduled Substances

	Schedule I	Schedule II	Schedule III	Schedule IV	Schedule V
Potential for Abuse	High potential for abuse	High potential for abuse	Potential for abuse is less than substances in Schedules I and II	Low Potential for abuse relative to drugs in Schedule III	Low potential for abuse relative to drugs in Schedule IV
Medical Uses	No currently accepted medical use in treatment	Has currently accepted medical use in treatment or currently accepted medical use with severe restrictions	Has currently accepted medical use in treatment	Has currently accepted medical use in treatment	Has currently accepted medical use in treatment
Consequences for Abuse	Lack of accepted safety for use	Abuse of drug may lead to severe psychological or physical dependence	Abuse of drug may lead to moderate or low physical dependence or high psychological dependence	Abuse of drug many lead to limited physical or psychological dependence	Abuse of drug may lead to limited physical or psychological dependence

irresponsible, mentally ill and, even dangerous, the committee found just the opposite: that most marijuana users tended to be drowsy, lethargic, and passive. Further, the committee report stated that there was no evidence of danger of either physical or psychological harm from those who used cannabis. Finally, the Commission members recommended that while the government's policy should discourage heavy marijuana use, they should also decriminalization simple possession of the drug.

Even though the Shafer Commission recommended decriminalizing possession of marijuana, President Nixon made it clear that he would not do that. In a televised news conference on May 1, 1971, Nixon said,

> As you know, there is a Commission that is supposed to make recommendations to me about this subject; in this instance, however, I

have such strong views that I will express them. I am against legalizing marijuana. Even if the Commission does recommend that it be legalized, I will not follow that recommendation … I can see no social or moral justification whatever for legalizing marijuana. I think it would be exactly the wrong step. It would simply encourage more and more of our young people to start down the long, dismal road that leads to hard drugs and eventually self-destruction.[47]

A few days later, at a press conference on June 17, 1971, President Nixon declared a War on Drugs. He said,

America's public enemy number one in the United States is drug abuse. In order to fight and defeat this enemy, it is necessary to wage a new, all-out offensive. I have asked the Congress to provide the legislative authority and the funds to fuel this kind of an offensive. This will be a worldwide offensive dealing with the problems of sources of supply, as well as Americans who may be stationed abroad, wherever they are in the world … I have brought Dr. [Jerome H.] Jaffe into the White House, directly reporting to me [as Special Consultant to the President for Narcotics and Dangerous Drugs], so that we have not only the responsibility but the authority to see that we wage this offensive effectively and in a coordinated way.[48]

While this debate was going on, and immediately after the 1970 law was passed, the National Organization for the Reform of Marijuana Laws, or NORML, petitioned the DEA to reschedule marijuana. In 1972, the organization filed documents with the government to reclassify marijuana as a Schedule II drug. This would enable physicians to legally prescribe the drug to patients. Officials in the government refused to act on the petition until years later.

1970s

The war against medical marijuana continued throughout the 1970s. In 1973, President Nixon reorganized any existing bureaucracies that dealt with drugs (primarily the Bureau of Narcotics and Dangerous Drugs and the Office of Drug Abuse Law Enforcement) and created the Drug Enforcement Administration (DEA). The idea was that one agency could focus their resources more effectively to fight all illicit drug use, including marijuana use.[49]

The next year (1974), the National Institute on Drug Abuse (NIDA) was established. One of the responsibilities of the new agency was to administer the contracts with those groups that grew marijuana for federal government's research projects. At that time, The University of Mississippi was the source for the only legal cannabis in the U.S. The University had a contract with NIDA to grow cannabis, depending on research demand. They also had a contract to manufacture and distribute cannabis cigarettes through The Research Triangle Institute (RTI) for the Compassionate Use program.[50]

The Compassionate Use program was established in November, 1976, after the U.S. Supreme Court ruled that Robert Randall's use of marijuana was a "medical necessity." He suffered from glaucoma. After a petition by Randall, the government began providing him with government-grown marijuana. He was the first American to receive marijuana for treatment of a medical disorder (See Chapter 5).

1980s

In 1980, Marinol, synthetic THC, was tested on cancer patients by the National Cancer Institute. The results of the experiments showed that patients responded well to the new drug. At the same time, however, six states conducted similar studies and found that thousands of patients reported that marijuana was safer and more effective than the synthetic THC. In the end, government officials approved Marinol as a legitimate medical drug. In 1981, the government sold the patent for Marinol to Unimed Pharmaceuticals.

Anti-Drug Abuse Acts of 1986 and 1988

As part of President Reagan's War on Drugs, Congress passed the Anti-Drug Abuse Act of 1986 that, among other things, increased minimum sentences and fines for possessing and dealing in large amounts of drugs, including marijuana. The sentences depended on the amount of drug involved. A person possessing 100 marijuana plants would receive an equal penalty as a person possessing 100 grams of heroin. The potential sentences could be up to life in prison for certain offense, and a $10 million fine. The penalties were doubled for those offenders who used minors to sell drugs, or for selling drugs to minors. An amendment to the Act created a "three strikes and you're out" provision that required a life sentence for repeat drug offenders. It also established the death penalty for anyone convicted of being a "drug kingpin."

Two years later, Congress again passed an Anti-Drug Abuse Act. Like the 1986 version of this Act, the new law increased penalties for drug possession and trafficking, but also provided money for educational and treatment programs. The nation's drug czar was established through this act.

Also in 1988, the DEA's chief administrative law judge, Francis Young, conducted hearings about medical marijuana. He ruled that the therapeutic use of marijuana was recognized by a minority of the medical community, and that it met the standards of other legal medications. Saying that marijuana was safe and had medical benefits, he then recommended that the drug be reclassified as a Schedule II drug. His recommendation was ignored by government officials, and in 1989, the Director of the DEA ordered that marijuana not be reclassified.

1990s

In June, 1991, the government decided to suspend the Compassionate Use Medical Marijuana Program. The Bush administration considered the program to be a contradiction to the administration's position opposing illegal drugs. They were also concerned that the number of applications from potential recipients would skyrocket as a result of the AIDS epidemic. The few patients still receiving marijuana as part of the program would continue to receive their shipments, but others would be encouraged to try synthetic forms of the drug. At the time the program was halted, twenty-seven patients who had received approval for marijuana were canceled, whereas thirteen patients who were already receiving medical cannabis would continue to receive supplies.

That fall, on November 5, 1991, the first ballot initiative for medical marijuana was passed by the voters in San Francisco. Called "Proposition P," it passed by 79 percent of the vote. The initiative required state officials and the California Medical Association to put medical marijuana to the list of available medicines in California, and not to penalize those physicians who chose to prescribe marijuana to patients for medical purposes.

Voters in the entire state of California had the opportunity to vote for medical marijuana in 1996. That year, California voters passed Proposition 215, becoming the first state to legalize medical marijuana. The law, also called the Compassionate Use Act of 1996, would allow patients and their caregivers, with a physician's recommendation, to possess and cultivate marijuana for the treatment of diseases such as AIDS, cancer, muscular spasticity, migraines, and several other disorders. The initiative also protected doctors from punishment if they recommend marijuana to their patients.

Because the local and state laws were in violation of federal laws, questions arose about how they would be implemented and enforced. Officials in the Office of National Drug Control Policy issued a statement indicating that the decision to enforce the federal law would be decided on a case-by-case basis. However, in December, 1996, the Clinton administration announced its plan to institute criminal prosecution of any physician who recommended or prescribed marijuana. Then, in April 1997, federal agents with the DEA raided

Flower Therapy, a medical marijuana dispensary in California, but made no arrests. This was the first federal action after California voters passed Proposition 215.

In July 1994, the Assistant Secretary of Health announced a decision not to reopen the Compassionate Use Medical Marijuana. The official claimed that the program did not generate sufficient data that could be submitted to the FDA to either support or reject the hypothesis that smoked marijuana was not only safe but had medical properties.

The push to have marijuana reclassified continued through the mid 1990s. In February, 1994, the U.S. District Court rejected a petition to review a request pertaining to the rescheduling of marijuana. A ruling by the U.S. Court of Appeals (D.C. Circuit) upheld the DEA's decision to keep marijuana in Schedule I.

In July 1995, Jon Gettman, former National Director of the National Organization for the Reform of Marijuana Laws (NORML), filed another legal challenge to marijuana's Schedule I status. Although the drug was not rescheduled, the DEA restricted synthetic THC (Marinol) in 1999 to a Schedule III drug. This made the drug subject to less regulatory controls, and lowered criminal sanctions for those who used it illegally. The drug would also be more available to patients. The rescheduling was approved after the DEA and the Department of Health and Human Services found that there were few instances of illicit abuse of the drug.

Research into the potential effects of cannabis continued during this time. From January 1997 through March, 1999, the Institute of Medicine (IOM) conducted a comprehensive study on the possible medical effects of marijuana. The study, commissioned by the federal drug czar, requested the IOM to review the scientific evidence on the potential benefits and risks of marijuana and cannabinoid use. The final report, *Marijuana and Medicine: Assessing the Science Base*, was released in March 1999. The report provided evidence on both sides of the debate. It concluded that there was evidence to show that marijuana is a safe and effective medicine, but emphasized the need for continued, scientific research into the long-term effects of the drug on patients. They argued that patients should have access to the drug, if recommended. In the end, the federal government ignored the findings and did not act on the recommendations.

Towards the end of the 1990s, more legislation was proposed allowing for medical marijuana. This time, Representative Barney Frank (D-MA) introduced legislation to eliminate federal restrictions that interfered with a state's decision to allow patients to use the medical use of marijuana.

Executives also got in on the debate. In October 1998, Presidents Ford, Carter, and Bush urged voters to reject medical marijuana proposals. Before the November 1998 election, the former Presidents released a statement in which they urged voters to reject state initiatives, arguing that the proposals circumvented the process by which the Food and Drug Administration (FDA) uses to test new medicines to ensure their safety and effectiveness for consumers. Despite their pleas, the medical marijuana initiatives passed in every state in which they appeared on the ballot, including Alaska, Oregon, and Washington State.

Other states continued to support new medical cannabis laws. In November 1999, voters in Maine passed an initiative to remove state-level criminal penalties for medical marijuana use, possession and cultivation. In June 2000, the legislature in Hawaii supported a bill to remove state-level criminal penalties for medical marijuana use, possession and cultivation (see chapter 3).

2000s

In the 2000s, states continued to pass laws to allow for medical marijuana. In November 2000, such laws passed in Nevada and Colorado. These both removed state-level criminal penalties for medical marijuana use, possession and cultivation. They became the seventh and eighth States to legalize medical marijuana. In 2004, two states passed medical marijuana. One of those was Vermont, which passed a law through legislative action, and the second was Montana. In January 2006, Rhode Island became the 11th state to legalize medical marijuana. New Mexico's governor signed the legislation in April of 2007. This made New Mexico the 12th state to legalize medical marijuana. Voters in Michigan approved a ballot measure allowing severely ill patients to use medical marijuana in November 2008. The measure removed state-level penalties for registered patients using medical marijuana. Many other states have followed (see chapter 3).

By this time, the question regarding the inconsistencies between federal and state enforcement was making its way through the courts. In May, 2001, the U.S. Supreme Court made a ruling that was a start in answering this question. In this case, the Oakland Cannabis Buyers' Cooperative, a dispensary that distributed medical marijuana to qualified patients in California, was sued by the U.S. government as a way to force the dispensary to shut down. The Cooperative claimed that marijuana was medically necessary for certain patients and they should be permitted to remain open. Their argument was rejected, which was then overturned by the Ninth Circuit. The Supreme Court ruled that "there is no medical necessity exception to the Controlled Substances Act's prohibition on manufacturing and distributing marijuana" (see chapter 7).

That same year, the DEA again denied a petition by NORML's Jon Gettman to have marijuana removed as a Schedule I drug and placed into a different category. DEA officials stated that there was overwhelming evidence that there was a high potential for abuse of marijuana.

There were multiple court decisions after that regarding the status of medical marijuana. In July 2002, the California Supreme Court upheld Proposition 215. In September, the D.C. federal appeals court blocked a proposed medical marijuana initiative in the District. The court overturned a previous court ruling that would permit a medical marijuana initiative to be considered by the voters. And in October 2002, the U.S. 9th Circuit Court of Appeals ruled in *Conant v. Walters* that the federal government could not revoke a doctor's license to dispense medications, nor could they investigate a physician, after he or she recommended a patient use medical marijuana.

A study of the remaining IND patients was released in 2002. Overall, the study concluded that the patients reported that medical marijuana provided to them improved the quality of their lives. The study noted that the quality of the marijuana provided to the patients was very poor, but barring that, smoking the drug gave the patients at least some relief of their symptoms. However, they also noted that there was evidence that pointed to some mild pulmonary risk in chronic users. The authors of the study recommended reestablishing the Compassionate IND program or amending laws to allow access to clinical cannabis.[51]

October 2003, the U.S. Supreme Court rejected an appeal of this decision, denying a request from the Bush administration that the justices consider whether the federal government could punish any doctor who recommended that a patient use medical marijuana. The 9th Circuit Court of Appeals made another ruling in December 2003 in which they indicated that those who use marijuana for medical purposes could not be prosecuted by federal officials as long as they grew their own marijuana or obtained it from other growers without charge.

In June 2005, the Supreme Court justices declared that federal officials may prosecute any patient who smokes cannabis, even if the use was based on a recommendation from their physician. This ruling, in *Gonzalez v. Raich*, verified that state medical marijuana laws do not protect users from possible prosecution by the federal government. In that decision, the justices noted that California's 1996 medical marijuana law conflicted with the federal Controlled Substances Act (CSA) of 1970, which bans possession and use of marijuana.

Because of the courts' decisions, the federal government continued to enforce federal laws against cannabis. On December 12, 2005, federal and local law enforcement officers raided medical marijuana dispensaries in California. Agents from the DEA and local law enforcement cooperated to carry out raids on eleven marijuana dispensaries in San Diego and two in San Marcos. While they questioned employees and customers and seized documents and an unknown quantity of marijuana, no arrests were made. Authorities said the purpose of the investigation was to determine how much marijuana was being sold and who was supplying it.

On March 16, 2006, DEA agents arrested twelve people and charged them with distribution of marijuana. As a result of searches conducted at the same time, law enforcement seized thousands of marijuana plants, a large amount of U.S. currency, two semi-automatic weapons, one revolver, and candy and soft drinks made with cannabis.[52]

On February 25, 2009, Attorney General Eric Holder stated that the DEA would end its raids on state-approved marijuana dispensaries. During the Bush presidency, DEA agents shut down between thirty to forty marijuana dispensaries.[53] This was followed up with a memo from the Department of Justice from October 2009, also known as the Ogden memo, that was intended to "provide clarification and guidance to federal prosecutors in States that have enacted laws authorizing the medical use of marijuana." In the memo, the DOJ announced that law enforcement should not target "individuals whose actions are in clear and unambiguous compliance with existing state laws providing for the medical use of marijuana." Specifically, individuals who are suffering from cancer or other serious illnesses and who have chosen to use medical marijuana and the caregivers who provide the medical marijuana in accordance with state law should not be the focus of federal prosecution. Further, the memo clarified that "prosecution of commercial enterprises that unlawfully market and sell marijuana for profit continues to be an enforcement priority." It is also explicitly stated that the memo "does not 'legalize' marijuana or provide a legal defense to a violation of federal law."[54]

2010s

In March, 2011, the DEA placed five synthetic cannabinoids into Schedule I category of the CSA, citing as a reason the "imminent hazard" of the drugs to the public's safety. They reported that the popularity of the synthetic drugs had increased significantly throughout the United States, and that they were being abused for their psychoactive properties. Some of the product names include "Spice" and "K2."[55] However, in July, 2011, the DEA denied a request to reclassify marijuana out of Schedule I. It declared that marijuana has "no accepted medical use" and should remain illegal under federal law in Schedule I, even though many states had passed legislation to permit medical marijuana use. The DEA Administrator, Michele Leonhart, stressed that marijuana "has a high potential for abuse," "has no currently accepted medical use in treatment in the United States" and "lacks accepted safety for use under medical supervision."

State governors took a different perspective. The governors of Washington and Rhode Island requested that medical marijuana be reclassified by the DEA from Schedule I to a Schedule II substance. The petition, filed on November 30, 2011 by Democratic Governor Christine Gregoire of Washington and independent Governor Lincoln Chafee of Rhode Island, declared that the Schedule I classification of cannabis is "fundamentally wrong and should be changed."[56]

Between March 23 and May 16, 2011, U.S. Attorneys sent threatening letters to officials in states with legal medical marijuana, including Arizona, Colorado, Montana, Rhode Island, Vermont, Hawaii, New Hampshire, Maine, and Washington. In the letters, officials threatened to prosecute those who implemented cultivation and distribution programs.[57]

In October 2012, the U.S. Court of Appeals reviewed the DEA's refusal to reclassify marijuana in the Controlled Substances Act. In the past, many groups who sought to reclassify the drug have argued that the DEA demonstrated a "bias" against marijuana by downplaying its medicinal qualities and at the same time focusing on its alleged dangerous qualities. The three-justice panel on the court considered if they had the authority to overturn the DEA's rejection of the petition.[58]

Conclusion

Throughout history, marijuana has been used to treat medical conditions of all kinds. Today, using, selling, possessing and cultivating marijuana for medical reasons remains illegal in the United States by federal law. However, many individual states (as well as other nations) have passed legislation to allow for such use. The debate over the enforcement of the law will more than likely continue until the state and federal governments agree as to the benefits of marijuana (if there are any) and the most appropriate way to categorize the drug. These issues will continue to be clarified by courts on the federal and state levels.

Review/Discussion Questions

1. How was medical marijuana used in cultures prior to its use in the U.S.?
2. Describe the Harrison Tax Act and the Marijuana Tax Act and their impact on marijuana use in the U.S.

3. What are the five categories of drug schedules as defined in the 1970 Comprehensive Drug Abuse and Prevention and Control Act of 1970 (the Controlled Substances Act)? How are drugs placed into each category?
4. Describe the Drug Abuse Acts passed by Congress in the 1980s.
5. What are some of the key events regarding medical marijuana in the 1990s? The 2000s? 2010s?

Key Terms

William Brooke O'Shoughnessy
Pure Food and Drug Act of 1906
Harrison Tax Act of 1914
Harry Anslinger
Marijuana Tax Act of 1937
Food, Drug and Cosmetic Act of 1938
Boggs Act 1951
Narcotics Control Act of 1956
Bureau of Narcotics and Dangerous Drugs
Comprehensive Drug Abuse and Prevention and Control Act of 1970
Anti-Drug Abuse Act of 1986 and 1988

Chapter 3

States with Medical Marijuana Laws

Overview: Regardless of federal laws that outlaw medical marijuana, many states have passed laws allowing certain patients to use medical marijuana under specific situations. This chapter describes these state laws, with their similarities and differences.

Introduction

Medical marijuana use is illegal in the U.S. as defined through the Controlled Substances Act, which classifies marijuana as a Schedule I drug. The federal government maintains that marijuana has no accepted medical value in the treatment of any disease (see chapter 2). However, some states have passed laws permitting patients to grow, possess, and use cannabis to relieve symptoms of illnesses without fear of punishment. These laws were passed on a state-by-state basis, and at different times, so there is no consistency between them. In general, the state laws remove any criminal penalties from patients who use medical cannabis within the boundaries determined by the individual state law, and from the doctors who prescribe or recommend the drug to their patients.

Some state laws require that every patient, before being allowed to use cannabis, have written documentation from a licensed doctor affirming that the person suffers from a debilitating condition and might benefit from the medical use of the drug. Other states require patients present this documentation, or a "marijuana ID card," prior to receiving marijuana from a dispensary, or even prior to an arrest. Other provisions may include limits on the type of conditions for which medical marijuana can be used. State laws also vary in terms of the amount of marijuana that a person (or their caretaker) may possess, use, or grow. Some states have other provisions, such as employee restrictions on the medical use of marijuana at the workplace, or the fees to register as a patient or be issued an ID card.

Individual states also differ as to how patients will obtain marijuana. The majority of the laws do not establish mechanisms for dispensing the drug or for regulating the quality and safety. This leaves patients on their own for obtaining their marijuana. However, other states have passed legislation to establish state-licensed institutions to sell medical marijuana to patients. While some states call them dispensaries, others refer to them as "compassion centers," or "alternative treatment centers." Some are for profit and others not-for-profit.[1]

In 1996, California was the first state to pass a bill to legalize medical marijuana when voters passed Proposition 215, the Compassionate Use Act. The law allows for the possession and cultivation of marijuana for medical purposes upon a doctor's recommendation. Immediately upon its passage, the Clinton Administration's response to the new law was to take a hard line against it. The Director of the Office of National Drug Control Policy, the Drug Czar, said in one press conference, "Nothing has changed. Federal law is unaffected by these propositions." Clinton's Secretary of Health and Human Services, Donna Shalala, expressed concern that the law reinforced the belief that marijuana was a benign drug. Clinton's Attorney General, Janet Reno, announced that she would begin reallocating federal law enforcement resources in a way that would target physicians in the state who went so far as to recommend marijuana to their patients. She threatened to revoke their registration with the Drug Enforcement Administration (DEA), and then prohibit them from participating in Medicare and Medicaid programs.

The reaction to Clinton's response was not always popular. One group of physicians, patients, and nonprofit agencies filed a complaint to prevent the federal government from punishing those physicians who recommended marijuana to their patients. The complaint, which later became *Conant v. McCaffrey*, was heard by the courts in September of 2000. The decision by the U.S. District Court for Northern California (a federal judiciary) limited the ability of federal officials to punish any physician who prescribed medical marijuana under the new law. In May 2004, the California Medical Board issued a statement in which they indicated that those physicians who recommended medical marijuana to their patients as part of their practice would not face any repercussions if they followed sound or accepted medical practice.

On October 19, 2009, the U.S. Deputy Attorney General, David W. Ogden, issued a memorandum to U.S. Attorneys that was intended to provide guidance to federal prosecutors in the states that passed medical marijuana laws.

Table 3.1: States with Medical Marijuana Laws

State	Year Passed	Method
Alaska	1998	Ballot Measure 8 (58%)
Arizona	2010	Proposition 203 (50.13%)
California	1996	Proposition 215 (56%)
Colorado	2000	Ballot Amendment 20 (54%)
Connecticut	2012	House Bill 5389 (96–51 House, 21–13 Senate)
DC	2010	Amendment Act B18-622 (13–0 vote)
Delaware	2011	Senate Bill 17 (27–14 House, 17–4 Senate)
Hawaii	2000	Senate Bill 862 (32–18 House; 13–12 Senate)
Maine	1999	Ballot Question 2 (63%)
Massachusetts	2012	Ballot Question 3 (63%)
Michigan	2008	Proposal 1 (63%)
Montana	2004	Initiative 148 (62%)
Nevada	2000	Ballot Question 9 (65%)
New Jersey	2010	Senate Bill 119 (48–14 House; 25–13 Senate)
New Mexico	2007	Senate Bill 523 (36–31 House; 32–3 Senate)
Oregon	1998	Ballot Measure 67 (55%)
Rhode Island	2006	Senate Bill 0710 (52–10 House; 33–1 Senate)
Vermont	2004	Senate Bill 76 (22–7) HB 645 (82–59)
Washington	1998	Initiative 692 (59%)

Ogden provided seven criteria to guide federal prosecutors and agents to ascertain whether a patient's use, or their caregiver's provision, of medical cannabis represents a recommended treatment regiment consistent with applicable state law. In the memo, Ogden recommended against prosecuting those patients who were using medical cannabis according to state laws. Ogden declared that if prosecutors and agents did not use those criteria, it would be a waste of federal resources. Nonetheless, the raids against dispensaries continued as the DEA enforced federal laws against dispensaries and patients alike.

Despite federal raids, states continue to pass laws allowing for medical use of cannabis. To date, eighteen states and the District of Columbia have legalized medical marijuana for certain patients suffering from various medical conditions. Table 3.1 shows the states where medical marijuana is legal, the year it became legal, and if the law was voted in through a ballot measure (popular vote) or legislative action (by a state legislature). More specific information on each state law is provided in this chapter.

Alaska

Voters in Alaska approved Ballot Measure 8, the "Alaska Medical Uses of Marijuana for Persons Suffering from Debilitating Medical Conditions Act" on November 3, 1998, by 58 percent of the vote. In doing so, they became the fourth state to pass a medical marijuana law. The new law became effective on March 4, 1999 and removed state-level criminal penalties on the use, possession and cultivation of marijuana by those patients who possessed written documentation from their physician stating that they would benefit from the use of cannabis. The state now allows the compassionate use of marijuana by patients who have been diagnosed with debilitating and chronic ailments. Some of the medical conditions for which the drug can be used include cachexia, cancer, chronic pain, epilepsy and other seizure disorders, glaucoma, HIV/ AIDS, multiple sclerosis and other disorders characterized by muscle spasticity, and nausea. Other medical conditions for which the drug could be used would need the approval of the Alaska Department of Health and Social Services.

Under the law, patients or their primary caregivers can legally possess no more than one ounce of usable marijuana, and may cultivate no more than six marijuana plants, of which no more than three may be mature. In order to grow marijuana, patients and caregivers must register with the state. The state also has dispensaries to distribute marijuana to patients. The law creates a confidential, state-run patient registry that has the obligation to issue identification cards to those patients who meet the qualifications and seek to use marijuana.

In 1999, the Alaska legislature passed Senate Bill 94 to require that all patients who use medical marijuana enroll in the state-run registry program and hold a valid picture identification card. Those patients who choose not to enroll will not be able to argue the "affirmative defense of medical necessity" if they are arrested on marijuana charges.[2] The bill became effective on June 2, 1999.

Individuals seeking to become a caregiver for medical marijuana patients in Alaska must be at least 21 years old and cannot have any felony drug offenses on their record. This caregiver may receive one of two titles: primary caregiver or alternate caregiver. The patient must decide which title is most appropriate.

Arizona

Arizona was the 15th state to pass a ballot initiative to allow the compassionate use of medical marijuana by residents who have been diagnosed with chronic and debilitating medical conditions. Ballot Proposition 203 was passed on November 2, 2010, by 50.13 percent of the vote. Under the new law, any resident who has been diagnosed with an "approved" medical condition and has a written recommendation from a physician would be allowed to legally use marijuana. The medical conditions for which an individual can receive a prescription for medical marijuana in Arizona include Alzheimer's disease, cancer, Crohn's disease, glaucoma, HIV/AIDS, hepatitis C, Lou Gehrig's disease, cachexia (wasting syndrome), severe and chronic pain, severe nausea, seizures, epilepsy and multiple sclerosis.

The new law requires the Arizona Department of Health Services to establish and maintain a registration and renewal application system that oversees both patients and non-profit dispensaries.[3] A web-based verification system would be established to allow law enforcement officials and dispensary employees to verify registry identification cards. The Department of Health Services would issue identification cards to those qualifying patients and their designated caregiver. All registration cards are good for a one-year period. Registration by patients is mandatory, and patients must pay a $150 registration fee.

Qualified medical marijuana patients or their designated caregivers may not have over 2.5 ounces of marijuana on their person at any time, and can only receive up to 2.5 ounces of the drug from a dispensary in a fourteen day period. They are permitted to grow twelve plants, which must be in a locked and enclosed facility. If the patient lives within a 25-mile radius of a dispensary, they are not permitted to grow their own marijuana. A caregiver must be at least twenty-one years old and has agreed to assist a patient with their use of medical marijuana. A caregiver must not have been convicted of a felony and be assisting no more than five patients at one time.

Patients in Arizona cannot possess or use marijuana on a school bus, on the grounds of a school, in a correctional facility, on a form of public transportation or any public place. Patients who are under the influence of marijuana cannot operate a motor vehicle, aircraft or motorboat. Other provisions of the Act provide more clarifications. For example, the law specifies that those who employ medical marijuana patients may not penalize those patients if they test positive for marijuana in drug tests, although the law does not authorize patients to use, possess, or be impaired by marijuana on the employment premises or during the hours of employment.

The Department of Health Services is required to oversee dispensaries, which are non-profit. All dispensaries must be registered with the Department, and information on each officer and dispensary agent must be reported. The procedures for issuing and suspending the registration of dispensaries were to be determined by the Department. They should maintain records related to the operation and oversight of the dispensary. The Department will define minimum security requirements. For example, dispensaries should have one secure entrance and should have appropriate security measures to deter and prevent the theft of marijuana. Individual cities/towns/counties may enact zoning regulations that limit the location of the dispensaries. The total number of dispensaries cannot exceed 10 percent of the number of pharmacies in the state (which would cap the number of dispensaries around 124).

California

On November 5, 1996, California voters supported Proposition 215, the Compassionate Use Act, with 56 percent of the vote. In doing so, California became the first state to create a legal framework for medical marijuana. Under the new initiative, seriously ill residents would have the right to obtain and use marijuana for medical purposes as recommended by a physician. The patients and their caregivers could no longer be prosecuted for use, possession or cultivation of marijuana on the state level, and doctors could not be punished for recommending that their patients use marijuana. The approved conditions for use of marijuana include AIDS, anorexia, arthritis, cachexia, cancer, chronic pain, glaucoma, migraine, persistent muscle spasms, multiple sclerosis, seizures, epilepsy, severe nausea or other chronic or persistent medical symptoms. Patients can possess eight ounces of usable, dried marijuana. They are also allowed to have six mature or twelve immature plants. The law became effective the day after the election.[4]

The original law was amended in 2003, when the California legislature passed Senate Bill 420, the Medical Marijuana Protection Act. It was signed into law by Governor Gray Davis and became effective on January 1, 2004. The legislation filled in some of the gaps in the existing law and clarified some of the terms. For example, it expanded the definitions of "patient" and "primary caregiver" and created guidelines for identification cards. Further, it defined the amount of marijuana that patients and their primary caregivers could possess. Under SB 420, patients could possess larger amounts of marijuana if recommended by a physician. They could now have up to eighteen plants, only six of which could be flowering, and up to eight ounces (half-pound) of marijuana in their possession. This amount could be higher if a physician recommended it. The legislation also allowed counties and municipalities to adopt their own local ordinances permitting patients to possess larger quantities of medicinal pot than allowed under the new state guidelines, or to ban it altogether. S.B. 420 also provided for establishing dispensaries to provide marijuana to patients, and granted legal protection to dispensaries. It further clarified the method for providing identification cards for patients so that the cards would be issued through the California Department of Public Health's Medical Marijuana Program (MMP).

After SB 420 was passed, law enforcement was asked to accept a medical marijuana card from a patient as a defense upon arrest unless the officers believed that the card was fraudulent. Further, no employer or penal institution was obligated to accommodate a medical marijuana patient. Inmates in those institutions were permitted to apply for a medical marijuana card, and penal facilities could allow inmates to use medical marijuana if it did not endanger the health and safety of other prisoners or security of the facility. Additionally, health insurance companies would not be obligated to reimburse patients for their marijuana use. Patients may not smoke medical marijuana within a school zone, on a school bus, while in a vehicle that is moving, or while driving a boat.

In August, 2008, the then-Attorney General of California, Jerry Brown, issued a directive for law enforcement and medical marijuana patients as a way to provide more clarification about the state's marijuana laws. The non-binding, eleven-page document stated, "In light of California's decision to remove the use and cultivation of physician recommended marijuana from the scope of the state's drug laws, this Office recommends that state and local law enforcement officers not arrest individuals or seize marijuana under federal law when the officer determines from the facts available that the cultivation, possession, or transportation is permitted under California's medical marijuana laws."[5] The guidelines stated that dispensaries and cooperatives sell only to legitimate patients, operate as non-profit agencies, and only buy cannabis from fellow cooperative members.

On January 21, 2010, the California Supreme Court affirmed that the amendments to Proposition 215 (in SB 420) violated the California constitution and were therefore illegal. They ruled that the voter-approved Proposition 215 could only be amended by the voters.

Currently, California law allows dispensaries throughout the state to sell medical cannabis to patients. Since the Compassionate Use Act was passed, numerous dispensaries have opened. The dispensaries offer patients different types, or grades, of marijuana, and employees will often make a recommendation about what type of marijuana would be best for a patient's symptoms. Some also sell edible products that contain marijuana. The items cannot be sold to patients since the businesses are prohibited by law from doing so, but a donation is acceptable. A patient can go to any dispensary they choose, and some visit different dispensaries on the same day or subsequent days to find the product they need. The dispensaries and cooperatives are all subject to search and closure under federal law.

The dispensaries throughout the state can be regulated by individual municipal governments. For example, in Riverside County, California, four dispensaries operate: the Healing Nations Collective in Corona, Compassionate Caregivers in Palm Springs, C.A.P.S. in Palm Springs and CannaHelp in Palm Desert. On the other hand, the members of the El Cerrito City Council voted on July 17, 2006, to put a ban on all medical marijuana facilities because of a report that showed a rise in crime in the area near the dispensaries. The crimes included robberies, assaults, burglaries, murders and attempted murders.

Officials in the City of West Hollywood also passed a similar moratorium. In 2007, they became concerned when there was a 2,350 percent increase in the number of medical marijuana dispensaries in LA during a one-year period. The City Council members passed an ordinance that prevented any new medical marijuana stores and limited their hours of operation and their proximity to schools, churches, parks, and other dispensaries. Then in January, 2010, the Los Angeles City Council approved an ordinance to close hundreds of dispensaries and set strict rules on the operation and locations of the dispensaries. The ordinance put a limit on the number of operational dispensaries at seventy.

However, new stores continued to open. It was estimated that there were 762 stores registered, with 200 more planning to open in LA. So, in July 2012, the LA City Council placed bans on medical marijuana dispensaries. Under the ban, all of the 762 dispensaries that have registered with the city were sent a letter in which they were ordered to close within 30 days. They were also warned that if they chose to remain open, they could face legal action from the city.[6]

In the case of *Gonzales v. Raich*, the U.S. Supreme Court ruled that the United States Supremacy Clause renders California's Compassionate Use Act of 1996 and Medical Marijuana Program Act of 2004 illegal. No state has the power to grant its citizens the right to violate federal law. Despite the ruling, patients in California continue to distribute and use medical marijuana.

Colorado

Laws to allow for the use of medical marijuana were passed in Colorado on November 7, 2000, through ballot amendment 20, making Colorado the eighth state to allow medicinal cannabis. It succeeded with 54 percent of the vote and became effective on June 1, 2001. A patient or primary caregiver who has been issued the appropriate registry identification card can possess up to two ounces of usable marijuana, and up to six plants (three mature, three immature) in this state.[7]

As approved by voters, the law removes state-level criminal penalties on the use, possession and cultivation of marijuana by those patients who possess a written note from a licensed physician declaring that the patient suffers from a debilitating condition that they might benefit from the medical use of marijuana. The approved conditions for the use of medical marijuana include cancer, glaucoma, HIV/AIDS, cachexia, severe pain, severe nausea, seizures, epilepsy, or persistent muscle spasms from multiple sclerosis. Other conditions are subject to approval by the Colorado Board of Health.

The original bill was amended through House Bill 1284 and Senate Bill 109, effective June 7, 2010. The bill was intended to prevent fraud and abuse surrounding medical marijuana, and included measures to ensure that those physicians who authorize medical cannabis for their patients actually performed a physical exam. Also, the law seeks to prevent physicians with a financial relationship with a dispensary from advising patients to use the drug. The then-governor of Colorado, Bill Ritter, signed the bill into law. He stated, "House Bill 1284 provides a regulatory framework for dispensaries, including giving local communities the ability to ban or place sensible and much-needed controls on the operation, location and ownership of these establishments. Senate Bill 109 will help prevent fraud and abuse, ensuring that physicians who authorize medical marijuana for their patients actually perform a physical exam, do not have a DEA flag on their medical license and do not have a financial relationship with a dispensary."[8]

In Colorado, medical marijuana patient must register with the state, and must pay a registry fee of $35. Patients can get their marijuana through dispensaries or grow their own. In order to grow and use marijuana under the Colorado medical marijuana law, patients and caregivers need to register with the state health agency (Colorado Department of Public Health). Only Colorado residents can be on the registry. After being processed, a medical marijuana card will be provided to each patient.

A physician in Colorado is not subject to arrest or prosecution for advising a patient to use medical marijuana or for providing a written recommendation to a patient. Law enforcement cannot harm, injure, neglect or destroy any property seized from a caregiver or patient. Any marijuana and paraphernalia seized by law enforcement shall be returned if it is determined that the person is a legal, registered patient or caregiver. A patient may not use marijuana in a way that endangers the health or well-being of anyone else. They may not use marijuana in plain view, nor in a place open to the public. A marijuana dispensary cannot be located within 1,000 feet of a school.

A state task force was established to create rules for implementing the new law, including criminal enforcement, taxes, and product labeling. The Amendment 64 Implementation Task Force proposed that marijuana should be grown only indoors and would be prohibited from use in bars, restaurants and social clubs. It could be sold to people visiting from out of state, though. It could be given away to adults an ounce at a time. State regulators would oversee the sale of the drug.[9] The Task Force made fifty-eight recommendations in a 265 page report.

Connecticut

On May 31, 2012, Connecticut became the 17th state to legalize medical marijuana when Governor Dannel P. Malloy signed HB 5389 into law. The bill was passed by the state House of Representatives by a vote of 96–51 and by the Senate membership by a vote of 21–13. The law, "an act concerning the palliative use of marijuana," allows licensed physicians to certify an adult patient's use of medicinal marijuana if it is determined that the patient has a debilitating disease or other medical condition and could potentially benefit from using the drug.[10] According to the new law, those patients who possess a written document and who register with the Department of Consumer Protection may obtain marijuana from certified pharmacists at a licensed dispensary, who has obtained it from a licensed producer.[11]

The conditions for which medical marijuana can be used in Connecticut include cancer, glaucoma, HIV/AIDS, Parkinson's disease, multiple sclerosis, damage to the nervous tissue of the spinal cord with objective neurological indication of intractable spasticity, epilepsy, cachexia, wasting syndrome, Crohn's disease, posttraumatic stress disorder, or any medical condition or disease that has been approved by the Department of Consumer Protection.[12] As written, the bill allows patients to possess a one month supply of medical marijuana.[13] Patients must be residents of the state and at least eighteen years of age. Prison inmates and others under the supervision of the Department of Corrections do not qualify, regardless of their medical condition.

Dispensaries were to be used to distribute marijuana, but the exact number of dispensaries was not determined in the law. State officials indicated that the Commissioner of Consumer Protection would determine the number of dispensaries that would be most appropriate to meet the needs of the patients in the state. Additionally, the patient registry fee was not determined in the law. Instead, the Commissioner of Consumer Protection was given the task of establishing a "reasonable fee," although patient registration was mandatory.

Delaware

Delaware became the 16th state to legalize medical marijuana on May 13, 2011, when Governor Jack Markell (D) signed SB 17 into law. It was approved by the House by a vote of 27–14 and the Senate's vote was 17–4. The law, which became effective on July 1, 2011, allows qualifying patients in Delaware (or their caregivers) who have been diagnosed with certain debilitating conditions to possess up to six ounces of marijuana with a doctor's recommendation, but cannot possess any plants.[14] The purpose of the law was to protect patients who have debilitating medical conditions, as well as their physicians and providers, from arrest and prosecution, criminal and other penalties, and property forfeiture if such patients engage in the medical use of marijuana. The patient or their designated caregiver must receive their medical marijuana from a state certified non-profit compassion center.

Under the law, patients in Delaware are protected from arrest if they can show written documentation from their physician showing that they have been diagnosed with a specified, debilitating medical condition, and that they would receive therapeutic benefit from using medical marijuana. The approved conditions for using medical marijuana in Delaware include cancer, HIV/AIDS, decompensated cirrhosis, ALS, Alzheimer's disease, post-traumatic stress disorder, a condition that produces wasting syndrome, severe debilitating pain that has not responded to other treatments for more than three months or for which other treatments produced serious side effects, severe nausea, seizures, or severe and persistent muscle spasms. If a patient is diagnosed with one of these conditions and seeks to use marijuana as a treatment, they must send a copy of the written certification to the state's Department of Health and Social Services, and the Department will issue an ID card after verifying the information. As long as the patient is in compliance with the law, there will be no arrest.

While the law does not allow patients or caregivers to grow marijuana at home, it does allow for distribution of medical marijuana by compassion centers. All compassion centers must be approved by the state. To be certified, a center must pay a fee, provide the name and address of the center, the names of the board members, operating bylaws (including procedures for accurate record keeping), and a statement about the suitability of the center's location. A registered compassion center may not dispense more than 3 ounces of marijuana to a registered patient in any fourteen-day period, and a patient may register with only one compassion center.

Patients are required to register with the state, and pay a fee of $125. Delaware will accept ID cards from other states, so that a visiting qualifying patient would not be subject to arrest for possessing marijuana. A designated caregiver must be at least 21 years old, has not been convicted of a felony and assists no more than five patients with their medical use of marijuana.

The law does not protect people who undertake any task while under the influence of marijuana if doing so would constitute negligence or professional malpractice. It also does not protect people who possess marijuana in a school bus or on the grounds of any preschool or primary or secondary school, or in a correctional facility. It also cannot be smoked in a public place, or while operating a motor vehicle, aircraft or motorboat. A private health insurer is not required to reimburse a person for costs associated with use of medical marijuana; employers are not required to allow for employees to use marijuana in a workplace. Employers are permitted to discipline an employee for ingesting marijuana in the workplace.

After he signed the new law, Governor Jack Markell (D) asked officials in the federal government for some clarification on their possible response to the state's new law. The federal officials responded with:

> Growing, distributing and possessing marijuana, in any capacity, other than as part of a federally authorized research program, is a violation of federal law regardless of state laws permitting such activities.... Moreover, those who engage in financial transactions involving the proceeds of such activities may also be in violation of federal money laundering statutes.... State employees who conduct activities mandated by the Delaware Medical Marijuana Act are not immune from liability under the Controlled Substances Act.[15]

Governor Markell responded this way:

> I am very disappointed by the change in policy at the federal department of justice, as it requires us to stop implementation of the compassion centers. To do otherwise would put our state employees in legal jeopardy and I will not do that. Unfortunately, this shift in the federal position will stand in the way of people in pain receiving help. Our law sought to provide that in a manner that was both highly regulated and safe.

The Governor then suspended implementation of the compassion centers.

Hawaii

A law allowing for medical marijuana passed in Hawaii in 2000 as Senate Bill 862. The state was the first to allow medical marijuana through legislation rather than a ballot initiative. The vote in the House was 32–18 and in the Senate 13–12. The law, which became effective on December 28, 2000, established guidelines for medical use of marijuana by those patients who had been diagnosed with debilitating ailments. It permitted a patient to have three ounces of usable marijuana, and seven plants (three mature, four immature). The law was signed by Governor Ben Cayetano on June 14, 2000.

The new law removed state-level criminal penalties for the use, possession and cultivation of marijuana by those patients who possess a signed statement from their physician affirming that the patient suffers from a debilitating condition and that the potential benefits of medical marijuana would likely outweigh the health risks. The conditions given approval for medical marijuana include cancer, glaucoma, HIV/AIDS, cachexia, severe and chronic pain, severe nausea, seizures, epilepsy, muscle spasms, multiple sclerosis, or Crohn's disease. Other conditions can be approved by the Hawaii Department of Health.

The law establishes a mandatory, confidential state-run patient registry that issues identification cards to qualifying patients. To register, patients must pay $25. Other state registration cards are not accepted in Hawaii. Only a Hawaiian medical marijuana card allows patients and their caregivers to legally grow, possess and use marijuana.[16]

A patient may not use medical cannabis in any public areas, including a school bus or any moving vehicle, at work, on school property, any public park, beach, recreation center or youth center. A patient or primary caregiver may assert the use of medical marijuana as an affirmative defense from any prosecution involving marijuana, provided they were in compliance with the state laws. No physician can be subject to arrest or prosecution for providing a written prescription to a patient, given that they have described the potential benefits and risks associated with the use of the drug.

Marijuana, paraphernalia, and other related property seized from a patient or caregiver in connection with the claimed use of medical marijuana under the law shall be returned once the court determines that the patient or caregiver is covered under the law. However, law enforcement personnel are not responsible for the care and maintenance of live plants seized.

Maine

Maine was the fifth state to pass medical marijuana laws through a ballot initiative on November 22, 1999. Voters passed Ballot Question 2 by a vote of 61 percent, establishing laws and guidelines for the medical use of marijuana. As of December 22, 1999, patients can now use medical cannabis to treat certain medical conditions. Some of the conditions for which an individual may be approved for medical marijuana use are Alzheimer's Disease, chemotherapy (for treating severe nausea), Crohn's Disease, epilepsy, glaucoma, hepatitis C, multiple sclerosis, and HIV/AIDS. Medical marijuana patients in Maine (and their caregivers) are allowed to possess up to 1.25 ounces of marijuana and up to six mature plants. There are no limits as to how many plants can be in the immature state. Medical marijuana patients from outside states are allowed to use and possess their medicine for up to thirty days after entering the state. They are not, however, permitted to obtain cannabis in Maine. In order to grow and use marijuana under the Maine medical marijuana law, patients and caregivers need to register with the Department of Health and Human Services.

The medical marijuana laws in Maine were amended in 2002 with Senate Bill 611, which was signed into law on April 2, 2001. The definition of a "usable" amount of marijuana for medical use was increased to 2 1/2 ounces or less of harvested marijuana. The act also expanded the list of qualifying illnesses for which a person may receive a medical marijuana card.

A second amendment, Question 5, was passed on November 3, 2009, when it received 59 percent approval by voters. This amendment again expanded the list of conditions for which someone could obtain a medical marijuana permit. These included cancer, glaucoma, HIV, AIDS, hepatitis C, amyotrophic lateral sclerosis, Crohn's disease, Alzheimer's, nail-patella syndrome, chronic intractable pain, cachexia or wasting syndrome, severe nausea, seizures (epilepsy), severe and persistent muscle spasms, and multiple sclerosis. Question 5 also instructed the Department of Health and Human Services to establish a registry as well as setting provisions for the operating of nonprofit dispensaries.

Under the laws in Maine, a patient may possess and use medical marijuana if it has been prescribed, sold or dispensed by a physician. The medical marijuana must be kept in the container that it was in when it was sold or received by the patient, except when "in use." Patients can also obtain marijuana through dispensaries. The dispensaries are not-for-profit and were licensed and regulated by the Maine Department of Health and Human Services.[17] It is voluntary for a patient to register, and there is no patient registry fee to use a dispensary; however, caregivers must pay $300 per patient, with a limit of five patients.[18]

Massachusetts

In November, 2012, voters in Massachusetts were asked to vote on a proposal allowing for medical marijuana. The final wording of the bill was:

A 'yes' vote would enact the proposed law eliminating state criminal and civil penalties related to the medical use of marijuana by patients meeting certain conditions. The marijuana will be produced and distributed by new state-regulated centers or, in specific hardship cases, patients will be allowed to grow marijuana for their own use.[19]

On November 6, 2012, Massachusetts became the eighteenth state to legalize medical marijuana for certain individuals when Ballot Question 3 passed with 63 percent of the public vote. After January 1, 2013, licensed physicians could prescribe marijuana to patients diagnosed with serious medical conditions. By voting for the proposal, the citizens of the state showed their preference that there would be no state punishment for qualifying patients, physicians and health care professionals, personal caregivers, or treatment center employees for the medical use of marijuana. After the law passed, a doctor who has a 'bona fide' relationship with a patient could certify that the patient suffered 'a debilitating medical condition, such as cancer, glaucoma, HIV/ AIDS, hepatitis C, Crohn's disease, Parkinson's disease, ALS, or multiple sclerosis.[20] The law allows patients to have a sixty day supply of marijuana for personal medical use, but no more than is necessary for their personal use. Patients are required to register with the state.[21]

The law set forth criminal penalties for fraudulent or nonmedical use of marijuana, including possible jail sentences. It also required checks for those people who handled marijuana at treatment centers, and put a limit on the number of treatment centers allowed to dispense marijuana across the state (the limit is thirty-five). The ballot initiative also prohibited smoking marijuana in public.[22]

The law stipulated that in the first year after the law became effective, the state would issue registrations for up to thirty-five non-profit medical marijuana treatment centers, as long as there is at least one treatment center located in each county, and not more than five in any one county.

Michigan

Medical marijuana was made legal in Michigan on November 4, 2008 when Proposal 1, the Michigan Medical Marijuana Act, was approved by 63 percent of the vote. This made Michigan the 13th state to pass a medical marijuana law. As of December 4, 2008, certain patients can have up to 2.5 ounces of usable marijuana and twelve plants if they are diagnosed with a debilitating medical condition such as cancer, glaucoma, HIV, AIDS, hepatitis C, amyotrophic lateral sclerosis, Crohn's disease, agitation of Alzheimer's disease, nail patella, cachexia or wasting syndrome, severe and chronic pain, severe nausea, seizures, epilepsy, muscle spasms, or multiple sclerosis. Under the law, a patient or caregiver who is in possession of an identification card will not be subject to arrest, penalty or prosecution as long as they possess an amount of useable marijuana that is within the law. Further, a physician may not be prosecuted for providing a MMJ recommendation to a prospective patient after the doctor has examined the person, diagnosed a debilitating medical condition and discussed the pros and cons of the use of medical marijuana with the patient.

In order to become a medical marijuana patient in Michigan, an individual must visit a state-approved doctor who may prescribe treatment. If they choose to grow and use marijuana, patients and caregivers are required to register with the Bureau of Health Professions, Department of Community Health. Those patients who wish to cultivate their own marijuana are required to keep the plants in an enclosed and locked facility. When grown outdoors the plants must not be visible from ground level or from any permanent structure. The plants may be kept by the patient only if he or she has not specified a primary caregiver to cultivate the marijuana for them. Caregivers must be of at least 21 years old and are not permitted to provide medicine for more than five patients.

Even though medical marijuana is legal in the state, an employee can still be fired if they test positive on a drug test, despite having a doctor's recommendation. Employers are not required to accommodate the ingestion of medical marijuana by any employee.

Marijuana, paraphernalia, or licit property possessed under this Act shall not be seized. Out of state registry identification cards are accepted in Michigan.

Using medical cannabis is legal as long as nothing is done while under the influence of marijuana that would constitute negligence or professional malpractice. It is not legal to possess or use medical marijuana in a school bus, on the grounds of a school, or in a correctional facility. It is not allowable to smoke marijuana on public transportation, in any public place, or to operate or control any type of motor vehicle. Insurance companies are not required to cover the costs of the use of medical marijuana.

The original law was amended recently in House Bill 4856, effective December 31, 2012. The new law made it illegal to transport or possess usable marijuana by car unless the marijuana is "enclosed in a case that is carried in the trunk of the vehicle." Violation of the law is a misdemeanor punishable by imprisonment for not more than 93 days or a fine of not more than $500.00, or both. It was again amended by House Bill 4834, effective April 1, 2013. This time, the amendment required a patient show proof of Michigan residency when applying for a registry ID card (driver license, official state ID, or valid voter registration) and makes cards valid for two years instead of one. In another change (found in HB4851), also effective April 1, 2013, the "bona fide physician-patient relationship" is more clearly defined. Under the law, this is one in which the physician "has created and maintained records of the patient's condition in accord with medically accepted standards" and "will provide follow-up care."

In February 2013, The Michigan Supreme Court ruled in *Michigan vs. Mc-Queen* in a 4–1 vote that dispensaries are illegal. The justices ruled that the transfer of medical marijuana between patients in dispensaries is not included in the original Michigan Medical Marijuana Act passed in 2008. As a result, medical marijuana patients in Michigan were then forced to grow their own marijuana or get it from a designated caregiver who is limited to five patients. In response, the Michigan House of Representatives proposed a bill that would allow for medical marijuana dispensaries to be established so that patients have safe access to the drug. The Medical Marijuana Provisioning Center Regulation Act would allow cities to permit or deny dispensaries in their community.[23]

Montana

A ballot initiative allowing for medical marijuana in Montana was passed on November 2, 2004, through Initiative 148 with 62 percent of the vote. They became the 11th state to pass a medical marijuana law. The initiative gave certain patients under medical supervision and with defined medical conditions the right to alleviate their symptoms through the use of marijuana. The Medical Marijuana law went into effect immediately after passage. In addition to legalizing the use of marijuana for patients, the law also allows a registered patient and their caregiver to grow and/or possess a limited number of marijuana plants. Patients are allowed to have 1 ounce of usable marijuana and four mature plants and twelve seedlings. The conditions for which a patient could receive a prescription for medical marijuana in Montana include cancer, glaucoma, HIV/AIDS, cachexia, severe or chronic pain, severe nausea, seizures, including seizures caused by epilepsy, or severe or persistent muscle spasms, including spasms caused by multiple sclerosis or Crohn's disease, or any other medical condition or treatment for a medical condition adopted by the department by rule.

Montana has created dispensaries to sell medical cannabis to its patients. In order to receive marijuana, patients must register by paying a fee of $25 for a new application, or $10 for a renewal application. They do not accept ID cards from other states. In order to receive a registration card, patients must have a doctor's certification; pay the application or renewal fee; provide their name, address and date of birth; their caretakers name, address and date of birth; and physicians name, address and date of birth. The Department shall issue a registry identification card to the caregiver. A caregiver in Montana cannot have a previous conviction for a felony drug offense.

A qualifying patient or caregiver possessing a valid registration card may not be arrested, prosecuted or penalized in any manner for their medical use of marijuana as long as it is within the law. Possession of a registration card or an application for a card does not alone give a law enforcement officer the probable cause to conduct a search. Montana does not permit driving a motor vehicle under the influence, smoking on a school bus or any public transportation, smoking in jail, smoking at any public park, public beach, recreation center or youth center. A government agency or an employer is not required to accommodate the medical use of marijuana.

The ballot initiative was amended with Montana Senate Bill 423, which was passed on April 28, 2011, signed by the Governor on May 3, 2011, and took effect on July 1, 2011. The new law required patients to be residents of the state. Patients must provide proof of their chronic pain by a second physician to qualify for a registration card. They must also carry their registration cards at all times. The number of mature marijuana plants allowed per patient was lowered from six to four, and the plants cannot be grown in view of the street or a public place.[24] In order to grow and use marijuana under the Montana medical marijuana law, patients and caregivers need to register with Quality Assurance Division of the Department of Public Health and Human Services. On November 6, 2012, Montana voters chose to uphold SB 423 in referendum No. 124 by a vote of 56.5 percent to 43.5 percent.

Nevada

Voters in Nevada agreed to allow medical marijuana on November 7, 2000, when they voted for Ballot Question 9, with 65 percent of the voters agreeing to the proposal. The law became effective on October 1, 2001. It removes state-level criminal penalties on the use, possession and cultivation of marijuana by patients who have written documentation from their physician of a chronic or debilitating medical condition, and that marijuana may alleviate the condition. The approved conditions for use of medical marijuana in Nevada include AIDS, cancer, glaucoma, cachexia, persistent muscle spasms or seizures, severe nausea or pain. Other conditions are subject to approval by the health division of the state Department of Human Resources. Patients or their primary caregivers are legally permitted to have up to one ounce of usable marijuana, as well as seven plants (three mature, four immature).

Other requirements to become a patient include residency within the state and registration as a patient. The registry is a state-run, confidential program that issues identification cards to patients. All patients must pay a $50 application fee, plus $150 for the card (new or renewal), plus $15–42 in additional related costs. A person who holds a registry card is not exempt from state prosecution for driving or operating a vehicle or a vessel under power or sail while under the influence of marijuana; possessing a firearms; possessing marijuana in violation of the law; engaging in marijuana use in any public place, or any local detention facility (jail state prison, or reformatory), providing marijuana for another person who does not hold a registry card.

Possession of a registry card is not grounds for search or inspection by law enforcement in Nevada. It is not probable cause to search a person or their property. If any property is seized by state or local law enforcement, the law enforcement agency should ensure that the property is not destroyed. The property should be returned immediately.

The law establishes a program for evaluation and research of medical marijuana at the University of Nevada School of Medicine. This involves research on the treatment of people who have been diagnosed with chronic or debilitating medical conditions.

The original ballot initiative was amended in Assembly Bill 453, which became effective on October 1, 2001. This amendment created a state registry for patients whose physicians recommend medical marijuana and tasked the Department of Motor Vehicles with issuing identification cards. The program was to be funded entirely by donations.

New Jersey

On January 11, 2010, the New Jersey legislature approved a proposal (Senate Bill 119) to make the state the 14th state in the nation to legalize the use of medical marijuana by patients with chronic illnesses. The vote on the Compassionate Use of Medical Marijuana Act was 48–14 in the House of Representatives and in the Senate it was 15–13. Patients diagnosed with illnesses such as cancer, AIDS, Lou Gehrig's disease, muscular dystrophy and multiple sclerosis would be permitted to have access to marijuana grown and distributed through state-regulated dispensaries. Governor Jon S. Corzine signed the bill into law on January 18, 2010, and it became law six months later.[25]

The new law protects patients who use medical marijuana as a way to alleviate suffering from debilitating medical conditions, as well as their physicians, primary caregivers, and those who are authorized to produce marijuana for medical purposes from arrest, prosecution, property forfeiture, and criminal and other penalties. Medical conditions that would apply in this case include seizure disorders (i.e. epilepsy), intractable skeletal muscular spasticity, glaucoma, severe or chronic pain, severe nausea or vomiting, cachexia, HIV/AIDS, cancer, amyotrophic lateral sclerosis (Lou Gehrig's disease), multiple sclerosis, muscular dystrophy, or inflammatory bowel disease, including Crohn's disease, or any terminal illness. If a physician would like to consider treatment for another disease or condition, he or she must get approval from the Department of Health and Senior Services. Physicians can determine how much marijuana a patient needs, depending on their specific disease, and then give written instructions to be presented to a treatment center. The maximum amount for a 30-day period is two ounces.

Since the law does not allow for patient cultivation of marijuana, there will be alternative treatment centers created throughout the state. The first two centers issued a permit in each region will be nonprofit agencies, and centers created after that may be either nonprofit or for-profit entities. In order to use a dispensary's services, a patient must register with the state. The registry fee for patients is $200, which is valid for two years. There are reduced fees for patients who qualify for state or federal assistance programs. The name and address of the physician and caregiver must be provided. New Jersey dispensaries do not accept other states' registry ID cards.

However, a caregiver can grow cannabis. Caregivers must be at least eighteen years of age and have a clean drug background. This person must pay a $200 fee and pass a background check before they are permitted to begin growing medical cannabis. Patients and caregivers need to register with the Department of Health and Senior Services.

Someone using medical marijuana cannot operate, navigate or be in control of any vehicle, aircraft, train, heavy equipment or vessel while under the influence of marijuana. A person cannot smoke marijuana in a school bus or other form of public transportation, in a private vehicle while being operated, at any public park or beach, or any recreation center.

On February 3, 2011, the Department of Health and Senior Services proposed new rules to streamline the permit process for cultivating and dispensing marijuana. It also prohibited home delivery of marijuana by the treatment centers, and required that the medical conditions listed in the original law be revised to include the stipulation that the diseases must be resistant to conventional medical therapy in order to qualify as a debilitating medical conditions.

The patient registration system for the New Jersey Medical Marijuana Program was opened on August 9, 2012. In order to register as a patient, a person must have a physician's recommendation, a government-issued ID, and proof of residency.

The first dispensary permit was issued in New Jersey on October 16, 2012, to Greenleaf Compassion Center, allowing it to operate as an Alternative Treatment Center and dispense medical marijuana to qualified patients. The center opened on December 6, 2012. At the same time, five other treatment centers were in various stages of finalizing their locations or background examinations of their employees.

New Mexico

A law permitting the use of medical marijuana received enough votes to pass the New Mexico legislature in 2007, making it the 12th state to pass a medical marijuana law. Senate Bill 523, the Lynn and Erin Compassionate Use Act, was approved on March 13, 2007, when the House voted 36–31 to support the bill and the Senate voted 32–3 in favor. The bill became effective on July 1, 2007, after Governor Bill Richardson signed it. The Act removes state-level criminal penalties related to the use and possession of marijuana by ailing patients who used the drug to alleviate the symptoms caused by debilitating medical conditions and their medical treatments. The New Mexico Department of Health was designated as the agency responsible for the implementation of the program, particularly the registration of patients, caregivers, and providers.[26]

According to the law in New Mexico, there are fifteen qualifying conditions for medical cannabis. They include severe chronic pain, painful peripheral neuropathy, intractable nausea/vomiting, severe anorexia/cachexia, hepatitis C infection, Crohn's disease, Post-Traumatic Stress Disorder, ALS (Lou Gehrig's disease), cancer, glaucoma, multiple sclerosis, damage to the nervous tissue of the spinal cord with intractable spasticity, epilepsy, HIV/AIDS, and hospice patients. These patients, once identified by a physician, are permitted to possess up to six ounces of usable cannabis, four mature plants and 12 seedlings. A primary caregiver may provide services to a maximum of four qualified patients under the Medical Cannabis Program.

While patients can apply for a license to produce their own medical cannabis, New Mexico also utilizes dispensaries to sell medical cannabis. To use a dispensary, patients must first register. New Mexico does not charge a fee to register. It also does not accept registration cards from other states. Dispensaries get their marijuana from commercial growers who are registered with the state to cultivate up to 150 cannabis plants, to be distributed to dispensaries.

Those who legally use medical marijuana under the Compassionate Use Act (or their caregivers) are not immune from criminal prosecution for activities not authorized in the Act. It is illegal for patients to operate a vehicle while under the influence of cannabis, or to use it in a school bus or public vehicle, or on school property, a public park or recreation center.

The law also stipulates that the Secretary of Heath should create an advisory board of eight practitioners who specialize in neurology, pain management, medical oncology, psychiatry, infectious disease, family medicine and genecology. The board members will review petitions to add medical conditions to the list of conditions that qualify for medical marijuana.

Oregon

A medical marijuana law passed in Oregon on November 3, 1998, with Ballot Measure 67, the Oregon Medical Marijuana Act. It passed with 55 percent of the vote and became effective one month later, on December 3, 1998. The law removes state-level criminal penalties on the use, possession and cultivation of marijuana by patients who possess a signed recommendation from their physician stating that marijuana "may mitigate" his or her debilitating symptoms. Approved conditions for medical marijuana in Oregon include cancer, glaucoma, HIV/AIDS, a medical condition or treatment for a medical condition that produces cachexia, severe pain, severe nausea, seizures, including seizures caused by epilepsy, or persistent muscle spasms, including spasms caused by multiple sclerosis. Other conditions are subject to approval by the Health Division of the Oregon Department of Human Resources.[27]

In order to qualify to be a medical marijuana patient, a person must possess valid, written documentation from a physician indicating that the person has a debilitating medical condition and that medical marijuana may help relieve the symptoms of the condition. The patient must also provide their address and date of birth; the name of the physician; and identification of the caregiver. They must pay the required fees of $200 for a new applicant or a renewal applicants, or $100 for a renewal application, or for those receiving SNAP (food stamp). If a person is receiving SSI benefits, the cost is only $20. If a person grows their own marijuana, they must pay an additional $50 grow site registration fee.

Patients approved to use medical marijuana can have up to 24 ounces of usable marijuana and up to twenty-four plants (six mature, eighteen immature). Grow sites will also be established by the Department of Human Services. Cardholders can register and be authorized to produce marijuana. Once a grow site is approved, the registration card must be displayed at all times while the marijuana is being produced.

An eleven-member advisory Committee on Medical Marijuana was established within the Department of Human Services. The members will be people who possess registry cards, designated primary caregivers and advocates of medical marijuana and will advise the director on administration of the act, review current rules and make suggestions for changes.

A person who has been given a registry card may use medical marijuana only as justified to mitigate their symptoms. The patient and their caregiver is exempted from the criminal laws of Oregon for possession, delivery, or other offenses related to the use of marijuana. However, they are not permitted to drive under the influence of marijuana, smoke marijuana in a public place or in a correctional facility or youth facility. They cannot manufacture marijuana in a place other than the authorized grow site.

The original law was amended (effective July 21, 1999) in House Bill 3052. The amendment mandates that patients (or their caregivers) may only cultivate marijuana in one location. This bill also states that law enforcement officials who seize marijuana from a patient pending trial do not have to keep those plants alive. Additionally, the amendment adds "agitation due to Alzheimer's disease" to the list of debilitating conditions qualifying for medical marijuana use.

The 2005 Oregon Legislature passed Senate Bill 1085, which took effect on January 1, 2006, that again amended the original bill. This new bill raised the quantity of cannabis that authorized patients may possess from seven plants (with no more than three mature) and three ounces of cannabis to six mature cannabis plants, eighteen immature seedlings, and twenty-four ounces of usable plant. The bill also changed the penalty for exceeding the amount allowed for state-qualified patients. The new guidelines no longer give patients the ability to argue an "affirmative defense" of medical necessity at trial if they exceed the allowed number of plants. But patients who are within the limits retain the ability to raise an affirmative defense at trial even if they fail to register with the state.

On November 2, 2010, 55.79 percent of Oregon Voters rejected Measure 74, which would have allowed for the creation of state-regulated dispensaries.

Rhode Island

The legislature in Rhode Island legalized medical marijuana in 2006 by passing Senate Bill 0710, the Edward O. Hawkins and Thomas C. Slater Medical Marijuana Act. When it was passed, Rhode Island became the 11th state to pass medical marijuana laws. The law simply spelled out how much marijuana patients and their caretakers could possess and grow, but did not include provisions about consumption and distribution. The bill was approved by the House (52 to 10) and Senate (33 to 1), but vetoed by Governor Donald Carcieri on June 29, 2005. The veto was over-ridden by the House and Senate and the law went into effect on January 3, 2006.[28]

The legislation outlines the conditions for which medical marijuana can be prescribed. These include cancer, glaucoma, HIV/AIDS, Hepatitis C, a chronic or debilitating disease or medical condition or its treatment that produces cachexia or wasting syndrome; severe, debilitating, chronic pain; severe nausea; seizures, including but not limited to, those characteristic of epilepsy; or severe and persistent muscle spasms, including but not limited to, those characteristic of multiple sclerosis or Crohn's disease; or agitation of Alzheimer's Disease; or any other medical condition or its treatment approved by the state Department of Health. In order to use medical marijuana, patients must have written approval from a doctor stating that the medical benefits of cannabis will outweigh the potential health hazards.

The law limits the amount of marijuana that can be possessed and grown to up to twelve marijuana plants or 2.5 ounces of cultivated marijuana. Primary caregivers may not possess an amount of marijuana in excess of twenty-four marijuana plants and five ounces of usable marijuana for qualifying patients to whom he or she is connected through the Department's registration process.

Medical marijuana patients in Rhode Island must register and pay a registry fee of $75, or $10 for applicants on Medicaid or Supplemental Security Income (SSI). If a person has medical marijuana registry identification card from any other state, U.S. territory, or the District of Columbia, they can use it in Rhode Island. It has the same force and effect as a card issued by the Rhode Island Department of Health.

In 2009, changes to the original bill were made in House Bill 5359. The amendment, which became effective on June 16, 2009, allows for the creation of state-approved compassion centers, which may acquire, possess, cultivate, manufacture, deliver, transfer, transport, supply, or dispense marijuana, or related supplies and educational materials, to registered qualifying patients and their registered primary caregivers. However, in 2011 the governor put a halt on the implementation of those dispensaries, because of the threats from the federal government. In essence government officials informed the leadership in Rhode Island that they would become the new target of federal raids and prosecution, if they allowed these dispensaries to operate. In late spring of 2012, the governor decided he would allow three dispensaries to open, but they would not be permitted to cultivate more than 99 mature cannabis plants, or 150 total plants.

Under the new legislation, three Compassion Centers will be licensed by the Department of Health. They would be not-for-profit agencies that will acquire, possess, cultivate, manufacture, deliver, transfer, transport, supply or dispense marijuana to registered patients and their caregivers. Patients wanting marijuana need a registration card. In order to be issued a registry identification card, patients must submit an application fee; their name, address, and date of birth; name, address, and phone number of the physician and the caregiver, if any. A person may not serve as a primary caregiver if he or she has a felony drug conviction. The information submitted is confidential, and it is a punishable crime (up to 180 days in jail and a $1,000 fine) to breach that confidentiality.

Currently in Rhode Island, it is illegal to smoke marijuana in a school bus or other form of public transportation, on school grounds, in a correctional facility, or where exposure to marijuana smoke could significantly adversely affect the health, safety or welfare of children. No government program or private health insurer will be forced to reimburse a person for costs associated with medical use of marijuana.

Vermont

Medical marijuana was legalized in 2004 in Vermont through Senate Bill 76 and House Bill 645, an Act Relating to Marijuana Use by Persons with Severe Illness. Governor James Douglas (R) allowed the act to turn into a law unsigned on May 26, 2004 and the law became effective on July 1, 2004. The Act grants patients who have chronic or debilitating medical conditions the right to legally alleviate their symptoms through the use of marijuana. With this law, a patient with written documentation and a registry identification card to legally use marijuana. The law also allows patients and caregivers to obtain marijuana for medical use without fear of sanctions or criminal prosecution. The conditions for which medical marijuana can be used include cancer, AIDS/HIV, multiple sclerosis, or the treatment of these conditions if the disease or the treatment results in severe, persistent, and intractable symptoms; or a disease, medical condition, or its treatment that is chronic, debilitating and produces severe, persistent, and one or more of the following intractable symptoms: cachexia or wasting syndrome, severe pain, nausea or seizures.

Vermont medical marijuana patients can have no more than two mature marijuana plants, seven immature plants, and two ounces of usable marijuana may be collectively possessed between the registered patient and the patient's registered caregiver. Patients must register with the state. To do so, they must pay a fee of $50. Patients can assign a caregiver, who must be at least 21 years of age, and never been convicted of a drug-related crime. A person can submit an application to the Department of Public Safety to become a caregiver. They can be a caregiver for only one patient at a time.

To become a registered patient, a person must be diagnosed with a chronic, debilitating condition by a licensed physician. The patient must submit documentation to the Department of Public Safety with identification and contact information for the patient, caregiver and physician. A statement must be attached that verifies that reasonable medical efforts have been made over a reasonable amount of time to relieve symptoms. A review board will be established comprised of three licensed Vermont physicians. The board members can hear appeals for denied registration applicants.

A person who has a valid registration card who is in compliance with the law is exempt from arrest or prosecution. However, a law enforcement officer shall not be required to return marijuana or other paraphernalia that has been seized from a registered caregiver. A patient can be arrested and/or prosecuted for being under the influence of marijuana while operating a vehicle, boat, or vessel, or for being in a workplace or place of employment, or for operating heavy machinery. They also cannot smoke marijuana in a school bus, public bus or other public vehicle, in a workplace or place of employment, on any school grounds, in a correctional facility or in a public park, beach or recreation center.

A registered patient or caregiver who chooses to grow marijuana must keep it in a secure, indoor facility. They must not transport the drug in public unless it is secured in a locked container.

Vermont's medical marijuana law was amended with Senate Bill 00007, effective May 30, 2007. This amendment increased the amount of marijuana a patient could cultivate from three plants (one mature, two immature) to nine (two mature, seven immature). However the amendment did not raise the amount a patient or caregiver could possess. This amendment also makes it possible for doctors in states that neighbor Vermont to prescribe medical marijuana to Vermont residents. Four medical marijuana dispensaries are also permitted in the state, and each allowed to serve up to a maximum of 1,000 patients.[29]

The law was again amended with Senate Bill 17, "An Act Relating To Registering Four Nonprofit Organizations To Dispense Marijuana For Symptom Relief." This was signed by Governor Peter Shumlin on June 2, 2011. The amendment established a framework for registering up to four nonprofit marijuana dispensaries in the state. A dispensary would be permitted to cultivate and possess at any one time up to 28 mature marijuana plants, 98 immature marijuana plants, and 28 ounces of usable marijuana.

Washington

Medical marijuana became legal in Washington on November 3, 1998 with Initiative 692, the Washington State Medical Use of Marijuana Act that passed with 59 percent of the vote. It became effective the same day. The law removes state-level criminal penalties on the use, possession and cultivation of marijuana by patients who possess "valid documentation" from their physician affirming that he or she suffers from a debilitating condition and that the "potential benefits of the medical use of marijuana would likely outweigh the health risks." Approved conditions for using medical marijuana include Cachexia; cancer; HIV or AIDS; epilepsy; glaucoma; intractable pain, and multiple sclerosis. Other conditions are subject to approval by the Washington Board of Health.[30]

Medical marijuana patients in Washington are allowed to possess, use and cultivate their own medication. Patients or their primary caregivers may legally possess or cultivate no more than a 60-day supply of marijuana. The Department of Health may permit certain individuals to grow/possess more than those amounts, on an as-needed basis. A caregiver must be at least 18 years of age and are only allowed to grow marijuana for one patient at a time. Washington law states that the caregiver is prohibited from consuming any of the cannabis that he/she grows for patients. The law does not establish a state-run patient registry.

The original law was amended with Senate Bill 6032, which became effective on July 1, 2008. This amendment added additional medical conditions to the list of approved conditions for medical marijuana. The added conditions are Crohn's disease, Hepatitis C with debilitating nausea or intractable pain, diseases, including anorexia, which result in nausea, vomiting, wasting, appetite loss, cramping, seizures, muscle spasms, or spasticity, when those conditions are unrelieved by standard treatments or medications.

To become a qualifying patient in Washington, a person must be a resident of the State of Washington, a patient under a licensed physician, and been diagnosed with a terminal or debilitating medical condition. A qualifying patient and designated provider may possess a total of no more than twenty-four ounces of usable marijuana, and no more than fifteen plants. This quantity became the state's official "60-day supply" on November 2, 2008.

On January 21, 2010, the Supreme Court of Washington ruled in *State v. Fry* that Ballot Initiative 692 did not legalize marijuana, but rather provided an authorized user with an affirmative defense if the user shows compliance with the requirements for medical marijuana possession.

On April 1, 2010, Washington State expanded the list of medical professionals who were authorized to recommend medical marijuana to patients. Under the new law, additional medical professionals will be allowed to authorize the use of medical marijuana for qualified patients under a measure signed into law by Governor Christine Gregoire. Gregoire signed the bill on April 1, 2010 and it took effect June 10, 2010. It adds physician assistants, naturopaths, advanced registered nurse practitioners and others to the list of those who can officially recommend marijuana for patients under the state's medical marijuana law. Under previous law, only physicians were allowed to write the recommendation. The medical marijuana measure is Senate Bill 5798.[31]

The original bill was again amended by SB 5073, effective July 22, 2011. Governor Gregoire signed sections of the bill and partially vetoed others. Gregoire struck down sections related to creating state-licensed medical marijuana dispensaries and a voluntary patient registry.

Even though it is legal in the state, an employee can still be fired if they test positive on a drug test, despite having a doctor's recommendation. Other limitations include that no health insurer can be required to pay for the medical use of marijuana; work, school busses, school grounds, youth facilities and correctional facilities are not required to accommodate the on-site use of medical marijuana; patients are not allowed to smoke in any public place in which smoking of any kind is prohibited under the Washington Clean Indoor Air Act. It is a misdemeanor to use or display medical cannabis in a manner or place that is open to the view of the general public. Health care professions are exempted from the state's criminal laws, and should not be penalized in any manner for advising a patient about the risks and benefits of using marijuana, or for providing a patient with valid documentation that marijuana may benefit a patient.

District of Columbia

In 1998 voters in the District of Columbia approved the compassionate use of medical cannabis by an overwhelming 69 percent majority in Initiative 59 (the Legalization of Marijuana for Medical Treatment Initiative). However, a Congressional ban on the issue prevented city lawmakers from implementing the law. Thus, patients were restricted from cultivating their own plants and there were no dispensaries in place, no one was able to take advantage of the law. However, medical marijuana passed in the District of Columbia in 2010 when Amendment Act B18-622, the "Legalization of Marijuana for Medical Treatment Amendment Act of 2010" was approved by the Council of the District of Columbia on May 4, 2010 by a 13–0 vote. It was signed by the mayor on May 21, 2010. After it was signed by the mayor, it underwent a 30-day Congressional review period. Neither the Democratically-controlled Senate nor the House acted to overrule the bill, so it became effective when the review period ended, which was July 27, 2010.

The law allows a patient to possess two ounces of dried marijuana. The limits on other forms of the drug will be determined. Those patients who qualify as low-income individuals to obtain their medical cannabis at a reduced-cost from the normal price.

The law allows patients with cancer, glaucoma, HIV/AIDS, multiple sclerosis, other conditions that are chronic, long-lasting, debilitating, or that interfere with the basic functions of life, serious medical conditions for which the use of medical marijuana is beneficial, patients undergoing treatments such as chemotherapy and radiotherapy to possess up to four ounces of the drug.[32]

The new law requires the DC Department of Health to oversee the creation of as many as eight facilities to distribute medical marijuana to qualified patients. These facilities are allowed to be either non-profit or for-profit but are limited to growing 95 plants or less per facility at any given time. Additionally, qualified patients are not permitted to cultivate marijuana within the safety and security of their own homes. In order for patients to obtain medical marijuana under the DC law, they must register with the District Department of Health.

Other regulations are listed in the law. Those include: a patient shall not administer medical marijuana at a dispensary or cultivation center; a patient shall not use medical marijuana in a place where smoke would adversely affect the health, safety or welfare of a minor; when transporting medical cannabis, it should be in a labeled container or sealed package. A patient cannot operate, navigate or control a motor vehicle, aircraft or motorboat while under the influence of medical marijuana.

A physician can recommend marijuana to a patient based on their medical history, current medical condition, and after considering other approved medications that may provide relief to the patient. The physician shall not be subject to arrest, prosecution or disciplinary proceeding for advising a patient about medical marijuana. A medical marijuana program will be established to regulate the manufacture, cultivation, distribution, dispensing, purchase, delivery, sale, possession, and administration of medical marijuana. The program will be administered by the mayor. All qualified patients and caregivers should be registered here, as are all dispensaries and cultivation centers. They will distribute registration cards.

There can be no more than five dispensary centers in the District, but they may increase that number to as many as eight if needed. All dispensaries and cultivation centers should maintain complete and current records of each employee, each transaction, the quantity of marijuana distributed, the need given for the marijuana, the recipient of the marijuana, the quantity of marijuana held at the center, and any other information required by the mayor. They must also keep records of each patient, including their name and address. Dispensary officials must develop educational materials about drug interactions that may occur when using medical cannabis. All dispensaries will be subject to both announced and unannounced inspections. They must also establish a system to provide medical marijuana for patients who are unable to afford a sufficient supply of medical marijuana based on their income and existing financial resources. They cannot dispense more than two ounces of marijuana to a patient in a thirty-day period. They can have no more than 95 plants at any time.

A dispensary shall not be visible from any public property, and it cannot be located within a residential district or within 300 feet of a preschool, primary or secondary school or recreation center. All dispensaries should not be for profit. Each center must develop a staffing plan, a security plan, a cultivation plan, and a product safety and labeling plan. The mayor would be required to establish a Medical Marijuana Advisory Committee that will monitor best practices in other states that allow medical marijuana and oversee scientific research on medical marijuana. The committee shall give a report to the mayor and council recommending changes, if needed.

Conclusion

Despite federal laws that outlaw the use of marijuana for any reason, many states have passed laws allowing the compassionate use of the drug for patients suffering from debilitating diseases. Some have passed through legislative action, whereas others have been passed by the voters. The specifics of the laws vary from state to states, as do the rights given to patients. But this shows that many people believe the possible health benefits to those who are suffering outweigh any possible risks that may occur from using the drug.

Review/Discussion Questions

1. How are state laws regarding medical marijuana similar and/or different?

2. What are some medical conditions for which medical marijuana can be used?
3. Choose one state and describe the law on medical marijuana. Choose another state and compare/contrast those two state laws.
4. Design the "perfect" state medical marijuana law.
5. Describe the different methods states have for providing marijuana to qualified patients. Which is the best method?

Key Terms

Marijuana ID Card
Compassion Centers
Dispensaries
Affirmative Defense of Medical Necessity
Qualified Patient
Caregiver

Chapter 4

States Considering Medical Marijuana Laws

Overview: Some states have successfully passed laws to allow for medical marijuana, whereas others have not been successful in this endeavor. The states in which marijuana laws have been considered, but not yet passed, are described here.

Introduction

While many states have passed laws to allow patients to use medical marijuana to alleviate symptoms of serious medical conditions, other states have considered or attempted such laws but have not been successful. This chapter shows what states have attempted yet failed to pass laws to legalize medical marijuana, and the status of their attempts.

Alabama

Legislators in Alabama have considered medical marijuana bills since 2005. That year, HB 703 was introduced into the state legislature to authorize medical marijuana for certain patients who have been diagnosed as having a debilitating medical condition. The bill was reintroduced in February of 2006 as House Bill 663. In 2007, the proposed bill included the phrase "would be regulated in the same manner as other controlled substances." The phrase was removed in the 2008 version (HB679).[1] In 2009, Representative Patricia Todd (D) proposed HB434, to allow for medical use of marijuana. None of these bills were given much attention by legislators.

In 2010, there were two bills concerning medical cannabis introduced: HB207 (The Michael Phillips Compassionate Care Act) and HB642.[2] Under the bills, patients suffering from cancer and other serious ailments could, with a doctor's recommendation, possess up to 2.5 ounces of marijuana and could grow their own medicine if they so chose. The bills made a distinction between medical and non-medical uses of marijuana. The medical conditions for which marijuana could be used included cancer, glaucoma, multiple sclerosis, chronic arthritis, cachexia, chronic pain, fibromyalgia, migraine, AIDS, anorexia, seizures, severe nausea and other symptoms that substantially limit the ability of a person to conduct major life activities.[3] The bills would also allow for licensed dispensaries where patients could obtain their medicine. Patients would first have to apply for and be granted a state-issued identification card. During this session, the House Judiciary Committee members voted "yes" on the bill. The bill went to the House floor, but the legislature adjourned before voting on the bill.[4] Even though it did not pass, it was the first time a medical marijuana bill passed the first step toward becoming law in the state of Alabama.[5]

In 2011, Representative Todd again proposed a bill to regulate medical marijuana (HB 386). Again called the Michael Phillips Compassionate Care Act, the bill did not pass. Todd tried again in 2012, this time as HB25. Another bill, HB 66, was proposed by Representative K.L. Brown (R), and was known as the Alabama Medical Marijuana Patients' Rights Act. It would create a safe and regulated program for marijuana use by patients as a way to relieve their pain and suffering. During this session, there was a letter writing campaign whereby supporters were asked to write letters to the officials in the House and Senate. The purpose was to bring the bill to the attention of legislators, discover their viewpoints as a way to focus their resources on those who supported the bill.[6] Both bills died when the legislative session ended.[7]

During the 2013 session, Representative Todd introduced a law for the medical exemption for use and possession of marijuana for certain patients who have been diagnosed by a physician as having a serious medical condition and been issued a valid medical marijuana identification card. The bill, HB 315, was also known at the Alabama Medical Exemption Act. Representative Todd also introduced HB2, The Alabama Medical Marijuana Patients' Rights Act, to authorize the medical use of marijuana only for certain qualifying patients who have been diagnosed by a physician as having a serious medical condition. This time, the Committee on Health voted 12–2 not to advance the bill, which killed the proposal.

Florida

On February 27, 2013, Senator Jeff Clemens (D) proposed Senate Bill 1250, to allow a qualifying patient to possess and administer medical cannabis, and/or authorizing the patient's caregiver to possess and administer medical cannabis to the qualifying patient. As defined in the law, the maximum amount of medical cannabis which a qualifying patient or the patient's caregiver could possess was four ounces of dried cannabis, eight mature marijuana plants, or eight immature plants. The Senate version, SB 1139, was introduced by Representative Katie Edwards (D) the next day. This bill died in the Health Policy Committee.

Idaho

In 2011, there was an informational hearing on a medical marijuana bill in the Committee on Health and Welfare in Idaho's House of Representatives. In that meeting, Representative Tom Trail (R) and some marijuana patients gave testimony about the need for a medical marijuana program in the state. But the bill went nowhere. In 2012, Representative Trail introduced House Bill 370, the Idaho Compassionate Use Medical Marijuana Act. The bill was a proposal to establish a distinction between medical and nonmedical uses of marijuana. The purpose was to protect users of medical marijuana from arrest, prosecution, property forfeiture, and criminal penalties. It would also cover their physicians, primary caregivers and those who are authorized to produce marijuana for medical purposes.[8] But it also did not pass.

Illinois

In 2009, Senate Bill 1381 was proposed by Senators William Haine (D), Iris Martinez (D), and Jeff Schoenberg (D) that would allow seriously ill patients with certain conditions to use medical marijuana in Illinois upon the recommendation of their physicians. The bill was passed by the Senate Public Health Committee by a vote of 6-2. In the House of Representatives, HR 2514 was passed by the House Human Services Committee. It was introduced by Lou Lang (D), Angelo Saviano (R), Karen Yarbrough (D), Cynthia Soto (D), Deb Mell (D) and Elizabeth Hernandez (D). Both bills went to the floor of their chambers, but they did not have enough support votes pass, despite a 68 percent approval rate by voters in the state.[9]

House Bill 30, The Compassionate Use of Medical Cannabis Pilot Program Act, was introduced by Representative Lang in 2010. It would allow state-registered patients who have been diagnosed by a physician as having a debilitating medical condition to cultivate medical marijuana or to obtain it from state-regulated dispensaries. Other provisions would repeal the program after three years, prohibit patients from driving for twelve hours after consuming marijuana, make it illegal for dispensaries to make campaign contributions, set a $5,000 non-refundable application fee and $20,000 certificate fee for dispensaries, and exclude public safety personnel from the definition of "qualifying patient."[10] The bill would have prohibited doctors from dispensing the marijuana to their patients. Instead, patients would be permitted to grow it themselves. They would be permitted to possess up to six cannabis plants, three of which could be mature plants. The patients would have to obtain the plants from a state-sanctioned supplier. The bill failed on a 53–59–1 vote (60 was needed for passage).[11]

On March 9, 2011, the Illinois House Human Services Committee voted, 6–5, to approve House Bill 30, the Compassionate Use of Medical Cannabis Pilot Program Act.[12] The Senate version of the bill was SB 1548, filed by Senator Haine (D) on February 9, 2011. Neither bill passed.

Indiana

In 2012, HB 1370 was introduced by Representative Tom Knollman (R), to require the state's Department of Health to adopt rules to regulate registered cardholders, dispensaries, and dispensary employees and to eliminate certain crimes pertaining to medicinal marijuana cardholders, dispensaries, and dispensary employees. The bill died in Committee when the legislative session ended.

Iowa

In 2009, Iowa legislators considered Senate File 293, a bill to create the Medical Marijuana Act, sponsored by Senator Joe Bolkcom (D). The law would allow for the possession and use of marijuana for therapeutic purposes, create compassion centers and provide for criminal and civil penalties for misuse. Those patients deemed qualified (i.e. patients with a medical condition like cancer, hepatitis C, Crohn's disease, AIDS, or other chronic medical condition) would be issued an identification card that would allow them to possess and use marijuana without prosecution or arrest.[13] Four public forums on medical marijuana, sponsored by the Iowa Board of Pharmacy, were held throughout the state.[14] The Board members were seeking both scientific evidence as well as testimony regarding whether marijuana should be allowed for medical purposes in Iowa.[15]

In 2010, most politicians in Iowa refused to discuss the issue of medical marijuana, even though over 60 percent of citizens in the state supported the policy. One activist, Carl Olsen, the director of Iowans for Medical Marijuana, announced he was going to sue the state's Board of Pharmacy over its refusal to issue rules that would allow pharmacies to distribute marijuana as medicine.[16] The Iowa Board of Pharmacy voted 6–0 to propose legislation to reclassify marijuana as a Schedule II drug so that it could be used for medical purposes.[17] However, the Governor-Elect of Iowa at the time, Terry Branstad (R), opposed the idea.[18] The board also recommended that the state create a task force of patients, medical professionals and law enforcement officers who would devise a procedure to implement a medical marijuana program.[19]

That year, Iowa state Representative Clel Baudler (R) (a 71-year-old retired state trooper) went to California to fraudulently obtain a prescription for medical marijuana as a way to show "how asinine it would be to legalize 'medical marijuana'" in Iowa. He was able to obtain a prescription for medical marijuana by telling a doctor in California that he suffered from hemorrhoids and depression, even though he did not. He wanted to show that medical marijuana was just about people who wanted to get high. Unfortunately, lying about a medical condition to a doctor in the state of California was illegal at that time and carried up to a $1,000 fine or six months in jail.[20]

In the 2011–12 legislative session, many bills were proposed concerning medical marijuana. Senator Joe Bolkcom (D) introduced a bill (SF 266) to allow for medical cannabis, including the creation of nonprofit dispensaries. This would allow certain patients to possess no more than two and one-half ounces of usable marijuana and six marijuana plants. The bill died in 2012 when it did not advance out of committee.[21]

Representative Baudler sponsored a bill opposing medical marijuana. HF 183 would deny marijuana's medical value by placing it only in Schedule I (it is currently also in Iowa's Schedule II) and remove the Board's ability to make medical marijuana rules. The bill did not make it out of committee. Similar legislation proposed by Governor Branstad (SSB 3031 and HSB 552) also did not make it out of committee.[22]

In 2013, Senator Bruce Hunter (D) proposed a new law, Senate File 79, to prevent a qualifying patient who has been issued and possesses a registry idenfication card from being arrested or prosecuted for the medical use of marijuana, provided that the marijuana is not under two and one-half ounces and does not exceed six plants, which are in an enclosed, locked facility. The same bill was proposed into the Senate as File 22.

Kansas

In 2008, a bill was considered in a Senate committee in the Kansas legislature that would allow judges to consider a medical condition as defense for marijuana possession. Under the proposal, those with a debilitating illness arrested for the drug's possession could present in court a doctor's written certification that marijuana would offer therapeutic benefits.[23] The bill was not acted on in that session.

Another proposal appeared in 2010 to legalize medical marijuana, but it did not to come to a vote. Representative Gail Finney (D) introduced a bill that would make marijuana legal with a doctor's prescription. The bill would also require all medical marijuana be grown in Kansas.[24]

The following year, in 2011, House Bill 2330, the Cannabis Compassion and Care Act, would provide for the legal growing, selling buying and using cannabis for certain debilitating medical conditions. These patients would be able to use medical cannabis without fear of reprisal under state law; it would protect patients' rights as employees, tenants, and parents. A patient registry system would be established, along with non-profit care centers and a board to oversee the entire program. Patients could legally possess up to six ounces of cannabis.[25] It would provide for the registration and operations of compassion centers, issuing identification cards for patients. The bill died because it did not meet a committee deadline.[26] A similar bill in the Senate, SB 345 was "An Act enacting the cannabis compassion and care Act." This provided for the legal use of cannabis for certain debilitating medical conditions, provided for the registration and functions of compassion centers, and issuing of identification cards. These bills did not receive any action. In January 2012, Senator David Haley (R) proposed the same bill (Senate Bill 9) to create the Cannabis Compassion and Care Act.[27] The proposal died when the legislative session ended.

New proposals were made in 2013, House Bill 2198 and Senate Bill 9, the Cannabis Compassion and Care Act. As proposed in 2012, they would provide for the legal use of cannabis for certain debilitating medical conditions, provide for the registration and functions of compassion centers, and authorize identification cards, and establish a compassion board.

Kentucky

A bill introduced by Senators Perry Clark (D) and Kathy W. Stein (D) in 2012, the Gatewood Galbraith Memorial Medical Marijuana Act (SB 129), would make medical marijuana a Schedule II drug in the state so it could be prescribed by a doctor. The bill was named after the late Gatewood Galbraith, a five-time candidate for Governor and outspoken proponent of ending marijuana prohibition. If passed, marijuana would be allowed for certain patients, with the limitation that a patient may not possess more than five grams of marijuana per month or have more than five marijuana plants for personal use. There was also a provision to require the Board of Pharmacy to establish a certification program for those pharmacies that sought to dispense marijuana to patients. The program would set up rules for prescribing and dispensing the drug. The bill also stipulated that any plants a patient is growing could not be taxed under state law.[28]

SB 129 was assigned to the Senate Judicial Committee, whose chair, Senator Tom Jensen (R), refused to call the measure before committee, effectively killing it. Observers argued the bill was largely symbolic and would not legalize medical marijuana because the bill included the word "prescribe" and federal law prohibits marijuana from being prescribed.

The proposal was made again in 2013, this time as Senate Bill 11. This time, the Gatewood Galbraith Medical Marijuana Memorial Act would to establish a comprehensive system for medical marijuana in Kentucky, including provisions for medical verification of need, persons allowed to cultivate, use, and possess the drug, organizations allowed to assist in providing the drug, regulation by the state Department for Public Health.

Maryland

In May, 2003, the governor of Maryland, Republican Robert Ehrlich, signed new medical marijuana legislation into law. This was the first time that a Republican governor signed a bill to protect medical marijuana patients. Many believed that the laws that then existed in Maryland, the Darrell Putman Compassionate Use Act, was not strong enough because it allowed patients to be a convicted even if they offered a medical necessity defense in court. This meant that even a successful defense would result in a permanent criminal record, which posed barriers to future financial aid, housing, and employment. They noted that Maryland's medical marijuana law was the only state medical marijuana law that did not protect patients from arrest.[29]

In 2007, HB 1040, The Maryland Compassionate Use Act, was introduced into the state legislature. The intent was to create provisions regarding the cultivation of medical marijuana, identification cards for patients, confidentiality issues, fees, transportation, and possession, of marijuana. The law was blocked by the Chair of the Judiciary Committee, Joseph Vallario (D), who refused to put the legislation up for vote.

On 2010, SB 308 was passed by the legislature. It would have provided patients with legal protections.[30] This did not pass, so in 2011, HB 15, the Maryland Medical Marijuana Act, was filed by Delegate Cheryl Glenn (D). The bill would allow for the medical use of marijuana under certain specified circumstances. It also would repeal criminal punishments for use of marijuana. This bill died because the legislative session ended before the bill could go to a vote in the Senate.

The Senate version of the bill, SB 995, was introduced by Senator David Brinkley (R). This bill would establish an affirmative defense to a prosecution for the possession of marijuana or paraphernalia that the defendant was a caregiver for a recognized patient. It would also establish that a specified qualifying patient who has been issued and possessed written certification would not be subject to prosecution, penalty, or denial of a right for the medical use of marijuana, under specified circumstances. The bill died because the legislative session ended before the bill could go to a vote in the House.

In 2012, there were three bills in the House proposing medical marijuana. However, Governor Martin O'Malley (D) was opposed to any bill that named a state agency as a regulatory body for the program because of the fear of threats that Maryland State employees will be federally prosecuted. One of the bills was House Bill 15, introduced by Delegate Glenn (D). It was a proposal to allow patients to cultivate marijuana for medical reasons. The Senate version was SB 995.[31]

In 2013, the House membership debated House Bill 302, the Maryland Medical Marijuana Act, introduced by Delegate Glenn. The law would authorize the medical use of marijuana under certain circumstances. It would repeal criminal provisions of previous laws that allow for the imposition of a fine or the use of an affirmative defense for use or possession of marijuana or possession of drug paraphernalia related to marijuana under specified circumstances.

They also considered House Bill 1100, introduced by Delegate Dan K. Morhaim (D) which would establish an independent Medical Marijuana Oversight Commission. The Commission would be required to issue a registry identification card to approved patients. They would also be responsible for creating a registration program for pharmacies and dispensing centers.

A third bill, House Bill 180, would create a Medical Marijuana Caregiver Affirmative Defense. This bill would confirm that it is an affirmative defense to a prosecution that the possession of marijuana or drug paraphernalia is intended for medical use by an individual with a specified debilitating medical condition for whom the defendant is a specified caregiver. This was introduced by Delegate Glenn. This bill would not legalize medical marijuana, but provide a defense for patient caregivers. This bill was approved by the governor and signed into law on April 9, 2013.

Minnesota

In House File 508, the Courts would be authorized to recognize a necessity defense for criminal, administrative, and civil cases involving Cannabis. Introduced by Representative Alice Hausman (Democratic–Farmer–Labor Party), the proposal would not legalize medical marijuana, but simply provide an affirmative defense for medical marijuana patients.

Mississippi

In 2012, Senator Deborah Dawkins (D) introduced Senate Bill 2252 to authorize the medical use of marijuana by seriously ill patients under a physician's supervision, to provide and exemption from criminal and civil penalties for the medical use of marijuana, and to provide a legal defense for patients and primary caregivers. The proposal died in committee.[32]

Senator Dawkins again introduced the bill in 2013. Senate Bill 2369 was referred to Judiciary committee on January 21, 2013, but again died in committee.

Missouri

In 2008, Missouri considered HB 1830. If this passed, patients would be required to obtain a written recommendation from their doctor before they could apply for an ID card from the state. Registered organizations would be allowed to provide patients with medical marijuana. Under the bill, those diagnosed with cancer, glaucoma, HIV/AIDS, hepatitis C, Alzheimer's disease, rheumatoid arthritis, fibromyalgia, severe migraines, and multiple sclerosis would be permitted to have marijuana. Those who were receiving treatment that produces side effects such as cachexia or wasting syndrome; severe pain; severe nausea; anorexia; seizures, including those characteristic of epilepsy; or severe and persistent muscle spasms, including those characteristic of multiple sclerosis (MS), Lou Gehrig's disease (ALS), or Crohn's disease would also be eligible. Patients would be able to have three mature and four immature plants, and one ounce of marijuana. If a patient was found to be in possession of more than these amounts, an affirmative defense would be available. The bill would protect patients, caregivers, and doctors from arrest, prosecution, and other penalties. A patient's medical marijuana property would be protected from seizure from law enforcement, and if property was seized, then law enforcement must maintain it until it is returned to the patient. The proposal did not have enough support to pass into law.

In 2012, HB 1421 was introduced by Minority Whip Representative Mike Colona (D). The bill was a proposal to change the laws regarding the classification of marijuana as a controlled substance and allows its use for medicinal purposes under certain conditions.

In 2013, House Bill 688 was introduced into the Missouri legislature by Representative Colona (D). This would allow a qualifying patient who possesses written certification from a physician that they shall not be subject to arrest, prosecution, or penalty in any manner for the medical use of marijuana, provided the quantity of marijuana does not exceed an adequate supply. Additionally, the proposal allows for a "nonprofit corporation registered with the state to sell, administer, deliver, dispense, distribute, cultivate, or possess marijuana."

New Hampshire

In 2011, HB 442 was introduced by Representative Evalyn Merrick (D) and then was passed by the House with a vote of 221–96. The purpose of this Act was to protect patients with debilitating medical conditions, as well as their physicians and designated caregivers, from arrest and prosecution, criminal and other penalties, and property forfeiture if such patients engage in the medical use of marijuana. The bill made it to the Senate but died for lack of support.

Senate Bill 309 was then introduced by Senator James Forsythe (R) to allow qualifying patients who possess a registration card to possess six ounces of marijuana and up to six plants (plus twelve seedlings if the patient does not have a designated caregiver). The bill was passed by both the House and Senate, and sent to Governor John Lynch (D), who previously vetoed medical marijuana legislation (HB 648) in 2009. Governor Lynch vetoed Senate Bill 309 on June 21, 2012. He stated in part, "I continue to believe that the most effective manner in which to facilitate the safe and controlled use of marijuana for medical purposes is to distribute the drug like any other controlled substance through a regulated prescription system. I recognize that such a system is unlikely as long as marijuana use for medicinal purposes remains illegal under federal law. As well intentioned as the efforts reflected in SB 409 are, I cannot support establishing a system for the use of medical marijuana that poses risks to the patient, lacks adequate oversight and funding, and risks the proliferation of a serious drug." On June 27, 2012, the Senate members voted

13–10 to override the governor's veto. This vote was three votes short of the sixteen needed to enact SB 409. As a result, the veto was sustained and the bill was considered dead.

In 2013, a bill that would allow New Hampshire citizens to use medical marijuana to treat symptoms of chronic, debilitating diseases was again introduced to the House (HB 573) by Representative Donna Schlachman (D). It was approved by a House committee by a vote of 14–1. The proposal would allow seriously ill patients to use medical marijuana if their doctors recommended it. Those patients who were approved would be permitted to grow up to three mature marijuana plants in their homes, or they could obtain marijuana through one of the five non-profit, state-licensed alternative treatment centers in the state. Governor Maggie Hassan (D) expressed support for the legislation.[33] She signed the bill on July 25, 2013.

New York

SB 2774 was introduced by Representative Tom Duane (D). It would legalize the possession, manufacture, use, delivery, transfer, transport or administration of marijuana by a certified patient or designated caregiver for a certified medical use. It also directs the Department of Health to monitor use of marijuana and establish rules and regulations for registry identification cards. The proposal set a possession limit of 2.5 ounces.

A bill that would legalize the use of medical marijuana in New York State (A 0576) was passed by the Health Committee. The bill had bipartisan support in the Democratic-dominated Assembly and the state's medical community but the governor, George Pataki (R), was opposed.[34]

In 2009, two bills, A 9016 and S 4041-B passed through several committees with support from both sides of the senate. Amendments requested by the Executive Branch were made, resulting in bills A. 11565 and S. 8427. There was an agreement that medical marijuana legislation would be included in the budget, but it was excluded at the last moment.[35]

In the 2011–12 Session, Assembly Bill A7347 was introduced by Assembly Health Committee Chair Richard Gottfried (D) on May 2, 2011. The bill would have legalized the possession, manufacture, use, delivery, transfer, transportation or administration of marijuana by a certified patient or designated caregiver for medical use. The bill was passed by the Assembly by a vote of 90-50 and then sent to the Senate. In the Senate, S 7283 was introduced by Senator Diane Savino (D). The law would have allowed a licensed practitioner to certify that a patient had a serious medical condition for which they were likely to receive benefit from treatment with medical marijuana. Moreover, the bill would allow a certified patient or caregiver who was registered with the state Department of Health to possess up to two and one half ounces of marijuana. The state Department of Health would license and regulate "registered organizations and producers" that would dispense medical marijuana for patients, and would issue registry identification cards to patients and caregivers.

In 2013, Senate Bill 1682 was proposed to legalize the possession, manufacture, sale, administration, delivery, dispensing and distribution of up to eight ounces of marijuana in connection with medical use thereof for certified patients.

North Carolina

House Bill 84, the North Carolina Medical Cannabis Act, was introduced in February, 2013, in the North Carolina legislature. If it was passed into law, qualified patients and their caregivers would not be subject to arrest, prosecution, or penalty for the possession or purchase of cannabis for medical use by the patient. The bill was introduced by Representatives Kelly M. Alexander, Jr. (D) and Pricey Harrison (D). The bill was defeated when the House Rules Committee gave it an unfavorable report.

Ohio

In 2012, HB 214 was introduced by Representatives Kenny Yuko (D) and Robert Hagan (D). Under the proposal, registered qualifying patients or visiting qualifying patient could use medical cannabis if they possessed a valid registry identification card or valid visiting qualifying patient identification card. The bill did not pass.

Oklahoma

In 2010, those who supported medical marijuana met with lawmakers to discuss the issue as part of Medical Marijuana Day at the state Capitol. They provided lawmakers with a copy of the proposed legislation that would set up a task force to study the effects of legalizing marijuana for medical purposes. Senate Bill 732 authored by Senator Constance Johnson (D), would create a commission that would study the diseases and conditions for which marijuana could be prescribed, how much patients could possess, and who could diagnose and prescribe marijuana for patients. Johnson's bill stated the commission would examine "the feasibility of legalizing Delta-9-Tetra-Hydrocannibinol in the State of Oklahoma." However, Senator Clark Jolley, (R), the chairman of the committee to which the bill would be introduced, did not bring the bill up for debate.[36]

The proposed legislation would have allowed for the use of medical marijuana in Oklahoma. Patients diagnosed with certain medical conditions would be included. The conditions were cancer, glaucoma, HIV/AIDS, and any chronic disease or condition that produces cachexia (or wasting syndrome), severe pain, severe nausea, seizures, epilepsy, muscle spasms, including those characteristic of multiple sclerosis or Crohn's disease. This list would also include any other medical condition that a patient's physician has determined would be appropriate.[37]

In 2011, SB 573 was introduced by Senator Johnson. Called the Compassionate Use Act of 2011, the law would remove criminal penalties for a patient who "possesses or cultivates marijuana for the personal medical purposes of the patient upon the written or oral recommendation or approval of a physician." In August of that year, the Democratic Party of Oklahoma passed a resolution in support of medical marijuana legislation. The resolution read, "The Oklahoma Democratic Party supports legislation protecting the doctor patient relationship by allowing medical marijuana with doctor's recommendation."[38] In the end, medical marijuana did not advance before the session ended and therefore failed in 2012.[39]

In 2013, Senate Bill 902 would legalize the possession, manufacture, sale, administration, delivery, dispensing and distribution of up to eight ounces of marijuana for medical use by certified patients. The law would have allowed registered organizations to sell, administer, or deliver, marijuana to certified patients or the caregiver for medical use. It was introduced by Senator Johnson on January 17, 2013.

In 2013, Senate Bill 710, the Compassionate Use Act of 2013 was proposed. This would have allowed qualified patients or their caregivers to possess up to eight ounces of dried cannabis and twelve cannabis plants (unless a doctor recommends a different quantity). It also exempted physicians from being punished for recommending the medical use of cannabis to a patient. The proposal was written by Senator Johnson. This bill failed in committee.

Pennsylvania

In 2009, State Representative Mark Cohen (D) announced his intention to introduce a bill to legalize medical marijuana in Pennsylvania. The bill would allow for prescriptions for marijuana to patients suffering from cancer, multiple sclerosis, and other diseases. Cohen described the bill as providing for benefits to the medical community, but also was a way to increase revenue for the state, up to $25 million a year through taxes.[40]

His bill, HB 1393, would have allowed doctors to legally prescribe marijuana to their patients. It also allowed for state-authorized "compassion centers" where patients could legally purchase the drug as well as provide patients with a registry identification card that identified them as legal medical marijuana users. As he introduced the bill, Cohen told the media, "When public hearings were held on making marijuana illegal by the federal government in the 1930s, the American Medical Association testified against it, pointing out the medical uses of marijuana. Prohibition has long since ended for alcohol. It is now time to end the prohibition of the medical use of marijuana.... Once word came out that I was planning to introduce this legislation, I began receiving phone calls and letters from patients telling me how much legal medical marijuana would greatly alleviate their suffering." He then added, "There are lots of people in every legislative district with cancer, wasting diseases, and HIV demanding we act to allow them to live their lives without pain. In listening to their stories, I know introducing this legislation is the right thing to do."[41] HB 1393 was debated, but never voted on prior to the end of the legislative session.

SB 1350 was introduced by Senator Daylin Leach (D) in 2009. The bill would allow people with some medical conditions to apply for a registry identification card that would permit them to possess up to an ounce of marijuana. Appropriate conditions for medical marijuana use included cancer, multiple sclerosis and epilepsy. Marijuana would be taxed and distributed at "Compassion Centers" run by the state Department of Health. Card holders could also grow up to six plants of their own marijuana.[42]

On April 25, 2011, Senator Leach introduced Senate Bill 1003, named the Compassionate Use Medical Marijuana Act, to allow seriously ill and debilitated citizens to use and possess medical marijuana free from the threat of arrest and prosecution at the state level so long as they have their physicians' recommendations. In addition, this bill would have created state regulated dispensaries so that Pennsylvania patients would have immediate, safe, and reliable access to their medicine. Introduced for the second time in a row, three co-sponsors were Larry Farnese (D), Jim Ferlo (D) and Wayne Fontana (D). Governor Raymond Shafer (R) said the Compassionate Use Medical Marijuana Act provided "for the medical use of marijuana; and repealing provisions of law that prohibit and penalize marijuana use." For the most part, the proposed bill was the same bill that was introduced in 2009–10 in both houses of the General Assembly. The bill included provisions for home cultivation and imposed a state sales tax on medical cannabis.[43]

Another bill was HB 1653, The Governor Raymond Shafer Compassionate Use Medical Marijuana Act, named after Raymond P. Shafer, the former Republican governor (1967–1971) and party leader in the state. He chaired a commission for President Nixon that recommended that marijuana not be placed on Schedule I of the Controlled Substances Act in 1970 and that it should be decriminalized at the federal level.[44]

This bill would have again provided for the medical use of marijuana and a repeal of provisions of state law that prohibited and penalized marijuana use. The bill was introduced by Representative Cohen. HB 1653 included restrictions that the above bill did not, such as limiting the number of dispensaries to one per 250,000 residents (not patients), and limiting a patients' purchases of marijuana to three ounces every two weeks. HB 1653 also mandated that the health department would monitor the possible contamination and potency of medical marijuana.[45] To date, no medical marijuana related bill has been passed in Pennsylvania, largely because the governor, Tom Corbett (R), has threatened to veto any medicinal cannabis legislation.[46]

South Dakota

On November 2, 2010, voters in South Dakota rejected Measure 13, which sought to legalize medical marijuana for people suffering from debilitating medical conditions, by a vote of 63 percent to 37 percent. Four years earlier a similar measure was voted down by a margin of 52 percent to 48 percent.[47]

In 2013, Representatives Dan Kaiser (R), Elizabeth May (R) and Betty Olson (R), and Senators Craig Tieszen (R), Stanford Adelstein (R), Jim Bradford (D) and Jason Frerichs (D) proposed HB 1227, to provide for an affirmative defense of medical necessity for certain marijuana offenses, in particular to the charge of possession of two ounces or less of marijuana. If the defendant could prove by a preponderance of the evidence, that the defendant had a medical necessity to possess or use marijuana, it could be used as a defense. The committee members voted to kill the bill by a vote of 7–6. HB 1227 would not legalize medical marijuana. Rather, it provided only for an affirmative defense for medical marijuana patients.

Tennessee

In 2011, House Bill 294 was introduced by Representative Jeanne Richardson (D). It was a proposal to establish the safe access program. To enroll in the program, a qualified patient must obtain a prescription for medical marijuana from a practitioner, stating that in the practitioner's professional opinion the potential benefits of the medical use of marijuana would likely outweigh the health risks for the qualifying patient. The prescription and safe access program enrollment completed at the participating pharmacy must specify the qualifying patient's debilitating medical condition. Since the bill used the word "prescribe" and federal law prohibits prescribing marijuana, the bill was considered by many to be largely symbolic and would not have legalized medical marijuana. The bill failed in Committee due to lack of support,[48] and in the end, proposals for medical marijuana for Tennessee failed in 2012.

Texas

In 2013, House Bill 594 was proposed to establish an affirmative defense to prosecution for marijuana offenses. If a person who possessed the marijuana was a patient of a physician who recommended the drug, the affirmative defense may apply. The bill was introduced by Representative Elliott Naishtat (D) on January 18, 2013. HB 594 would not legalize medical marijuana, but provide an affirmative defense for medical marijuana patients and protects physicians who recommend medical marijuana to patients.

West Virginia

In 2011, HB 3251, the Compassionate Use of Medical Marijuana Act was introduced by Representative Mike Moneypenny (D). Under the bill, a qualifying patient would not be subject to arrest, prosecution or penalty in any manner, or denied any right or privilege for the medical use of marijuana, provided that the patient possessed a registry identification card and no more than six marijuana plants and one ounce of usable marijuana. It also allowed for an affirmative defense, immunity for registered primary caregivers, protection for physicians, and the creation of compassion centers. Any physician-supervised patient with a chronic or debilitating medical condition could possess six marijuana plants and up to an ounce of usable marijuana for medical purposes. The measure also allowed for the compassion centers to dispense medical cannabis to those patients. This proposal failed to pass.

For the second consecutive year, Moneypenny introduced medical marijuana legislation in 2012. HB 4498 would allow patients with serious conditions to use medical marijuana if prescribed by their doctors. The bill was denied a public hearing in the House Health and Human Resources Committee in 2012. Moneypenny then offered a resolution, HCR 144, for the legislature to study the issue more thoroughly.[49] The bill did not advance before the session ended.

Wisconsin

In 2009, State Representative Mark Pocan (D) and Senator Jon Erpenbach (D) sponsored LRB 2517, the Jacki Rickert Medical Marijuana Act, named after a long-time patient and activist. Under the proposed legislation, terminally or seriously ill patients could obtain a doctor's recommendation to use marijuana. Possession of either the recommendation or a state ID issued by the Department of Human Services would protect patients and caregivers from arrest and prosecution. Patients and caregivers could grow up to twelve plants and possess up to three ounces of marijuana. The bill also provided for a dispensary system. This bill failed to move forward.[50]

In 2012, HB 371 was introduced by Senators Jon Erpenbach (D) and Lena Taylor (D). This bill would have established a medical necessity defense to marijuana-related prosecutions and forfeiture actions. A qualifying patient could invoke this defense if he or she acquired, possessed, cultivated, transported, or used marijuana to alleviate the symptoms or effects of his or her debilitating medical condition or treatment, but only if they possessed no more than the twelve marijuana plants and three ounces of marijuana leaves or flowers. The bill also prohibited the arrest or prosecution of a qualifying patient who possessed a valid registry identification card, a valid out-of-state registry identification card, or a written certification. In addition, the bill prohibited the arrest or prosecution of or the imposition of any penalty on a physician who provides a written certification to a patient. This proposal failed to move forward.

Conclusion

While medical marijuana laws have not been passed in these states, it is likely that some of them will eventually get the support needed to pass into law. Nonetheless, it is clear that opposition to medical cannabis still exists. Some state officials are resistant to approving laws allowing for medical marijuana because of the fear of federal enforcement against state employees who carry out state laws. Even if these laws pass on the state level, the possession, cultivation, and use of medical marijuana remains illegal and those who sell, transport or distribute it can be criminally charged and punished. There are also many legislators who are opposed to these laws simply because of the potential for harm by those who use marijuana. Whatever the reason, these states (and others) will more than likely continue to consider action to allow for medical cannabis in the years to come.

Review/Discussion Questions

1. What are some of the differences and similarities between the medical marijuana bills that have failed?
2. What are some of the reasons why these bills have failed whereas many others in different states have passed?
3. Choose a state and describe the events that resulted in the failure of the medical marijuana legislation.
4. What are some reasons that determine if a medical marijuana bill will pass?
5. Predict what will happen in these states in the future. Will more states allow medical marijuana?

Key Terms

Michael Phillips Compassionate Care Act
Alabama Medical Marijuana Patients' Rights Act
Cannabis Compassion and Care Act
North Carolina Medical Cannabis Act
Compassionate Use Act of 2013
Governor Raymond Shafer Compassionate Use Medical Marijuana Act
Jacki Rickert Medical Marijuana Act

Chapter 5

Executive Branch

Overview: Executives on the federal, state and local level have discussed their agenda for medical marijuana to different extents. When they do so, they can influence the policies that are adopted and how those policies are implemented.

Introduction

Over the past few years, executives on the federal, state and local levels (i.e. the U.S. president, state governors and local mayors) have opted to speak about medical marijuana in their speeches to varying degrees. When an executive speaks about an issue, he or she is communicating with the public about their ideas and positions on that issue and expounding upon their goals.[1] Beyond that, when executives choose to discuss an issue in their discourse, they are acknowledging that the public is concerned about that topic. Executives are recognizing that citizens are worried about that issue and at the same time demonstrating the need to address those concerns. Those executives who chose not to discuss an issue are indicating that other issues are more deserving of attention.[2]

Through their rhetoric, executives may also be encouraging action by legislators and others on both the federal and state levels. They can seek to influence the policy process and legislative action by drawing attention to a problem. Executives can recommend legislation to the legislative branches, although they do not have any other direct legislative authority. However, executives can prevent issues that s/he opposes from being placed on an agenda, or can show support for those that s/he favors.[3] Executives can also use their speeches to influence the content of legislation or the passage of it by establishing public support.[4]

Executives may also seek to change the public's opinion about an issue through their rhetoric. They attempt to sway the public's policy agenda and influence the issues about which the public is concerned, but also the accepted policy direction or solutions to those items. At the same time, executive action is often affected by public opinion. When the public expresses concern, executives must react. Many executives hope that their rhetoric will convey their concerns to the voters, therefore increasing their popularity ratings and electability.[5]

Executive rhetoric about issues varies over time as public concerns ebb and flow. Problems rise on agendas, and then fade away and are replaced with new problems. They may fade because government does not address the problem, or because conditions that created a problem may change. Possibly new items will emerge to replace old ones.[6] Executive rhetoric will also vary between office holders as some will talk about it more than others, or because they have different solutions.

Many of the statements made by executives are simply an attempt to make people feel better. Often, executives make public statements about a problem or solution that make it appear as if they are taking action when they may not be doing anything substantial. When this happens, it is considered to be a symbolic statement.[7] Edelman defined symbolic statements as those remarks or actions that do not provide any substantive or tangible proposal, benefit or reward; instead, they just make people feel good about what politicians are doing and saying. In other words, they reassure citizens that they are taking action to solve a problem.[8]

The following chapter will analyze executive rhetoric and action regarding medical marijuana to detect patterns of speech over time. It will show how federal executives (i.e. presidents) have responded to medical marijuana, followed by state executive (governors) responses and local (mayors). When it comes to medical marijuana, all of these executives have the potential to impact the direction of policy and public opinion.

Presidents

Presidential rhetoric on medical marijuana is limited to recent presidents (such as George H.W. Bush, Bill Clinton, George W. Bush, and Barack Obama). Earlier presidents (Johnson, Ford, and Nixon) only mentioned marijuana in general. Three former presidents relased a statement prior to the 1998 election in which they urged voters to vote against state initiatives that would permit medical marijuana. They believed that the proposals circumvented the FDA testing process to guarantee the safety and effectiveness of consumer goods.[9] Presidential action and statements on medical marijuana have varied, as shown below.

Johnson

The first president to mention marijuana was Lyndon B. Johnson. In the mid 1960s, President Johnson mentioned the drug in his "Special Message to the Congress on Crime and Law Enforcement" of March 9, 1966. In that speech, Johnson said, "Drug addiction has been a matter of federal concern for more than a half century. The Bureau of Narcotics has pursued its enforcement duties energetically and effectively. Seizure of illegal narcotics and marijuana rose 62 percent from 1962 to 1965."

Johnson made his views on marijuana clear in remarks given on March 1, 1968 in Beaumont, Texas. In his speech, Johnson said, "when talking about the real enemies of mankind," he said, "Human misery—broken homes, acquired bad habits, LSD, marijuana, poverty—between 20 and 30 percent of our people are still at the bottom of the ladder."[10]

It is obvious that President Johnson and the nation were unclear about the effects of marijuana during these years. This changed under his successor, Richard Nixon, who expanded the federal government's attention to marijuana in a very conservative way.

Nixon

In his campaign for the presidency, Nixon promised to be a president who was tough on drugs.[11] It was apparent from the start that Nixon was opposed to marijuana use in general. In a news conference on March 15, 1973, Nixon said, "As far as I am concerned, I oppose … the legalization of marijuana …" In a radio address about law enforcement and drug abuse prevention, Nixon again made his position obvious. He said, "In recent days, there have been proposals to legalize the possession and the use of marijuana. I oppose the legalization of the sale, possession, or use of marijuana. The line against the use of dangerous drugs is now drawn on this side of marijuana. If we move the line to the other side and accept the use of this drug, how can we draw the line against other illegal drugs? Or will we slide into an acceptance of their use as well? My Administration has carefully weighed this matter. We have examined the statutes. We have taken the lead in making sanctions against the use of marijuana more uniform, more reasonable. Previously, these sanctions were often unrealistically harsh. Today, 35 States have adopted our model statute on drugs, including marijuana. I hope others will. But there must continue to be criminal sanctions against the possession, sale, or use of marijuana."[12] In his March 14, 1973, State of the Union Message to the Congress on Law Enforcement and Drug Abuse Prevention, Nixon reiterated his thoughts on marijuana, "Finally, I want to emphasize my continued opposition to legalizing the possession, sale or use of marijuana. There is no question about whether marijuana is dangerous, the only question is how dangerous. While the matter is still in dispute, the only responsible governmental approach is to prevent marijuana from being legalized. I intend, as I have said before, to do just that."[13]

At the same time, he "advocated a more equitable type of punishment which will fit the crime" of marijuana use. He supported "mandatory criminal penalties with regard to hard drugs because I think we have to move vigorously in the area ..."[14] He informed the public that "mandatory sentences, as you know, only apply to hard drugs, heroin. It does not apply to marijuana. It does not apply to soft drugs, et cetera, et cetera."[15]

Nixon worked with leaders of other countries to reduce the importation of drugs into the U.S. On August 21, 1970, in a Joint Statement Following Discussions with President Diaz Ordaz of Mexico, it was reported that "President Diaz Ordaz and President Nixon reaffirmed their determination to suppress the illicit international traffic in marijuana, narcotics and dangerous drugs which has endangered the well-being of both countries."[16]

While doing this, Nixon worked to reduce the availability of drugs in the U.S. In March of 1973, he reported "Our domestic accomplishments are keeping pace with international efforts and are producing equally encouraging results. Domestic drug seizures, including seizures of marijuana and hashish, almost doubled in 1972 over 1971. Arrests have risen by more than one-third and convictions have doubled."[17]

During the Nixon administration, it is fair to say that the "War on Drugs" was initiated, in part because of Nixon's strong anti-marijuana stance. In succeeding administrations, the anti-drug policies continued.

Ford

In 1975, when President Ford was asked if he favored the decriminalization of the private use of marijuana, he said, "I do not believe we have sufficient evidence at the present time to warrant any recommendation in that regard."[18] When an audience member asked "How do you feel about your son's statement that he experimented with marijuana and your promise to say today whether or not you have tried it?" Ford answered, "Well, let me say I never have...."[19]

Ford did not have the same opinions about marijuana use as Nixon. Ford believed it was necessary for the federal government to admit that drug abuse existed. He convened a commission to look at the problem. The committee found that the marijuana was not a threat to society and that it was unlikely to eliminate drug abuse from society. They suggested that federal funds should be spent to attack international drug cartels as opposed to small-time domestic growers.[20]

Carter

President Carter was the only president to consider a reexamination of the country's marijuana laws, but his efforts were not successful.[21] When he entered the Oval office, it was America's policy to spray marijuana crops with paraquat, a herbicide that was actually dangerous if consumed by humans. Because of that, Carter stopped all funding for purchasing of paraquat.[22]

Reagan

Although President Reagan did not place the issue of medical cannabis on his agenda, it was clear that he was tough on drugs in general, and marijuana in particular. He called marijuana a dangerous drug, particularly for school-age youth.[23] In a radio address to the nation, Reagan described marijuana as an enemy of our children, calling it "cunning and treacherous."[24]

Reagan often announced his administration's successes when it came to controlling drug use in the U.S. For example, he announced that "drug-related arrests are up over 40 percent, the amount of marijuana seized is up about 80 percent."[25] In a message to Congress, he said, "…seizures of marijuana increased by 50 percent. I have every reason to believe that these and other administrative actions will continue to increase arrests and convictions of persons who violate Federal law."[26]

In his war against marijuana use, Reagan developed relationships with leaders of other nations, for example Colombia[27] and Belize.[28]

In 1982, he created the White House Drug Abuse Policy Office that was responsible for establishing a national strategy for reducing drug abuse throughout the nation. Reagan also supported the reintroduction of mandatory minimum sentences for drug offenses. First time offenders could receive a sentence of up to life imprisonment and the confiscation of their property. He also supported laws that made it illegal to own drug paraphernalia.

In contrast to President Carter, Reagan authorized the DEA to spray national forest areas in the U.S. with paraquat as a way to eradicate mass numbers of marijuana plants, despite the potential for harm.[29]

Reagan's wife, Nancy, also got involved in the pursuit of reducing drug use across America. She established a program with the phrase, "Just Say No" as a way to prevent youth from trying drugs. The president described her program as contributing to "an overwhelming change in consciousness that is taking place in America. The flippant attitude about drugs is changing."[30]

G.H.W. Bush

President Bush's opposition to medical marijuana (and his conservative approach) was made clear when, in October 2001, thirty DEA agents raided the Los Angeles Marijuana Resource Center, a group that provided medical marijuana to approximately 960 patients suffering from chronic health problems such as AIDS. Until then, the center was cooperating with the county sheriff's department and other city officials. The DEA agents uprooted 400 marijuana plants, seized growing equipment and computers that had the names and records of the patients, with the president's approval.

On September 5, 2002, federal agents armed with automatic weapons raided the WoMen's Alliance for Medical Marijuana, a similar clinic that was providing medical marijuana to about 150 patients. This time, DEA agents arrested its owners on charges of intent to distribute marijuana, and seized more than 100 marijuana plants, cutting down another 150, and confiscating more. California's Attorney General, Bill Lockyer, spoke out against the raid as a waste of law enforcement resources. He wrote a letter to Attorney General John Ashcroft to request a meeting to "discuss the federal government's unprecedented attacks on locally authorized medical marijuana operations." A DEA official reminded him that it is against the law to distribute illegal drugs. Three days later, the DEA raided other medical marijuana dispensaries in Sonoma County. Then on February 14, 2003, other federal agents raided L.A.-based marijuana clubs and businesses in ten states as part of a nationwide "Operation Pipe Dream." They also raided private homes and businesses, arresting fifty-five people for possession of drug paraphernalia.[31] Throughout his term, the Bush administration enforced the federal laws that ban marijuana use, even if states had laws to the contrary.

President Bush enforced his policies in other ways. After officials in Alaska declared that marijuana possession by adults in their own homes was protected under the constitutional right to privacy President Bush threatened to withhold federal funds from the state if they did not reverse the decision. They ended up doing so.[32]

Clinton

It was expected that President Clinton, a Democrat, would support more liberal policies regarding medical marijuana. However, this was not the case. Throughout his presidency, President Bill Clinton supported a "zero tolerance" policy toward illicit drugs, including marijuana. Clinton believed that the benefits, and safety, of medical marijuana were unproven. Additionally, if the government were to legalize marijuana for medical purposes, it would send the wrong message to the public, and especially to children, that marijuana is acceptable for recreational use and even beneficial for one's health.[33]

In 1998, after Arizona voters passed Proposition 200 and California passed Proposition 215, administration officials said that the federal government did not recognize California state law or any other state law that legalized medical marijuana. President Clinton threatened to prosecute those physicians who recommended marijuana to their patients, and also announced that the initiatives would not result in a decreased enforcement of federal laws outlawing marijuana. Clinton made it very clear that federal drug statutes were the primary legal authority when it came to medical marijuana.

Federal law enforcement agencies under Clinton regularly reminded Californians that drug activities remained federal crimes, despite being legal under state laws.[34] However, there were federal agents who admitted because of limited federal resources, it would be difficult, if not almost impossible, for federal agents to pursue many cases.[35] Consequently, Clinton proposed some alternate strategies to enforce the law, including suspending medical licenses of those doctors who opted to prescribe medical marijuana to patients. Because of these threats, many physicians in the state agreed that they were likely to stop recommending marijuana.[36]

Clinton's Drug Czar, General Barry McCaffrey, reinforced Clinton's policies and labeled the initiatives in California and Arizona simply a way to legalize drugs and drug use in those states. He stated that as the nation was trying to educate teenagers about the dangers of psychoactive drugs, the initiatives were sending the message that marijuana is good, and that it is medicine. He predicted that as a result of the referenda, the country would see increased drug abuse. McCaffrey reiterated the possible prosecution of physicians who recommended marijuana as a treatment.[37]

Clinton's Secretary of Health and Human Services, Donna Shalala, also stated that the California and Arizona laws would only serve to reinforce the belief that marijuana was a harmless drug. She repeated that the Clinton administration was opposed to legalizing marijuana. A month after voters passed the initiatives in California and Arizona, Shalala reinforced Clinton's threats to punish any doctors who prescribed marijuana by taking away their power to write prescriptions, which would affect their ability to practice medicine.[38]

On May 21, 1999, Clinton seemed to support a more liberal perspective when he announced that he would work to ease restrictions on research surrounding medical marijuana. He proposed selling government-grown marijuana to researchers, who in turn would seek their own research funding. Until then, there were only a small number of researchers who were looking into possible benefits of marijuana.[39]

From this, it is clear that Clinton was a president who supported conservative policies when it came to medical marijuana, despite belonging to the Democratic Party.

G.W. Bush

As a candidate for the presidency, Republican George W. Bush said he thought the federal government should respect state decisions on medical marijuana. However, his drug czar, John Walters, DEA chief Asa Hutchinson, and DEA Administrator John B. Brown III, sought to intensify federal efforts to suppress marijuana use and fight states that allow medical marijuana. Walters considered marijuana to be a "pernicious" drug with "destructive effects" and argued that medical marijuana supporters are involved in a "cynical campaign (that) is part of the drug legalization agenda."[40] During the Bush administration, the federal government started to bring more criminal charges against those who grew medical marijuana.[41]

Obama

During the 2008 presidential campaign, Candidate Obama promised not to order federal raids against medical marijuana dispensaries. This is supported in the following statement:

> When it comes to medical marijuana, I have more of a practical view than anything else. My attitude is that if it's an issue of doctors prescribing medical marijuana as a treatment for glaucoma or as a cancer treatment, I think that should be appropriate because there really is no difference between that and a doctor prescribing morphine or anything else. I think there are legitimate concerns in not wanting to allow people to grow their own or start setting up mom and pop shops because at that point it becomes fairly difficult to regulate. I'm not familiar with all the details of the initiative that was passed [in Oregon] and what safeguards there were in place, but I think the basic concept that using medical marijuana in the same way, with the same controls as other drugs prescribed by doctors, I think that's entirely appropriate. I would not punish doctors if it's prescribed in a way that is appropriate. That may require some changes in federal law. I will

tell you that … the likelihood of that being real high on my list is not likely. What I'm not going to be doing is using Justice Department resources to try to circumvent state laws on this issue simply because I want folks to be investigating violent crimes and potential terrorism. We've got a lot of things for our law enforcement officers to deal with.[42]

During his first few years as president, medical marijuana was addressed only twice by President Barack Obama. Both of these statements were in response to audience members' questions. On September 26, 2011, in a session in West Hollywood, California, an audience member yelled "Don't forget medical marijuana!" to which Obama replied, "Thank you for that."[43] Then a similar incident occurred on August 15, 2011, at a town hall meeting, in which an audience member asked the President, " … if you can't legalize marijuana, why can't we just legalize medical marijuana to help the people that need it?" The president replied: "Well, a lot of States are making decisions about medical marijuana. As a controlled substance, the issue, then, is it being prescribed by a doctor as opposed to—well, I'll leave it at that."[44] In another interview, President Obama said that recreational users of marijuana should not be a "top priority" of federal law enforcement in those states that have legalized its use. He said, "We've got bigger fish to fry."[45]

In 2009, shortly after he took office, the Department of Justice (Attorney General Eric Holder) issued a memorandum to its 93 U.S. Attorneys informing them that prosecuting individuals who use medical marijuana in compliance with state laws should not be a priority. The memo came from Deputy Attorney General David Ogden. In the memo, the White House indicated that the President was not going to use resources in the Justice Department to carry out raids on state-approved marijuana dispensaries. He explained that Obama's campaign promises about medical marijuana were the basis of the new policy. However, he made clear that marijuana use for non-medical purposes would remain illegal, and that authorities should remain on the lookout for anyone posing as medical marijuana operators who might be selling pot illegally. The memo is presented in Table 5.1.

Table 5.1: Ogden Memo

October 19, 2009
MEMORANDUM FOR SELECTED UNITED STATES ATTORNEYS
FROM: David W. Ogden, Deputy Attorney General
SUBJECT: Investigations and Prosecutions in States Authorizing the Medical Use of Marijuana

This memorandum provides clarification and guidance to federal prosecutors in States that have enacted laws authorizing the medical use of marijuana. These laws vary in their substantive provisions and in the extent of state regulatory oversight, both among the enacting States and among local jurisdictions within those States. Rather than developing different guidelines for every possible variant of state and local law, this memorandum provides uniform guidance to focus federal investigations and prosecutions in these States on core federal enforcement priorities.

The Department of Justice is committed to the enforcement of the Controlled Substances Act in all States. Congress has determined that marijuana is a dangerous drug, and the illegal distribution and sale of marijuana is a serious crime and provides a significant source of revenue to large-scale criminal enterprises, gangs, and cartels. One timely example underscores the importance of our efforts to prosecute significant marijuana traffickers: marijuana distribution in the United States remains the single largest source of revenue for the Mexican cartels.

The Department is also committed to making efficient and rational use of its limited investigative and prosecutorial resources. In general, United States Attorneys are vested with "plenary authority with regard to federal criminal matters" within their districts. USAM 9-2.001. In exercising this authority, United States Attorneys are "invested by statute and delegation from the Attorney General with the broadest discretion in the exercise of such authority." Id. This authority should, of course, be exercised consistent with Department priorities and guidance.

The prosecution of significant traffickers of illegal drugs, including marijuana, and the disruption of illegal drug manufacturing and trafficking networks continues to be a core priority in the Department's efforts against narcotics and dangerous drugs, and the Department's investigative and prosecutorial resources should be directed towards these objectives. As a general matter, pursuit of these priorities should not focus federal resources in your States on individuals whose actions are in clear and unambiguous compliance with existing state laws providing for the medical use of marijuana. For example, prosecution of individuals with cancer or other serious illnesses who use marijuana as part of a recommended treatment regimen consistent with applicable state law, or those caregivers in clear and unambiguous compliance with existing state law who provide such individuals with marijuana, is unlikely to be an efficient use of limited federal resources. On the other hand, prosecution of commercial enterprises that unlawfully market and sell marijuana for profit continues to be an enforcement priority of the Department. To be sure, claims of compliance with state or local law may mask operations inconsistent with the terms, conditions, or purposes of those laws, and federal law enforcement should not be deterred by such assertions when otherwise pursuing the Department's core enforcement priorities.

Typically, when any of the following characteristics is present, the conduct will not be in clear and unambiguous compliance with applicable state law and may indicate illegal drug trafficking activity of potential federal interest:

- unlawful possession or unlawful use of firearms;
- violence;
- sales to minors;
- financial and marketing activities inconsistent with the terms, conditions, or purposes of state law, including evidence of money laundering activity and/or financial gains or excessive amounts of cash inconsistent with purported compliance with state or local law;
- amounts of marijuana inconsistent with purported compliance with state or local law;
- illegal possession or sale of other controlled substances; or
- ties to other criminal enterprises.

Of course, no State can authorize violations of federal law, and the list of factors above is not intended to describe exhaustively when a federal prosecution may be warranted. Accordingly, in prosecutions under the Controlled Substances Act, federal prosecutors are not expected to charge, prove, or otherwise establish any state law violations. Indeed, this memorandum does not alter in any way the Department's authority to enforce federal law, including laws prohibiting the manufacture, production, distribution, possession, or use of marijuana on federal property. This guidance regarding resource allocation does not "legalize" marijuana or provide a legal defense to a violation of federal law, nor is it intended to create any privileges, benefits, or rights, substantive or procedural, enforceable by any individual, party or witness in any administrative, civil, or criminal matter. Nor does clear and unambiguous compliance with state law or the absence of one or all of the above factors create a legal defense to a violation of the Controlled Substances Act. Rather, this memorandum is intended solely as a guide to the exercise of investigative and prosecutorial discretion.

Finally, nothing herein precludes investigation or prosecution where there is a reasonable basis to believe that compliance with state law is being invoked as a pretext for the production or distribution of marijuana for purposes not authorized by state law. Nor does this guidance preclude investigation or prosecution, even when there is clear and unambiguous compliance with existing state law, in particular circumstances where investigation or prosecution otherwise serves important federal interests.

Your offices should continue to review marijuana cases for prosecution on a case-by-case basis, consistent with the guidance on resource allocation and federal priorities set forth herein, the consideration of requests for federal assistance from state and local law enforcement authorities, and the Principles of Federal Prosecution.

cc: All United States Attorneys

Lanny A. Breuer
Assistant Attorney General Criminal Division

B. Todd Jones
United States Attorney
District of Minnesota
Chair, Attorney General's Advisory Committee

Michele M. Leonhart
Acting Administrator
Drug Enforcement Administration

H. Marshall Jarrett
Director
Executive Office for United States Attorneys

Kevin L. Perkins
Assistant Director
Criminal Investigative Division
Federal Bureau of Investigation

Obama's position on medical marijuana seemed to change during his first term in office. On October 7, 2011, federal prosecutors in California announced efforts to crack down on medical marijuana dispensaries with "significant commercial operations." In recent years, federal law enforcement agencies have conducted raids on marijuana dispensaries, demonstrating a commitment to enforcing the federal Controlled Substance Act. Deputy Attorney General James Cole issued a memo in which the Justice Department was given the ability to enforce federal law, even in states where medical marijuana had been made legal. This was seen as a way to undermine state laws. Some felt the Cole memo[46] (Table 5.2) was permission to attack on the medical cannabis community.

Table 5.2: Memo from U.S. Department of Justice

June 29, 2011
MEMORANDUM FOR UNITED STATES ATTORNEYS
FROM: James M. Cole Deputy Attorney General
SUBJECT: Guidance Regarding the Ogden Memo in Jurisdictions Seeking to Authorize Marijuana for Medical Use

Over the last several months some of you have requested the Department's assistance in responding to inquiries from State and local governments seeking guidance about the Department's position on enforcement of the Controlled Substances Act (CSA) in jurisdictions that have under consideration, or have implemented, legislation that would sanction and regulate the commercial cultivation and distribution of marijuana purportedly for medical use. Some of these jurisdictions have considered approving the cultivation of large quantities of marijuana, or broadening the regulation and taxation of the substance. You may have seen letters responding to these inquiries by several United States Attorneys. Those letters are entirely consistent with the October 2009 memorandum issued by Deputy Attorney General David Ogden to federal prosecutors in States that have enacted laws authorizing the medical use of marijuana (the "Ogden Memo").

The Department of Justice is committed to the enforcement of the Controlled Substances Act in all States. Congress has determined that marijuana is a dangerous drug and that the illegal distribution and sale of marijuana is a serious crime that provides a significant source o f revenue to large scale criminal enterprises, gangs, and cartels. The Ogden Memorandum provides guidance to you in deploying your resources to enforce the CSA as part of the exercise of the broad discretion you are given to address federal criminal matters within your districts.

A number of states have enacted some form of legislation relating to the medical use of marijuana. Accordingly, the Ogden Memo reiterated to you that prosecution of significant traffickers of illegal drugs, including marijuana, remains a core priority, but advised that it is likely not an efficient use of federal resources to focus enforcement efforts on individuals with cancer or other serious illnesses who use marijuana as part of a recommended treatment regimen consistent with applicable state law, or their caregivers. The term "caregiver" as used in the memorandum meant just that: individuals providing care to individuals with cancer or other serious illnesses, not commercial operations cultivating, selling or distributing marijuana.

The Department's view of the efficient use of limited federal resources as articulated in the Ogden Memorandum has not changed. There has, however, been an increase in the scope of commercial cultivation, sale, distribution and use of marijuana for purported medical purposes. For example, within the past 12 months, several jurisdictions have considered or enacted legislation to authorize multiple large-scale, privately-operated industrial marijuana cultivation centers. Some of these planned facilities have revenue projections of millions of dollars based on the planned cultivation of tens of thousands of cannabis plants.

The Ogden Memorandum was never intended to shield such activities from federal enforcement action and prosecution, even where those activities purport to comply with state law. Persons who are in the business of cultivating, selling or distributing marijuana, and those who knowingly facilitate such activities, are in violation of the Controlled Substances Act, regardless of state law. Consistent with resource constraints and the discretion you may exercise in your district, such persons are subject to federal enforcement action, including potential prosecution. State laws or local ordinances are not a defense to civil or criminal enforcement of federal law with respect to such conduct, including enforcement of the CSA. Those who engage in transactions involving the proceeds of such activity may also be in violation of federal money laundering statutes and other federal financial laws.

The Department of Justice is tasked with enforcing existing federal criminal laws in all states, and enforcement of the CSA has long been and remains a core priority.

cc: Lanny A. Breuer Assistant Attorney General, Criminal Division

B. Todd Jones United States Attorney District of Minnesota Chair, AGAC

Michele M. Leonhart Administrator Drug Enforcement Administration

H. Marshall Jarrett Director Executive Office for United States Attorneys

Kevin L. Perkins Assistant Director Criminal Investigative Division Federal Bureau of Investigations

July 1, 2011, "Medical Marijuana memo: DOJ Cracks Down on Pot Shops" Huff Post Politics, http://www.huffingtonpost.com/2011/07/01/medical-marijuana-memo-doj_n_888995.html.

After that, there were additional raids on dispensaries. Federal officials seized property from dispensaries and landlords, demanded that patient records be released, used the Internal Revenue Service to bankrupt legitimate dispensaries, told banks to purge medical cannabis clients, evicted patients from low-income housing and denied a petition to recognize the well-established medical value of cannabis.[47] In 2011, federal prosecutors also sent letters to dozens of landlords and owners of marijuana dispensaries in California, accusing them of using the Compassionate Use law to hide illegal drug sales. They proceeded to warn the landlords that if they did not halt from selling marijuana, their property could be seized and other penalties could be incurred. Further, federal attorneys California announced they would begin to prosecute offenders in that state.[48]

In 2011, a group of medical marijuana advocacy groups filed a suit to force the Obama Administration to act on a nine-year-old petition to reclassify medical marijuana. The Coalition for Rescheduling Cannabis (CRC) originally filed a petition in 2002. In 2006, the Department of Health and Human Services recommended that the DEA (the final arbiter in the rescheduling process) review the drug schedules. Other groups in the suit included Americans for Safe Access (ASA), Patients Out of Time, and some medical cannabis patients. The suit claims the government has been "unreasonably" delaying the review process, a violation of the Administrative Procedures Act. In the lawsuit, the advocacy groups presented evidence that cannabis is not a dangerous drug and that it has proven therapeutic value. If the petition was rejected, the CRC could challenge the government's allegation that marijuana has no medical value. The CRC blamed the Obama administration for a lack of action and for stalling.[49]

Clearly, the Obama administration has shifted its policies toward medical marijuana since the 2008 campaign. At first, it seemed to be accepting of state laws that made it legal, but in recent years has stepped up raids and arrests at dispensaries as a way to enforce federal laws against medical cannabis.

Other Federal Action

In addition to presidential rhetoric, there has been other federal action on medical marijuana, beginning in 1972 when The National Commission on Marihuana and Drug Abuse, otherwise known as the Schafer Commission, released their final report. The report indicated that the previously held beliefs about the potential harmfulness of marijuana were exaggerated, and that reports of dependence upon and psychosis related to marijuana use was rare. They indicated that there was a symbolic role that marijuana played in a cultural conflict. In the end, the Commission members supported more research to explore the possibilities of marijuana for medicinal uses, as well as a reduction in criminal penalties for possession of marijuana.[50]

In 1975, three years after this report was made public, a glaucoma patient, Robert Randall, was arrested for growing his own marijuana. He defended his action in court (in *Randall v. U.S.*) by using a medical necessity defense. Table 5.3 provides more information about Mr. Randall.

Table 5.3: Robert Randall

Robert Randall was diagnosed with glaucoma at age 24. Doctors told him that the disease would cause him to be totally blind before he turned 30. His medical doctors gave him prescription drugs to help the pain, but nothing worked. He soon discovered that his symptoms were relieved after smoking marijuana. He began to grow marijuana plants as a way to supply himself with the drug, and was arrested in August 1975 for possession and cultivating marijuana. Using the Common Law Doctrine of Necessity to defend his actions in court (i.e. claiming that there was a justification for breaking the law and that there was no reasonable alternative; he should not be held liable for his actions because the act was necessary to prevent a greater harm), he convinced a federal Superior Court that it was a medical necessity for him to use marijuana to treat his medical condition. In 1976, he brought charges against the Food and Drug Administration, the DEA, and National Institute on Drug Abuse, the Department of Justice, and the Department of Health, Education and Welfare.

The criminal charges against Randall were eventually dropped, and in 1976 he became the first American to gain legal access to marijuana for medical purposes. At that time, the federal government began providing him with FDA-approved medical marijuana. With that, he became the first American to receive marijuana from the government for the treatment of a medical disorder. He received his first shipment of government cannabis in November 1976. The marijuana was sent through the U.S. mail to a doctor's office. The doctor purchased a 250-pound safe in which the marijuana was stored. Randall would go to the doctor's office when he needed the drug.

Two years later, the federal government tried to halt the shipments of marijuana to Randall, but he sued and won. He became a long-term user of marijuana, and over those years, the marijuana use helped to prevent Randall from going totally blind. Randall was diagnosed with AIDS in November 1994, and died on June 2, 2001 at the age of 52 because of complications related to the disease.

Randall felt obligated to help others who suffered from glaucoma and other diseases such as cancer. He worked to expand the right for other ill people to have access to medical marijuana. He assisted doctors and other groups learn more about the medical effects of marijuana. He worked with UCLA's Marijuana Research Project, and Johns Hopkins and Chapel Hill Duke University Eye Center. Through this research, he discovered that oral THC and smoked marijuana had different effects on the body. He often appeared in the media and gave interviews as a way to educate the public and to get support for medical marijuana. He fought for state ballot initiatives that would allow for medical marijuana, including ones in New Mexico, Florida, Louisiana, Illinois, West Virginia and Virginia. He also joined the fight to change the federal law to recognize medical marijuana.

Randall and his wife, Alice O'Leary, founded the Alliance for Cannabis Therapeutics and the Marijuana AIDS Research Service.

Source: Robert C. Randall and Alice M. O'Leary 1998 Marijuana Rx: The Patients' Fight for Medicinal Pot New York: Thunder's Mouth Press.

Largely because of the report of the National Commission and the Randall case, the federal government instituted an Investigational New Drug (IND) (or the Compassionate IND) program to explore the potential for medical use of marijuana. The program allowed chosen physicians to prescribe medical marijuana to patients on a trial basis only. Because there was an extensive process for patients to enroll in the program, there were only twelve patients accepted at first. Those accepted into the program had to follow strict protocols. All patients in the program received 300 low-potency marijuana cigarettes per month, or about 10.75 ounces (300 grams).[51]

The marijuana used in the program was grown at the University of Mississippi, which could provide patients with marijuana that was pesticide-free and of a standard potency. The Research Triangle Institute in North Carolina is allocated $62,000 a year from the Federal government to roll and packaged the marijuana cigarettes and ship them to the patients' doctors and pharmacists. All of the patients in the program were provided with a document from the FDA which granted them permission to use the marijuana.[52]

Today, the program is administered by the National Institute of Drug Abuse (NIDA). Between 1976 and 1988, there were only about six patients who qualified for the IND program. By 1989, largely because of the HIV/AIDs epidemic and patients seeking to relieve the nausea, the FDA became overwhelmed with applications. President Bush was forced to halt accepting new patients into the program in 1992, claiming that it sent the wrong message and contradicted the position of the Administration concerning illicit drug use. Efforts to reinstate the program under the Clinton Administration failed in 1994. In a court brief, Clinton's Justice Department acknowledged that the program's use of medical marijuana "was bad public policy." As of 2003, the program remained closed to new patients.[53] While at one time the program had thirty patients, at this time, there are only four surviving patients who remain in the program.[54]

White House Commission

On March 17, 1999, a report was issued by a committee established by the White House to study the medical literature about marijuana. The committee was comprised of eleven experts who were appointed to serve by the Institute of Medicine and funded by the White House Office of National Drug Control Policy. The committee met for two years. The conclusion of their final report stated that "the benefits of smoking marijuana were limited by the toxic effects of the smoke, but nonetheless recommended that the drug be given under close supervision to patients who do not respond to other therapies."[55] In other words, the panel members advised that marijuana could be given on a short-term basis to patients who did not respond well to other medications. The authors also wrote that there was no clear evidence that prescribing marijuana to ill patients would increase illicit drug use by the general population, nor would it serve as a "gateway drug" that encourages further drug use including cocaine and heroin.[56]

In the end, the report found that there was scientific data to show that there was potential value of marijuana use for controlling some forms of pain, alleviating nausea and vomiting, treating weight loss due to AIDs, and combating muscle spasms associated with multiple sclerosis.[57] However, it was not useful in treating glaucoma in the long-term. Additionally, the real benefits of marijuana were masked by the smoke, but that if capsules, patches and inhalers could be developed as a means to deliver the active components, or cannabinoids, the true positive effects of the drug would be seen.[58]

Presidents: Summary

To date, there has been a great deal of rhetoric and action on the federal level concerning medical marijuana. Presidents have taken different approaches to the issue, and various committees have also spent time to understand the problem better. The issue has also become a concern to governors, as shown below.

States

In addition to presidents, executives on the state level (governors) have also spoken about medical marijuana throughout the past five to ten years. In some ways, when governors discuss particular issues, their impact potentially is stronger than when presidents do so. Governors may have more direct impact on policies that affect the daily lives of citizens because governors are closer to the people.[59]

Like presidential rhetoric, gubernatorial rhetoric changes over time as issues change and develop. They also vary from state to state. The discussion below provides examples of what governors have said about medical marijuana in their individual state.

Arizona

After voters approved medical marijuana in Arizona, thirteen out of fifteen sheriffs in the state asked Republican Governor Jan Brewer to delay the implementation of medical marijuana in the state, which would require that the state provide dispensary licenses to almost 100 people. However, Brewer replied that there would be "no change" in carrying out the law because it was approved by the voters. Governor Brewer later asked the court to rule on whether federal law prevented the state from implementing a medical marijuana law, but a federal judge dismissed the suit.[60] In her letter to the court, she wrote that she understood the concerns about legalizing marijuana for medical reasons, and that the state of Arizona has the right to follow its own state law.[61]

Colorado

Colorado's Governor, Bill Ritter, Jr. (D), supported medical marijuana in Colorado. He said: "Another place where we need to find balance is medical marijuana. We need to uphold the will of the voters while reigning in abuses and bringing common sense to the chaos that now exists. Together, we can achieve bipartisan solutions that clarify the doctor-patient relationship and address the proliferation of dispensaries. I urge the General Assembly to act quickly in this area."[62]

Connecticut

The Republican Governor of Connecticut, M. Jodi Rell, voted against legislation that would have legalized medical marijuana. Although she described the authors of the bill as well-intentioned, she felt the proposal was flawed. The legislation would have allowed those patients suffering from specific medical conditions to grow up to four marijuana plants in their homes if they had a doctor's prescription. But the governor said, "I am troubled by the fact that in essence, this bill forces law-abiding citizens to seek out drug dealers to make their marijuana purchases."[63]

In 2012, the subsequent Governor of Connecticut, Dannel P. Malloy (D) signed a law that would approve the use of medical marijuana in the state. However, patients would be able to obtain marijuana only from certified pharmacists, and the number of marijuana producers across the state would be limited to ten. While discussing the law, the Governor said, "We don't want Connecticut to follow the path pursued by some other states, which essentially would legalize marijuana for anyone willing to find the right doctor and get the right prescription. In my opinion, such efforts run counter to federal law."[64]

At the same time, the Governor was concerned that the new legislation would send the wrong message about drug use to youth living in the state. It also did not specify where patients and their caregivers would obtain the marijuana.

Delaware

In 2012, the Deputy Attorney General in Delaware warned the Governor, Jack Markell (D), that state employees who regulated the medical marijuana industry in that state might not be safe from federal prosecution. To clarify that position, Markell questioned a U.S. Attorney about his attitude toward the state's law on medical marijuana. Not long after, Markell suspended the licensing process for the state's medical marijuana dispensaries, claiming that he was uncomfortable with putting state employees at risk of being punished. This act essentially ended medical marijuana in the state.[65]

Maine

The Governor of Maine, Paul LePage (R), signed a law (LD 1296) that would expand privacy protection for those patients accepted into the state's medical marijuana program. The new law would eliminate the requirements that doctors disclose information about patients who were using medical marijuana to state officials. It also required law enforcement, within seven days of its seizure, to return any property that was seized from patients using marijuana legally.[66]

Maryland

The Governor of Maryland, Martin O'Malley, a democrat, was described as being "likely" to veto any legislation that would legalize medical marijuana in Maryland. This is because of his concerns about whether such a law would stand up to federal scrutiny.[67]

New Hampshire

In New Hampshire, Governor John Lynch (D) vetoed medical marijuana legislation even though there was strong support in both the legislature and the voters. The bill, SB 409, was intended to protect the right of sick patients to grow their own marijuana plants, or designate a caregiver to do so.[68] The Governor stated that the proposed bill did not provide sufficient restrictions on the cultivation and prescription of the drug, and opposed provisions in the law that would allow ailing teenagers to use marijuana for treatment. He said, "I cannot support establishing a system for the use of medical marijuana that poses risks to the patient, lacks adequate oversight and funding, and risks the proliferation of a serious drug."[69]

New Jersey

In 2012, the out-going governor of New Jersey, Jon Corzine (D), and other members of the Democratic-controlled legislature at the time, supported medical cannabis and passed legislation to make marijuana legal for those citizens of the state who suffered from certain medical conditions. Upon leaving office, Corzine signed a bill making medical marijuana legal. He told state legislators, " … you all courageously eased the suffering of many New Jerseyians, present and future, by giving them the opportunity to legally access medical marijuana."[70] The bill included a provision that the new provisions had to be put into effect within six months.

The candidate chosen to be the next governor of New Jersey, Chris Christie (R), opposed medical marijuana. Once governor, Christie attempted to delay the implementation of the bill. His administration asked the state senate for a delay until January of 2013, claiming that many provisions of the bill remained unclear, including who would be permitted to grow marijuana, how those people would be chosen, and what the limits would be for possession of marijuana and the doses for patients.[71]

Despite his concerns, Governor Christie publicly announced his support for the bill and stated that he would allow the state to begin dispensing medical marijuana to patients who qualified, even though there was a concern that federal officials could prosecute state employees or state-approved growers. Because of these concerns, Christie sought assurances from federal officials that they would not pursue criminal charges against those in the state medical marijuana programs. Even though Christie did not get that assurance, he didn't believe federal authorities would prosecute people who were obeying the state law. Consequently, he supported implementation of the law by the Commissioner of Health in the state to implement the medical marijuana program in New Jersey.

Pointing out that Corzine signed the legislation the day before he left office, Christie said, "We were left with very little instruction in the end about how to implement this law and how to do it in a very complex legal environment, with conflicting and intersecting federal and state legal requirements and opportunities. And so we set out from the beginning to try to set up a scheme from a regulatory perspective that would allow us the greatest protection from federal intervention, because my goal in all of this from the beginning was pretty simple. I made clear during the campaign that this is not a law that I would have signed if I were governor at the time."[72] However, Governor Christie also said that he would not force any towns to allow medical marijuana if they were opposed to it. He said, "I absolutely believe this should be determined by local elected officials. If they want a dispensary or a growing facility in their town, that's up to them. If they don't, I will not as governor force them to take it."[73]

New Mexico

New Mexico's governor Gary Johnson, a member of the Libertarian Party, told the public that there were five bills pertaining to drug policy reform that would be before the state legislature, one of which was on the topic of medical cannabis. He believed that if the bills were passed, the state would be able to focus on providing treatment for those citizens who need it while at the same time providing better education regarding drugs to young people. In this way, he was sure that the "death, disease, and crime associated with drug abuse" would be reduced. Another benefit would be a savings in money.[74] Johnson claimed that, between 2005 and 2008, he smoked marijuana.[75] He said, "Rather than using painkillers, which I have used on occasion before, I did smoke pot, as a result of having broken my back, blowing out both of my knees, breaking ribs, really taking about three years to recover."[76]

New York

The Governor of the state, Andrew Cuomo, stated that while he understood the potential benefits of medical marijuana, he still thought the risks outweighed those benefits. In his 2010 campaign, Cuomo rejected legalizing marijuana for medical use, but later said he was reconsidering that position. He called it a complicated issue[77] and that more research needed to be conducted before medical marijuana could make the ballot.[78] He acknowledged that he would not sign such a bill because of the tremendous risks involved.[79]

Rhode Island

Lincoln Chafee (I), The Governor of Rhode Island, halted a plan that would allow state-run medical marijuana dispensaries because he was afraid that it was illegal under federal law. Even though he supported the plan early on, he later noted that the dispensaries across the state could violate federal law and become targeted by federal law enforcement. He said, "Federal injunctions, seizures, forfeitures, arrests and prosecutions will only hurt the patients and caregivers that our law was designed to protect." This means that patients in Rhode Island would be forced to grow their own marijuana, buy it off dealers in the street, or acquire it from one of over 2,500 licensed caregivers in the state.[80]

Vermont

Democratic presidential candidate Howard Dean blocked a medical marijuana bill from becoming law when he was governor of Vermont. The bill would have protected seriously ill patients from arrest if they were using medical marijuana with the approval of their doctors. Howard Dean said there's no proof that medical marijuana is effective medicine.

Washington

The Governor of Washington, Christine Gregoire (D), also expressed concerns that legalizing medical marijuana dispensaries in the state would put employees at risk of federal prosecution. She said, "We cannot presume to assure protections to one group of people—patients, providers and health care professionals—in a way that subjects another group, Department of Health and Department of Agriculture employees to federal arrest or criminal liability."[81]

She said she hoped that marijuana would be reduced to a Schedule II narcotic by the federal government. In November 2011, Gregoire filed a petition with the DEA asking the agency to reclassify marijuana as a Schedule II drug. The petition would require the FDA to conduct a new scientific review and analysis of the drug to determine if there were any potential medical benefits. Governor Lincoln Chafee (I-RI) also signed the petition.[82]

Other State Action

The federal compassionate Program in the 1970s prompted some states to implement similar programs on the state level. By the early 1980s, thirteen states approved laws that would allow for the distribution of medical marijuana by the state public health department. However, by 2000, none of the state programs was in effect, largely because of the legal concerns in obtaining marijuana from the federal government's source of marijuana in Mississippi.[83]

New York created such a program. It began in 1980 after the New York state legislature and its Governor, Hugh Carey, passed a medical marijuana law, becoming one of the first state programs. The methods to obtain and distribute the marijuana in the state never came to fruition because of federal bureaucracy.

In other compassionate user states, similar things happened. Any prospect that the state officials would receiving marijuana from the government for medical reasons diminished, primarily because the reasons for supplying the marijuana was a contradiction of official government policy. On December 14, 1999, as Vice President Al Gore was campaigning for the presidency, he admitted to reporters that his sister received medical marijuana while receiving chemotherapy for cancer in 1984 under the Tennessee program.[84] This brought more attention to the growing problem of medical cannabis.

The Tennessee law allowing the program was repealed in 1992. Laws like it either ran out or were repealed in ten other states. As of 2000, similar provisions still existed in thirteen states: Alabama, Georgia, Illinois, Massachusetts, Minnesota, New Jersey, New Mexico, New York, Rhode Island, South Carolina, Texas, Washington, and West Virginia. The marijuana was provided exclusively from the federal government's marijuana farm in Mississippi. But it became difficult to access the marijuana, so only seven state public health departments were able to keep their programs viable. Buried under the red tape lay a message: federal and state compassionate pot programs belied the official line on reefer by acknowledging the very opposite of government-anti-medical marijuana pronouncements.[85]

Mayors

Like presidents and governors, mayors of major cities also choose to put medical marijuana on their agendas, and talk about it in their speeches. Many mayors from major cities across the U.S. attended the 80th Annual Conference of Mayors in June 2012. At this conference, they adopted various resolutions concerning the administration and management of cities. One of the resolutions they adopted was to reclassify medical cannabis to Schedule II of the CSA. This is described in Table 5.4.

Table 5.4: 2012 Conference of Mayors Resolution

WHEREAS, 24 states, compromising almost one-third of the U.S. population, have passed or have under consideration law that either regulate or decriminalize the use of cannabis for medical or other purposes; and

WHEREAS, under the Controlled Substances Act (CSA), the Drug Enforcement Administration (DEA) has classified cannabis as a Schedule I substance, deeming it of no currently accepted medical use in treatment with a lack of accepted safety for use of the drug under medical supervision, instead of a Schedule II substance, a drug with a currently accepted medical use in treatment or a currently accepted medical use with severe restrictions; and

WHEREAS, the American Medical Association and the American College of Physicians support investigation and clinical research of cannabis for medicinal use and urged the federal government to reassess the Schedule I classification; and

WHEREAS, scientific evidence of the effectiveness of cannabis as a treatment for certain terminal or debilitating conditions is widely available, including four reviews of modern human clinical studies with cannabis and cannabinoids in the United States and elsewhere recently published in peer-reviewed publications; and

WHEREAS, in the past year, there have been numerous federal raids of locally sanctioned medical cannabis dispensaries, operating in accordance with state statutes, creating confusion about the legal status of these businesses; and

WHEREAS, the conflict between state statutes and federal regulation frustrates our citizens, costs cities significant time and resources to address, and prevents the establishment of a regulated and safe system to supply patients who may need medical cannabis; and

WHEREAS, in December of 2011, Washington State Governor Christine Gregoire and Rhode Island Governor Lincoln Chafee petitioned DEA to initiate a rulemaking for the reclassification of medical cannabis from Schedule I to Schedule II of the CSA,

NOW THERFORE, BE IT RESOLVED, that The United States Conference of Mayors supports the Gregoire-Chafee petition and urges the DEA to initiate rulemaking proceedings for the reclassification of medical cannabis from Schedule I to Schedule II of the Controlled Substances Act (CSA) so qualifying patients who follow state law may obtain the medication they need through the traditional and safe method of physician prescribing and pharmacy dispensing.

San Francisco

Mayor Lee of San Francisco supported medical marijuana, and even though he had been largely silent after the federal Justice Department shut down five city-licensed medical marijuana dispensaries,[86] he later became outspoken about the federal raids on dispensaries. His statement in Table 5.5 shows this.

Table 5.5: Mayor Lee's Statements

"It is important that San Franciscans who need medicinal cannabis can have safe access to it—there are oncology patients, HIV/AIDS patients, and people with debilitating pain who rely on this medicine to treat their conditions. Public Health Director Barbara Garcia continually advises me that legitimate use by people with certain medical conditions is an effective way to treat pain and ease end-of-life suffering.

And since 1996, when Proposition 215 first passed, the State of California and our City have reaffirmed many times over our support of legitimate medicinal use for people with serious illness. That's why I am concerned about recent federal actions targeting duly permitted Medicinal Cannabis Dispensaries, actions that aim to limit our citizens' ability to have safe access to the medicine they need.

Time and time again, the President of the United States has made it clear that the Justice Department has more important priorities than working to prevent patients from accessing this medicine. As long as San Francisco's dispensaries and patients are operating within the guidelines set by then-Attorney General Jerry Brown in 2008, I agree with our current Attorney General Kamala Harris that raids should not occur. She has said that 'an overly broad federal enforcement campaign will make it more difficult for legitimate patients to access physician-recommended medicine in California.'"

Source: "Mayor Lee's Statement on Medical Cannabis Dispensaries" County of San Francisco, Office of the Mayor, http://www.sfmayor.org/index.aspx?page=775; accessed 10/21/2012.

Los Angeles

Los Angeles Mayor Antonio Villaraigosa (D) supported a total ban on medical marijuana dispensaries. During a debate over the best way to regulate hundreds of dispensaries throughout the city, the mayor remained quiet. Many activists and local leaders believed that the number of dispensaries was out of control. At this time, a spokeswoman for the mayor reported that the mayor supported the ban. The ban would not permit storefront sales of marijuana, but would continue to allow small groups of patients and caregivers to grow it collectively.[87]

Newark

Mayor Cory Booker (D) described the government's war on drugs a "multibillion dollar failure," saying that it ruined many lives, but disproportionately affected African-Americans. In doing so, he called on New Jersey to legalize medical marijuana.[85]

Seattle

In the 2012 State of City speech, the Mayor of Seattle, Mike McGinn (D), stated that "Seattle is the kind of place that isn't afraid to try a different approach. We support safe access to medical marijuana and made enforcement of possession of marijuana for personal use our lowest enforcement priority."

Monrovia, CA

Monrovia, CA's mayor, Mary Ann Lutz (D), expressed her opinion that the federal government should reclassify medical marijuana so that it can be sold in pharmacies. She argued that it should be moved from a Schedule I drug to a Schedule II drug, which would recognize that it has medical purposes.[89]

Woodbridge, NJ

A medical marijuana clinic (one of six in New Jersey) was to be opened in Woodbridge. It would be run by the Compassionate Care Centers of New Jersey. Whereas the clinics faced opposition from the residents of other cities, the mayor of Woodbridge, John McCormac (D), welcomed the clinic. He said, "As long as it's legal, Woodbridge residents might as well get the benefit of it. If our residents need the products, it will be close by. It will be great."[90] He also said that it was just another retail store. "It's a retail use turning into another retail use."[91]

LA City Council

In July 2012, the members of the LA City Council voted to ban all marijuana dispensaries. They chose to send a letter to all of the 762 dispensaries ordering them to shut down immediately. If they did not, they were threatened with legal action from the city.[89] But by October, the City Council rescinded the prohibition. They were facing a long and costly battle, and would also lose electoral support. So supporters of the dispensaries collected almost 50,000 signatures seeking a referendum to overturn the ban.[90]

Conclusion

Executive rhetoric on an issue such as medical marijuana is growing, but remains infrequent. There has been very little action on part of presidents to guide the nation or give support to those who support medical cannabis. Not surprisingly, any discussion of medical marijuana by presidents has been by the more recent presidents. There has been some action by governors and mayors, but such rhetoric also remains scarce. However, the issue of medical marijuana is an emerging social and political issue, and there is likely to be more discussion of the issue by executives at all levels of government in the future.

Review/Discussion Questions

1. Why is executive rhetoric/action important at the federal, state or local level when it comes to medical marijuana?
2. What have different presidents said/done about medical marijuana?
3. What have different governors said/done about medical marijuana?
4. What have different mayors said/done about medical marijuana?
5. If you were an executive, what action would you take regarding medical marijuana?

Key Terms

Symbolic statements/actions
White House Drug Abuse Policy
Ogden Memo
Cole Memo
Coalition for Rescheduling Cannabis
National Commission on Marijuana and Drug Abuse
Schafer Commission
Robert Randall
Compassionate Investigational New Drug Program
National Institute on Drug Abuse (NIDA)

Chapter 6

Congressional Legislation

Overview: The U.S. Congress has considered many laws regarding medical marijuana. Some of these would allow for medical marijuana, whereas others would reschedule marijuana from Schedule I.

Introduction

The U.S. Constitution declares that the members of Congress shall "make all laws which shall be necessary and proper" to keep the country and its citizens safe. In a democratic system of government that exists in the United States, those laws should mirror the will of the people. In other words, the laws should be a reflection of the public's opinions.

The process by which a law is passed is complex and involves many actors, but includes many steps as a way to protect against biased or unfair laws from being passed. Every proposal for a new law must be introduced into both the House of Representatives and Senate for debate and editing, and must be voted upon and receive enough support in those bodies to move forward. If the bills are edited during the process and not similar upon passage, then a conference committee (made up of representatives from the House and Senate) must iron out the differences. If that is done, then the proposal moves on to the president for action. The president can sign a bill or veto it. If it is signed, it goes on to be implemented, or carried out. It vetoed, the proposal may return to the House and Senate for a re-vote. If enough members vote for the bill, it will become law despite the president's disapproval. If, at any point through the process, the bill does not receive enough support or is not acted upon, the proposal dies. This process must be completed within two years, as Congressional sessions begin every other year.

In addition to members of Congress and the president, many other actors can influence the content of a bill. Many interest groups seek to have input into what provisions a bill includes. These interest groups each want the law to reflect a particular policy perspective. Private citizens are also often involved in the legislative process, and can either get an issue enough attention to place it on the Congressional agenda, or can testify in front of Congress to provide vital information about a problem or possible new law. Sometimes bureaucracies (agencies) are very involved in the legislative process. Members of agencies can, like citizens, provide members of Congress information about a proposal. Each of the actors involved in the legislative process acts as a check on the behavior of the others. They ensure that a new law is not elitist, but reflects the will of the people, that it is fair to all, and that it is the best law that can be implemented.

When a new law is passed by Congress, it supersedes any laws passed in the states, because the federal Constitution is the "Supreme law of the land." This is important with regard to medical marijuana since many states have passed laws allowing for its use (see chapter 3). However, officials in the federal government have made it clear that the federal laws that forbid medical marijuana will not be influenced by state laws.[1] Agencies such as the DEA and FBI have continued to enforce laws that prohibit the use of marijuana, whether for recreation or medicinal purposes, regardless of the state provisions.

Congress has considered many laws regarding marijuana, beginning with the Harrison Narcotic Act of 1914 (see chapter 2). One of the most significant laws passed by Congress was the Controlled Substances Act of 1970, which classified marijuana as a "Schedule I" drug, indicating that it has no medicinal value. Congress has also relied heavily on the Commerce Clause as a source of its authority to regulate both inter-state and intra-state crime. Many people and organizations have attempted many different approaches to convince Congress to reclassify the drug, but those efforts have not been successful.[2]

The question surrounding the current federal policy of prosecuting medical marijuana patients and their providers, as outlined in the Controlled Substances Act of 1970, despite state laws that allow for medical cannabis, is one that remains unanswered. Should the current policy be maintained, or should federal laws be relaxed so that the medical use of marijuana can be permitted under certain circumstances? To date, the Congress has not seriously considered changing the federal law to reclassify marijuana from a Schedule I to a Schedule II drug, but they have considered many proposals to change the laws in some way. The following chapter provides an analysis of any recent proposals made in Congress regarding medical marijuana to show what proposals are being considered by that branch of government.

Recent Legislation on Medical Marijuana

Medical Marijuana first became the topic for Congressional legislation in 1995 and has been on the agenda of Congress ever since then. The following section gives an analysis of the more current legislation aimed at medical marijuana. A summary of this legislation is presented in Table 6.1, at the end of the chapter.

104th Congress (1995–96)

After medical marijuana bills were passed by the voters in Arizona and California in 1996, Republican Senator Orrin Hatch (UT), then chairman of the Senate Judiciary Committee, asked for a Congressional hearing into the results of the election. The hearing, called "A Prescription for Addiction? The Arizona and California Medical Drug Use Initiatives" included sessions where five opponents of medical marijuana and one supporter presented arguments about the laws. The opponents of the law complained that the voters were "duped" and did not understand the initiative for which they were voting. The sole supporter, Marvin Cohen, a former official in the Carter administration, stated that the allegation that the voters were duped was "absurd."[3]

Despite the negative allegations made about medical marijuana in the hearing, the entire Congress debated medical marijuana for the first time in the 104th Session (1995–96). A bill was introduced by Barney Frank (D-MA), and had eighteen co-sponsors. The proposal, HR 2618, would "provide for the therapeutic use of marijuana in situations involving life-threatening or sense-threatening illnesses and to provide adequate supplies of marijuana for such use." Under the proposal, the Controlled Substances Act (CSA) would be amended to authorize medical prescriptions of marijuana, subject to regulations that would be created by the Secretary of Health and Human Services. If the law passed, marijuana would be defined as a prescription drug that could be used for specified purposes. Only certain physicians would be certified and would be eligible to prescribe marijuana through a written prescription.The bill would also create an Office for the Supply of Internationally Controlled Drugs, which would be housed within the Department of Health and Human Services. The primary responsibility of the Office would be to regulate, administer, and supervise the domestic production of marijuana that would be distributed for medical, scientific, and research purposes.

Under the bill, bids would be accepted by those interested in growing and harvesting marijuana for the government. Within four months of their first harvest, officials working in the newly established Office would take possession of the harvested marijuana. If the marijuana supply was inadequate to meet the medical, scientific and research needs, the Secretary of Health and Human Services would declare a state of emergency. At that time, the Secretary would make other arrangements for importation of an adequate supply of marijuana. The Secretary of Health and Human Services would be required to secure and maintain a supply of marijuana that would be needed. The Secretary was also required to set a price for the drug that would allow for the costs incurred by the Government in producing, processing, and distributing marijuana to be covered.

The proposal created procedures for physicians interested in prescribing marijuana to their patients to file written application with the Office to be granted permission to do so. There were also provisions to allow hospitals and pharmacies to obtain adequate supplies of marijuana for their patients. Penalties would be established if the medicinal marijuana was used or distributed in a way that violated the new law.

At the end of the 104th Congress, the bill did not receive any action and died.

105th Congress (1997–98)

The Senate Judiciary Committee's hearings into the California and Arizona laws continued in this Congressional Session. Opponents of the new law, including the administration's Drug Czar, General Barry McCaffrey, made charges that the campaigns were run unfairly and that those who contributed to the campaigns had possibly violated federal statutes. They discussed their amazement at how the voters of those states could be so easily "duped" into voting for the proposals. On the other side were supporters of both the initiative and the campaign.[4]

During the 105th Congress, six bills were proposed on medical marijuana. One of those was HR 1265, the Medical Marijuana Deterrence Act of 1997, sponsored by Representative Gerald B. H. Soloman (R-NY). If passed, The Act would have provided that an individual who was convicted of a state-level drug trafficking or possession offense in a state where it is legal to use medical marijuana, would be ineligible for certain Federal benefits such as grants, contracts, loans, or licenses provided by a Federal agency or through appropriated funds.

Another proposed bill was HR 1310, the Medical Marijuana Prevention Act of 1997, also sponsored by Representative Soloman. This law would require that the Attorney General revoke the registration of any registrant to manufacture, distribute, or dispense a controlled substance or list I chemical who recommends to a patient a use which is illegal, under Federal law, of a controlled substance.

Representative Frank (and eleven co-sponsors) proposed a bill, HR 1782, the Medical Use of Marijuana Act. The bill would move marijuana from Schedule I to Schedule II of the Controlled Substances Act. It also declared that, in those states where marijuana may be prescribed or recommended by a physician for medical use, no provision of the Controlled Substances Act or the Federal Food, Drug, and Cosmetic Act (FDCA) shall stop a physician from prescribing the drug for medical reasons. Nor could an individual be stopped from obtaining and using marijuana if they had a prescription or recommendation from a physician. No pharmacy could be stopped from obtaining and holding marijuana for medical use by patients. The proposed bill also required the National Institute of Drug Abuse (NIDA) to make marijuana available for an investigational new drug study.

Senator Frank Riggs (R-CA) proposed HR 3184 that would clarify any doubts as to the application of Federal controlled substances laws in those states that passed laws to allow for the medical marijuana. Under the proposal, the Controlled Substances Act and the Controlled Substances Import and Export Act would apply according to their terms, notwithstanding any state law authorizing the use or distribution, by an individual or group, of marijuana or any controlled substance for medicinal or any other purpose.

The fifth law that was proposed during this session was S 15, the Youth Violence, Crime and Drug Abuse Control Act of 1997, sponsored by Senator Thomas A. Daschle (D-SD) and twenty-one co-sponsors. As part of a larger bill, the Office Director was required to conduct a study on the effects of the 1996 voter referenda in California and Arizona on the medicinal use of marijuana and other controlled substances on the general use of such substances in those States.

Finally, during that session, Senator John Ashcroft (R-MO) proposed the Drug Czar Responsibility and Accountability Act of 1998 (S 2028). This proposal would amend federal law and expand the responsibilities of the Director of National Drug Control Policy (the Drug Czar) to include taking necessary actions to oppose any attempt to legalize the use of a substance in any form that is listed in Schedule I of the Controlled Substances Act and that has not been approved for medical use by the FDA. This bill did not have enough support to pass.

106th Congress (1999–2000)

During this session of Congress there were eight bills relating to medical marijuana that were proposed or debated. One of those was HR 912, or the Medical Use of Marijuana Act, sponsored by Representative Frank and thirteen co-sponsors. The proposal would move marijuana from a Schedule I drug to a Schedule II drug under the Controlled Substances Act. Similar to Frank's proposal in the 105th Congress, this bill required that no provision of the Controlled Substances Act or the Federal Food, Drug, and Cosmetic Act (FDCA) shall restrict a physician from prescribing medical marijuana for medical use in those states where medical marijuana is allowed. Also in those states, an individual could not be restricted from obtaining and using marijuana through a prescription or recommendation by a physician for medical use. A pharmacy could not be halted from obtaining and holding marijuana for medical use by patients. Moreover, the law would require the National Institute of Drug Abuse to make marijuana available for an investigational new drug study under specified provisions of the FDCA.

The second bill offered this session was HR 2959, a proposal to prohibit the Legalization of Marijuana for Medical Treatment Initiative of 1998 from taking effect. It was sponsored by Representative Bob Barr (R-GA), with only one co-sponsor. Under the proposal, a proposition passed by voters in the District of Columbia, called the Legalization of Marijuana for Medical Treatment Initiative of 1998, would be prohibited from being implemented.

HR 3064, the District of Columbia Appropriations Act of 2000, sponsored by Representative Ernest Istook (R-OK), also provided that the Legalization of Marijuana for Medical Treatment Initiative of 1998, Initiative 59, approved by the electors of the District, would not be implemented. The same provision was found in HR 3194, the Consolidated Appropriations Act of 2000, also sponsored by Representative Istook, and in HR 4942, HR 5547, and HR 5633, all District of Columbia Appropriations Act of 2001.

A similar bill with the same intent was S 3041, District of Columbia Appropriations Act, 2001, sponsored by Senator Kay Bailey Hutchinson (R-TX). This proposal was another attempt to prohibit the Legalization of Marijuana for Medical Treatment Initiative of 1998, also known as Initiative 59, approved by the electors of the District from taking effect.

HJ Res 69, also known as the Disapproving the Legalization of Marijuana for Medical Treatment Initiative of 1998, was proposed by Representative Barr with no cosponsors. This bill demonstrated disapproval of the action of the District of Columbia Council and the Legalization of Marijuana for Medical Treatment Initiative of 1998. A similar resolution occurred in the Senate (SJ Res 35), sponsored by George Voinovich (R-OH). This was a joint resolution that showed disapproval for the Legalization of Marijuana for Medical Treatment Initiative of 1998.

107th Congress (2001–02)

Senator Frank and twenty co-sponsors supported HR 1344 and HR 2592, both referred to as the States' Rights to Medical Marijuana Act in the 107th Congress. These proposals would move marijuana from a Schedule I drug to a Schedule II drug under the Controlled Substances Act. As the same law in the 105th Congress, this bill required that no provision of the Controlled Substances Act or the Federal Food, Drug, and Cosmetic Act (FDCA) shall restrict a physician from prescribing medical marijuana for medical use in those states where medical marijuana is allowed. Also in those states, an individual could not be restricted from obtaining and using marijuana through a prescription or recommendation by a physician for medical use. A pharmacy could not be stopped from obtaining and holding marijuana for medical use by patients.

Many other bills were attempts to prohibit implementation of the Legalization of Marijuana for Medical Treatment Initiative of 1998, also known as Initiative 59, approved by the electors of the District of Columbia. One of these bills was HR 2944, the District of Columbia Appropriations Act of 2002, sponsored by Representative Joe Knollenberg (R-MI). Another was HR 5521, the District of Columbia Appropriations Act of 2003, also sponsored by Representative Knollenberg. Senator Mary Landrieu (D-LA) proposed S 1543, the District of Columbia Appropriations Act of 2002. She also introduced S 2809, the District of Columbia Appropriations Act of 2003, having provisions to prohibit the D.C. Initiative from taking effect.

Late in 2002, Representatives Frank and Ron Paul (R-TX) introduced legislation that would allow states to use marijuana for medical purposes. One of its supporters was Lyn Nofziger, who worked with President Reagan and supported his anti-marijuana policies. Nofziger claimed to have been convinced of the benefits of medical marijuana after his oldest daughter died from lymphoma.[5] This did not pass into law.

108th Congress (2003–04)

During the 108th Congress, HR 1717, or the Truth in Trials Act, was proposed by Representative Sam Farr (D-CA) with forty-two co-sponsors. The Act was a proposal to amend the Controlled Substances Act to create and allow an affirmative defense for any person facing prosecution or other legal proceeding for any marijuana-related offense when the activities in question complied with state laws regarding the medical use of marijuana. Specifically, the proposal would allow a defendant to be found guilty of a lesser offense if the defendant's marijuana-related activity was found to be for medical purposes. Moreover, any property seized as a result of an investigation would be returned. The same proposal was made in the Senate (S 2989) by Senator Dick Durbin (D-IL) and two co-sponsors.

Another bill proposed during the 108th Congress was HR 2086, the Office of National Drug Control Policy Reauthorization Act of 2003, introduced by Representative Mark Souder (R-IN) and one other sponsor. The proposal would allow the Director of the National Drug Control Policy Office (the drug czar) to conduct advertising and other activities that emphasize prevention of youth marijuana use. The proposal would also repeal the Drug-Free Media Campaign Act of 1998.

Again this session, Representative Frank and forty-four co-sponsors supported the States' Rights to Medical Marijuana Act (HR 2233). The proposal would move marijuana from a Schedule I drug to a Schedule II drug under the Controlled Substances Act. As the same proposal made in the 105th Congress, this bill required that no provision of the Controlled Substances Act or the Federal Food, Drug, and Cosmetic Act (FDCA) shall stop a physician from prescribing medical marijuana for medical use in those states where medical marijuana is allowed. Also in those states, an individual could not be restricted from obtaining and using marijuana through a prescription or recommendation by a physician for medical use; nor could a pharmacy be stopped from obtaining and holding marijuana for medical use by patients.

In HR 2673, the Consolidated Appropriations Act of 2004, sponsored by Representative Henry Bonilla (R-TX), there was a provision to provide that the Legalization of Marijuana for Medical Treatment Initiative of 1998, also known as Initiative 59, approved by the electors of the District on November 3, 1998, would not take effect. This same provision was found in HR 2765, the District of Columbia Appropriations Act sponsored by Representative Rodney Frelinghuysen (NJ), in HR 4850, the District of Columbia Appropriations Act of 2005, and in HJ Res 2, the Consolidated Appropriations Resolution of 2003, in S 1583, the District of Columbia Appropriations Act of 2004 sponsored by Senator Mike DeWine (R-OH), and in S 2826, the District of Columbia Appropriations Act of 2005, sponsored by Dewine.

House Amendment 297 (to amend HR 2799) was sponsored by Representative Maurice Hinchey (D-NY), would prohibit the use of funds to prevent the States of Alaska, Arizona, California, Colorado, Hawaii, Maine, Maryland, Nevada, Oregon, or Washington from implementing state laws authorizing the use of medical marijuana in those states. This same provision was found in House Amendment 646, which amends HR 4754 and was sponsored by Representative Farr.

109th Congress (2005–06)

During this session, Representative Frank and thirty-seven sponsors supported HR 2087, the States' Rights to Medical Marijuana Act. The proposal would move marijuana from a Schedule I drug to a Schedule II drug under the Controlled Substances Act. As the same law in the 105th Congress, this bill required that no provision of the Controlled Substances Act or the Federal Food, Drug, and Cosmetic Act (FDCA) shall restrict a physician from prescribing medical marijuana for medical use in those states where medical marijuana is allowed. Also in those states, an individual could not be restricted from obtaining and using marijuana through a prescription or recommendation by a physician for medical use; or a pharmacy from obtaining and holding marijuana for medical use by patients.

One proposal for a new law was introduced to the House, HR 3058, related to medical marijuana was the Transportation, Treasury, Housing and Urban Development, the Judiciary, the District of Columbia, and Independent Agencies Appropriations Act of 2006, sponsored by Representative Knollenberg. Under the law, officials would be prohibited from using funds from this Act to enact or carry out any law, rule, or regulation to legalize or otherwise reduce penalties associated with the possession, use, or distribution of any Schedule I substance under the Controlled Substances Act or any tetrahydrocannabinois (THC) derivative. It also had a provision to block the implementation of the Legalization of Marijuana for Medical Treatment Initiative of 1998, also known as Initiative 59, approved by the electors of the District on November 3, 1998.

The Truth in Trials Act was again proposed during this session. This time it was known as the Steve McWilliams Truth in Trials Act (HR 4272), and was sponsored by Representative Farr and nineteen co-sponsors. The Act created an affirmative defense for any individual who was charged with legal action related to a marijuana offense when the activities were in compliance with state law on the use of medical marijuana. In short, this proposal would make it possible for defendants in court to explain to jurors that their marijuana activity was related to their medical condition and legal under state law. The proposal would allow for a defendant to be found guilty of a lesser offense if the jurors decided that the activity was found to be related to a medical condition. Also, any property seized during the investigation would be returned.

House Amendment 272, sponsored by Representative Hinchey, would amend HR 2862. The amendment would prohibit any funds from this Act from being used to prevent the States of Alaska, California, Colorado, Hawaii, Montana, Nevada, Oregon, Vermont, or Washington from implementing State laws authorizing the use of medical marijuana in those States. The same provisions were part of House Amendment 1143, sponsored by Representative Hinchey, which was attached to 5672, and House Amendment 1144, also sponsored by Representative Hinchey.

A similar proposal was in S 1446, the District of Columbia Appropriations Act of 2006, proposed by Senator Sam Brownback (R-KS). This proposal would prohibit the use of funds to enact any law, rule, or regulation that would either legalize or reduce the penalties associated with the possession, use, or distribution of any schedule I substance under the Controlled Substances Act or any tetrahydrocannabinois (THC) derivative. There was also a provision to block the implementation of the Legalization of Marijuana for Medical Treatment Initiative of 1998, also known as Initiative 59, approved by the electors of the District on November 3, 1998. These words were part of S 3660, the District of Columbia Appropriations Act of 2007, made by Senator Brownback.

110th Congress (2007–08)

One bill proposed during the 110th Congressional session relating to medical marijuana was HR 2764, otherwise known as the Consolidated Appropriations Act of 2008. Part of this bill prohibited the use of funds to enact or carry out any law, rule, or regulation to legalize or reduce penalties associated with the possession, use, or distribution of any schedule I substance under the Controlled Substances Act or any tetrahydrocannabinois (THC) derivative. It would also prohibit the Legalization of Marijuana for Medical Treatment Initiative of 1998, also known as Initiative 59, from taking effect.

The same ideas were part of HR 2829, the Financial Services and General Government Appropriations Act of 2008, sponsored by Representative Jose Serrano (D-NY), and HR 7323, that provided for appropriations for financial services and general government for the fiscal year ending September 30, 2009, also sponsored by Representative Serrano, and in S 3260, the Financial Services and General Government Appropriations Act of 2009 sponsored by Senator Dick Durbin (D-IL).

HR 5842, the Medical Marijuana Patient Protection Act, was sponsored by Representative Frank with 23 co-sponsors. The proposed bill would move marijuana from a Schedule I drug to a Schedule II drug under the Controlled Substances Act. As the same law in the 105th Congress, this bill required that no provision of the Controlled Substances Act or the Federal Food, Drug, and Cosmetic Act (FDCA) shall restrict a physician from prescribing medical marijuana for medical use in those states where medical marijuana is allowed. Also in those states, an individual could not be stopped from obtaining and using marijuana through a prescription or recommendation by a physician for medical use. A pharmacy could not be stopped from obtaining and holding marijuana for medical use by patients.

Representative Hinchey proposed House Amendment 674, to amend HR 3093. The amendment would prohibit funds provided in this Act to the Department of Justice from being used to prevent certain States from implementing their own laws to authorize the use, distribution, possession, or cultivation of medical marijuana.

Senator Ted Kennedy (D-MA) proposed S 1082, the Food and Drug Administration Revitalization Act. In part of a long bill it would require the Secretary of the FDA to require that state-legalized medical marijuana be subject to the full regulatory requirements of agency.

In 2007, Congress passed legislation that expanded the FDA's regulatory powers. HR 3580/PL 110-85 made many changes to the responsibilities of the FDA. During the legislative process, Tom Coburn (R-OK) proposed an amendment to subject medical marijuana to the approval by the FDA, including an examination of its safety and efficacy. The amendment, while adopted in committee, was not included in the final bill.[6]

111th Congress (2009–10)

Once again, Representative Frank (D-MA) proposed the Medical Marijuana Patient Protection Act (HR 2835). The proposed bill would move marijuana from a Schedule I drug to a Schedule II drug under the Controlled Substances Act. As the same law in the 105th Congress, this bill required that no provision of the Controlled Substances Act or the Federal Food, Drug, and Cosmetic Act (FDCA) shall restrict a physician from prescribing medical marijuana for medical use in those states where medical marijuana is allowed. Also in those states, an individual cannot be restricted from obtaining and using marijuana through a prescription or recommendation by a physician for medical use; or a pharmacy from obtaining and holding marijuana for medical use by patients, or an organization that has been established by a state from producing and distributing marijuana for medical use.

The Truth in Trials Act (HR 3939) was again proposed by Representative Farr. The Act created an affirmative defense for any individual who was charged with legal action related to a marijuana-related offense when the activities were in compliance with state law regarding the medical use of marijuana. The proposal would allow for a defendant to be found guilty of a lesser offense if the defendant's marijuana-related activity was found to be related to medical purposes. Also, any property seized during the investigation would be returned.

H.J. Res. 93 was proposed, which disapproved of the action of the District of Columbia Council In approving the Legalization of Marijuana for Medical Treatment Amendment Act of 2010. It was sponsored by Representative Jason Chaffetz (R-UT) and with one co-sponsor. Similarly, HR 1105, the Omnibus Appropriations Act of 2009, proposed by Representative Dave Obey (D-WI) included a provision that attempted to prohibit the D.C. law from being enacted. This was also found in S 1432, the Financial Services and General Government Appropriations Act of 2010, sponsored by Representative Durbin.

112th Congress (2011–12)

During this session, Representative Frank, and 21 co-sponsors, introduced HR 1983, the States' Medical Marijuana Patient Protection Act. If passed, the new law would require the Secretary of Health and Human Services (HHS), within six months of enactment of this Act, to submit to the Administrator of the Drug Enforcement Administration (DEA) a recommendation on the listing of marijuana within the Controlled Substances Act (CSA) and to recommend listing it as other than a Schedule I or Schedule II substance.

Within twelve months, the Administrator of DEA, based upon the recommendation of the National Academy of Sciences, would issue a notice of proposed rulemaking for the rescheduling of marijuana within the CSA. This would include a recommendation to list marijuana as other than a Schedule I or Schedule II substance.

Further, the proposal makes it clear that no provision of the CSA or the Federal Food, Drug and Cosmetic Act should prohibit restrict, in a state in which the medical use of marijuana is legal under state law: (1) the prescription or recommendation of marijuana for medical use by a medical professional or the certification by a medical professional that a patient has a condition for which marijuana may have therapeutic benefit; (2) an individual from obtaining, manufacturing, possessing, or transporting within their state marijuana for medical purposes, provided the activities are authorized under state law.

Congressmen Frank and Paul also introduced a bill in 2011 that would make marijuana completely legal under Federal law. The "Ending Federal Marijuana Prohibition Act of 2011" (HR 2306) would end the schedules that were created in the CSA and remove all Federal penalties for its possession, sale, and cultivation of marijuana. Each state could then decide how to regulate (or even legalize) the drug. The goal of the proposed bill was not to legalize marijuana, but rather to remove marijuana from the list of federally controlled substances. This decision would then permit states to determine if they would legalize marijuana for recreation or medicine, and how they would regulate it. Doing this would end the confusion that patients, caregivers, and dispensary owners now have about whether they are following the laws.[7]

Representative Pete Stark (D-CA) and fourteen other sponsors proposed HR 1985, the Small Business Tax Equity Act of 2011. The proposal would amend the Internal Revenue Code to allow a tax deduction for expenses incurred in the trade or business of selling marijuana intended for patients for medical purposes pursuant to state law.

House Amendment 1084 was a proposal to amends HR 5326. It was sponsored by Representative Dana Rohrabacher (R-CA). The proposal would prohibit the use of funds to be used with respect to preventing the states of Alaska, Arizona, California, Colorado, Delaware, District of Columbia, Hawaii, Maine, Maryland, Michigan, Montana, Nevada, New Jersey, New Mexico, Oregon, Rhode Island, Vermont, and Washington from implementing their own State laws that authorize the use, distribution, possession, or cultivation of medical marijuana.

113th Congress (2013–14)

In the 113rd Congress, two members, Jared Polis (D-CO) and Earl Blumenauer (D-OR), introduced proposals aimed at "de-federalizing" marijuana policy but at the same time implementing federal taxes to cannabis that is used for either medical reasons or recreation. If passed, the first proposal (HR 499), entitled the Ending Federal Marijuana Prohibition Act of 2013, would remove marijuana from the Schedule I classification and give state officials the authority to regulate marijuana rather than the DEA. At that point, each state could choose to permit the use of marijuana. There were 16 co-sponsors for this proposal.

The second proposal, the Marijuana Tax Equity Act, would create a federal tax on the sale of marijuana.[8] HR 501 had 8 cosponsors. The bill would require that any person who engaged in a "marijuana enterprise" to obtain a permit to engage in that business. There would be both civil and criminal penalties for any violations of the law.

Representative Earl Blumenauer and twenty cosponsors introduced HR 689, the States' Medical Marijuana Patient Protection Act. The Secretary of Health and Human Services would, if this proposal passed, submit a recommendation to the DEA on the categorization of marijuana within the Controlled Substances Act (CSA), and to recommend changing it to a from a Schedule I drug.

The affirmative defense would be allowed for those arrested for federal marijuana-related offenses if a proposal introduced by Representative Farr was approved. HR 710, or the Truth in Trials Act, had twelve cosponsors. It would also require that any evidence gathered by law enforcement be preserved and returned in a defendant is acquitted of charges. A similar bill was HR 784, the States' Medical Marijuana Property Rights Protection Act, proposed by Representative Barbara Lee (CA) and six co-sponsors. Under the proposal, real property would be exempt from civil forfeiture if the offense was related to a medical marijuana-related conduct that is authorized under state law.

Conclusion

It is clear that Congress has considered many laws regarding medical marijuana in the past few sessions. However, as more states pass new referendums allowing patients to use the drug, more federal laws allowing for medical marijuana use may appear. This suggestion is supported by a statement made by the House Minority Leader Nancy Pelosi (D-CA) in 2012. She said that after the November 2012 elections, Democrats may seek changes in the federal laws that regulate medical marijuana. Specifically, she said, "I've been very clear on the subject of medical marijuana over time, in committee and on the floor as leader.... It would be hard for anyone to agree with the fact that someone who has HIV/AIDS or has cancer and they find relief from pain in medicinal marijuana that should be something that should be a priority to raid on the part of the Justice Department. Going along with that, we need to address some of the penalties for any nonviolent crimes that are out there." In the past, Pelosi has criticized the Obama administration for the raids on clinics in California.[9] Given this, is may be probable that more proposals to alter the current federal laws on medical marijuana will be introduced into Congress soon.

Table 6.1: Summary of Medical Marijuana Proposals

Congress	Bill Number	Topic	Name
104	HR 2618	Allow for therapeutic use of marijuana and to provide adequate supplies of such	
105	HR 1265	A person convicted of a state offense would be ineligible for federal benefits	Medical Marijuana Deterrence Act
105	HR 1310	The AG will revoke the registration of a manufacturer if they recommend its use by a patient	Medical Marijuana Prevention Act
105	HR 1782	Move marijuana from Schedule 1 to Schedule II	Medical use of Marijuana Act
105	HR 3184	The CSA will apply, notwithstanding any state law	
105	S 15	To conduct a study on effects of CA and AZ laws	Youth Violence, Crime, and Drug Abuse Control Act of 1997
105	S 2028	Expand the responsibilities of Drug Czar	Drug Czar Responsibility and Accountability Act
106	HR 912	Move marijuana from Schedule I to Schedule II	Medical use of Marijuana Act
106	HR 2959	To prohibit the Legalization of Marijuana for Medical Treatment Initiative from taking effect	
106	HR 3064	The Legalization for Marijuana for Medical Treatment Initiative will not take place	DC Appropriations Act
106	S 3041	To prohibit the Legalization of Marijuana for Medical Treatment Initiative from taking effect	DC Appropriations Act
106	HJ Res 69	To show disapproval of Legalization of Marijuana for Medical Treatment Initiative	Disapproving the Legalization of Marijuana for Medical Treatment Initiative
106	SJ Res	To show disapproval of Legalization of Marijuana for Medical Treatment Initiative	Disapproving the Legalization of Marijuana for Medical Treatment Initiative
107	HR 1344/ HR 2592	Move marijuana from a Schedule I to Schedule II	States' Rights to Medical Marijuana Act
107	HR 2944	To prohibit the Legalization of Marijuana for Medical Treatment Initiative from taking effect	

Congress	Bill Number	Topic	Name
107	HR 5521	To prohibit the Legalization of Marijuana for Medical Treatment Initiative from taking effect	DC Appropriations Act of 2003
107	S 1543	To prohibit the Legalization of Marijuana for Medical Treatment Initiative from taking effect	DC Appropriations Act
108	HR 1717	Allow for affirmative defense for marijuana offenses	Truth in Trials Act
108	S 2989	Allow for affirmative defense for marijuana offenses	Truth in trials act
108	HR 2086	Allow the Drug czar to advertise	Office of National Drug Control Policy Reauthorization Act
108	HR 2233	Move marijuana from Schedule I to Schedule II	States' Rights to Medical Marijuana Act
108	HR 2673	To prohibit the Legalization of Marijuana for Medical Treatment Initiative from taking effect	Consolidated Appropriations Act
108	HR 2765	To prohibit the Legalization of Marijuana for Medical Treatment Initiative from taking effect	DC Appropriations Act
108	HR 4850	To prohibit the Legalization of Marijuana for Medical Treatment Initiative from taking effect	DC Appropriations Act
108	HJ Res 2	To prohibit the Legalization of Marijuana for Medical Treatment Initiative from taking effect	Consolidated Appropriations Resolution of 2003
108	S 1583	To prohibit the Legalization of Marijuana for Medical Treatment Initiative from taking effect	DC Appropriations Act
108	S 2826	To prohibit the Legalization of Marijuana for Medical Treatment Initiative from taking effect	DC Appropriations Act
108	House Amend 297	To prohibit use of funds to prevent implementation of state laws	
108	House Amend 646	To prohibit use of funds to prevent implementation of state laws	
109	HR 2087	Move marijuana from a Schedule I to a Schedule II drug	States' Right to Medical Marijuana Act
109	HR 3058	To prohibit use of funds to carry out any law associated with CSA	Independent Appropriations Act

Congress	Bill Number	Topic	Name
109	HR 4272	Affirmative defense	Steve McWilliams Truth in Trials Act
109	House Amend 272	To prohibit use of funds to carry out any law associated with CSA	
109	House Amend 1143	To prohibit use of funds to carry out any law associated with CSA	
109	House Amend 1144	To prohibit use of funds to carry out any law associated with CSA	
109	S 1446	To prohibit use of funds to carry out any law associated with CSA	DC Appropriations Act
109	S 3660	To prohibit use of funds to carry out any law associated with CSA	DC Appropriations Act
110	HR 2764	To prohibit use of funds to carry out any law associated with CSA	Consolidated Appropriations Act
110	HR 2829/ HR 7323	To prohibit use of funds to carry out any law associated with CSA	Financial Services and Government Appropriations Act
110	HR 5842	To move marijuana from a Schedule I to a Schedule II drug	Medical Marijuana Patient Protection Act
110	House Amend 674	To prohibit funds from being used to prevent states from implementing their marijuana laws	
110	S 1082	Require that state laws be subject to full regulatory requirements of FDA	FDA Revitalization Act
110	HR 3580	To subject medical marijuana to the approval of FDA	
111	HR 2835	Move marijuana from a Schedule I to a Schedule II drug	Medical Marijuana Patient Protection Act
111	HR 3939	Creates an affirmative defense	Truths in Trial Act
111	HJ Res 93	Disapproved the Legalization of Marijuana for Medical Treatment Amendment Act	
111	HR 1105	Prohibits the Legalization of Marijuana for Medical Treatment Amendment Act	Omnibus Appropriations Act
111	S 1432	Prohibits the Legalization of Marijuana for Medical Treatment Amendment Act	Financial Services and General Government Appropriations Act

Congress	Bill Number	Topic	Name
112	HR 1983	To move Marijuana from a Schedule I to a Schedule II drug	States' Medical Marijuana Patient Protection Act
112	HR 1985	To Amend the IRS code to allow for a tax deduction for expenses related to marijuana trade	Small Business Tax Equity At
112	House Amend 1084	Prohibit use of funds to be used to prevent states from implementing their laws	
113	HR 499	Remove marijuana from Schedule I classification and give state officials the authority to regulate marijuana.	Ending Federal Marijuana Prohibition Act of 2013
113	HR 501	Creates a federal tax on the sale of marijuana.	Marijuana Tax Equity Act
113	HR 689	Require the Secretary of Health and Human Services to submit a recommendation to the DEA regarding the on the categorization of marijuana by the Controlled Substances Act	States' Medical Marijuana Patient Protection Act
113	HR 710	Would allow for the affirmative defense for those arrested on federal marijuana offenses. Any evidence gathered by law enforcement must be preserved and returned to defendant.	Truth in Trials Act
113	HR 784	Real property exempted from civil forfeiture if the offense was related to a medical marijuana-related conduct that is authorized under state law.	States' Medical Marijuana Property Rights Act

Review/Discussion Questions

1. Choose a session and describe the proposed laws made in Congress that year.
2. If you were to write a bill on medical marijuana for Congress to consider, what would that bill entail?
3. Who are the legislators who propose medical marijuana bills? Investigate their backgrounds and records in Congress.

Key Terms

Office for the Supply of Internationally Controlled Drugs
Youth Violence, Crime and Drug Abuse Control Act of 1997
Medical Use of Marijuana Act
Legalization of Marijuana for Medical Treatment Initiative of 1998
Legalization of Marijuana for Medical Treatment Initiative of 1998 (Initiative 59)
States' Rights to Medical Marijuana Act
Ending Federal Marijuana Prohibition Act of 2011
States' Medical Marijuana Property Rights Protection Act
Marijuana Tax Equity Act
Truth in Trials Act

Chapter 7

Court Decisions

Overview: Courts on the federal, state and local levels have all heard cases dealing with medical marijuana. These cases have helped to define the laws regarding medical marijuana and the rights patients have to use the drug.

Introduction

As the third branch of government, the judiciary branch, or courts, review the actions of legislative branches at all levels to determine the constitutionality of laws and the way in which they are implemented. In the U.S., the Supreme Court is the highest court in the land and their decisions are final and binding on all lower courts. Moreover, the U.S. Constitution is the Supreme Law of the nation. All legislation must be in agreement with the rights provided in that document. If a federal or state law is found to be in violation of the Constitution, the Supreme Court can declare it to be unconstitutional. Further, if a law is found to be implemented in a way that is contradictory to the U.S. Constitution, it can be declared unlawful.

The Constitution sets up a dual system of courts, which means that there are two court systems that operate simultaneously. There are courts on the federal level that hear questions regarding violations of federal law, and courts on the state level that preside over cases regarding violations of state laws. There are also local courts that hear cases on local laws. Differences also exist between trial courts and appellate courts. Trial courts are those that handle criminal cases where people are charged with violating a law. In these courts, a defendant is found to be guilty or not guilty of an accusation through a process that includes a judge, jury, prosecution and defense. The second type of court is an appellate court, which reviews the acts of lower courts and determine if the law was applied correctly. They also review laws passed by Congress to determine their Constitutionality.

The U.S. Supreme Court has relied on both the United States Supremacy Clause and the Commerce Clause in reaching its decisions regarding medical cannabis. The Supremacy Clause declares that all laws made in pursuance of the Constitution shall be the "supreme law of the land" and shall be legally superior to any conflicting provision of a state constitution or law. The Commerce Clause states that "the Congress shall have power to regulate Commerce with foreign Nations, and among the several States, and with the Indian Tribes." Another important legal concept used in cases related to medical marijuana is "medical necessity defense." Many marijuana patients claim that they should be legally permitted to defend themselves against criminal charges if they can demonstrate that their drug activities (i.e. possession, use, cultivation, transportation of marijuana) are necessary or appropriate based on their medical condition.

The issues surrounding medical marijuana have been heard by courts on the federal and state levels. The decisions of the courts help to define the status of the laws and how they are, or should be, implemented. The following chapter provides a description of the cases and issues heard in the courts revolving around medical marijuana.

U.S. Supreme Court

The U.S. Supreme Court has only addressed a few questions related to medical marijuana. This is simply because it takes time for cases to move up through the lower courts before appearing before the US Supreme Court. One of the earliest cases appeared as late as 2001.

United States v. Oakland Cannabis Buyer's Cooperative, 532 US 483 (2001)

In 1996, voters in California passed Proposition 215, the Compassionate Use Act, that made medical use of marijuana legal in the state. However, this law contradicted federal law, particularly the Marijuana Tax Act (1937) and the Comprehensive Drug Abuse Control Act of 1970. Officials in the federal government held the position that, despite the new state law, marijuana remained a Schedule I drug with no medical use, and that its use was illegal under federal law. Thus, patients who needed marijuana for medical treatment could use synthetic marijuana.

The Oakland Cannabis Buyer's Cooperative (OCBC) took the opposite position. They believed that the federal government had wrongly classified marijuana as a Schedule I drug, and that it had medicinal value. Further, under the new law, the Cooperative should be legally permitted to distribute cannabis to patients. Federal officials sought to close the OCBC and thirteen other medical marijuana distributors who were operating openly after Proposition 215 passed. Federal officials filed separate lawsuits against each of the centers.

In 1998, the case against the Cannabis Cultivator's Club was heard in the U.S. District Court (*United States v. Cannabis Cultivators Club*, 5 F. Supp. 2d 1086, 1992; ND Cal. 1998). While the Club argued that they should be permitted to use the medical necessity defense and remain open, the federal government argued that distributing marijuana was illegal and the centers should close. The court ruled that the medical necessity defense was not acceptable in this case and that by distributing marijuana to patients, the centers were violating the Comprehensive Drug Abuse Prevention and Control Act of 1970. Because of the decision, ten distribution centers shut down. The OCBC was also ordered to shut down, but it remained open. The OCBC filed two motions, one which claimed that the OCBC was immune from liability under federal law, and the second asking permission from the federal government to continue to distribute medicinal marijuana to those patients who had a doctor's certificate.[1]

District Court Judge Charles Breyer denied the OCBC's request to continue to operate, claiming that the Center did not prove that the federal government's actions were violating a patient's right to use marijuana. The Judge ruled that the OCBC violated a federal injunction by continuing to operate and distribute marijuana. Only two hours before federal marshals were going to lock the OCBC doors, employees voluntarily closed the agency, giving away trays of marijuana plants to patients.[2]

OCBC appealed the ruling. In 1999, the Ninth Circuit Court of Appeals reversed the decision and ordered the judge to review his original 1998 decision, stating that the medical necessity defense protected the patients and caregivers if they could demonstrate that marijuana was an indispensible part of their medical treatment. Justice Breyer, the presiding judge, amended his ruling, allowing cannabis centers to re-open. This time, the federal government appealed the Ninth Circuit's ruling to the U.S. Supreme Court. In doing so, the Supreme Court agreed to review the viability of the medical necessity defense in relation to medical marijuana.

While the Clinton administration indicated to the court that the medical necessity defense was contradictory to federal law, the justices on the Supreme Court unanimously overturned the Ninth Circuit's decision and upheld the District Court's ruling (*United States v. Oakland Cannabis Buyer's Cooperative*,

532 US 483, 2001). They decided in an 8-0 vote that the medical necessity defense could not be allowed in federal courts as a way to create a legal exception for the distribution of medical cannabis.[3] In essence, the Court stated that
federal drug laws take precedence over state laws, and that federal law prevents
states from legalizing the manufacture or distribution of marijuana for medical reasons.[4]

The court reasoned that because Congress had the ability to regulate illegal
drug use, the courts could decide if the action should be within the reach of
federal power. The court held that simply because the marijuana in question
was cultivated for medical purposes, it did not mean that the drug was not
transported in interstate commerce, nor did it mean that it was not purchased
as part of the larger, national drug market. Since the Club's conduct involved
distribution of marijuana, a commercial activity that invokes the authority of
the Commerce Clause, the Congress could regulate it.

In this case, however, the court did not rule on the possibility that the plaintiffs could legally use medical marijuana they had grown on their own.[5]

Conant v. Walters (309 F. 3d 629)

Dr. Marcus Conant was a physician in California who treated many HIV
and AIDS patients. Conant, a doctor for 33 years, prescribed Marinol (a synthetic form of marijuana) for his patients, but found that medical marijuana
was often more effective for some patients (and thus the only viable treatment
option for these patients). Because of federal law, Conant was legally unable
to prescribe medical marijuana to his patients. After Proposition 215 was passed
in California, Dr. Conant sought clarification about his right to recommend
to his patients that they use marijuana. Under federal law, those physicians
found to be recommending or writing prescriptions for medical marijuana in
California could be in violation of federal drug laws and could face harsh
mandatory sentences (up to life in prison) upon conviction. Under the law, if
a patient became involved in a medicinal marijuana distribution club with the
advice of a physician, that physician could be liable for all of the marijuana
that the patient and the marijuana distribution center ever bought or sold.

Conant believed that the federal government was violating his First Amendment right to free speech. Specifically, he argued that the First Amendment to
the U.S. Constitution protected him from federal attempts to prevent him from
discussing (and even recommending) marijuana as a form of treatment for
sick patients. The drug czar at the time, John P. Walters, argued that when Conant discussed medical marijuana with patients, he was violating federal law
because he was threatening the health and safety of the American public. In

return, Conant argued that as a physician, he should be able to discuss treatment options fully and honestly with his patients.

Conant brought a suit against the federal government, in particular the new drug czar General Barry McCaffrey, Attorney General Janet Reno, and Secretary of Health and Human Services Donna Shalala. Conant argued that the federal government's policy concerning medical marijuana was inconsistent and threatened his First Amendment rights to free speech. Additionally, the government and Bush administration officials (the DEA) were acting outside of their authority when they threatened to withdraw the ability of doctors to write prescriptions for those doctors who recommended medical marijuana to their patients.

Conant was not alone in his legal battle. The CEO of the California Medical Association, Dr. Jack Lewin, filed an amicus brief on Conant's behalf, presenting the argument that the Bush administration and the DEA were jeopardizing patients by preventing physicians from discussing all options open to them. At the same time, he argued that they were censoring the physicians' free speech. Also helping Conant was the ACLU, various medicinal marijuana advocacy groups, other activist doctors, and some patients using medicinal marijuana.

In July 2000, a U.S. District judge issued a permanent injunction against the federal government and their efforts to prosecute physicians for recommending marijuana (N.D. Cal. Sept. 7, 2000). The injunction forced federal law enforcement agencies to allow physicians to discuss treatment options such as medicinal marijuana with their patients. The federal government appealed the decision to the Ninth Circuit Court of Appeals, but lost (in *Conant v. Walters*, 309 F. 3d 629, 2002). The Circuit Court judges ruled that the federal government could not revoke the licenses of doctors who recommended marijuana to their patients, noting that doctors must be able to speak "frankly and openly" to their patients. The federal government then appealed the case to the Supreme Court. In October 2003, the Supreme Court refused to hear the government's appeal, letting the ruling of the lower court stand. This was a victory for the medical marijuana movement. Dr. Conant's free speech argument won and the decision protected a physicians' right to talk about medical marijuana with their patients.[6]

Raich v. Ashcroft

This case began in 2002 when some Californians were charged by federal law enforcement of violating federal drug laws. In August 2002, the DEA raided the residence of Diana Monson, where Angel Raich was living. Monson and Raich both suffered from serious medical diseases and used marijuana regularly to relieve their symptoms. Angel Raich was the wife of a lawyer for the

Oakland Cannabis Buyers Club, Robert Raich. Raich argued that the federal government violated the defendant's fifth, ninth and tenth Amendments, as well as violated their rights under the Commerce Clause of Article 1 of the Constitution. Raich argued that the Attorney General of the U.S., John Ashcroft, was wrong to have seized intrastate medical marijuana that was privately grown by patients and caregivers inside the state of California. Raich further argued that Ashcroft violated the civil rights and the law by harassing, raiding, arresting and prosecuting Raich and others.

Raich lost her case in District Court (248 F. Supp. 2d 918 (ND Cal. 2003). She then filed an appeal in March 2003 in the Ninth Circuit Court of Appeals. The Ninth Circuit Court reversed the decision by the district court (352 F. 3d 1222 (2003)). In 2004, the Supreme Court agreed to hear the case. In 2005, the Supreme Court ruled against Raich (545 U.S. 1) in a 6-3 vote (The case was now *Gonzales v. Raich* (Previously *Ashcroft v. Raich*, 545 U.S. 1 (2005).)). In the decision, it was noted that Congress has the right to regulate interstate commerce, and to prohibit possession of marijuana when state law permits medical use of the drug, and the substance is grown and used locally and non-commercially, through their power to regulate commerce. By banning growing marijuana for medical use, it was a way for Congress to prevent or limit access to marijuana use for other purposes. The justices held that Congress's commerce clause power extended to intrastate, noncommercial possession or cultivation of marijuana because of the potential impact that medical use of marijuana could have on the national market for the product.[7] The justices struck down the California law that exempted patients or caregivers from criminal prosecution if they possessed or grew marijuana for medicinal purposes if it was recommended or approved by a physician. Federal drug laws did not include such an exemption.[8]

The Court explained that under the Controlled Substances Act, marijuana is a Schedule I drug and is therefore strictly regulated by the federal government. They decided that the Commerce clause can be applied to individuals in California who grow marijuana for their own personal, medical reasons. Additionally, under the Supremacy Clause, the federal regulation of marijuana superseded any state laws. The Court found that the medical marijuana law in California did not provide a federal defense if an individual is arrested for growing or possessing marijuana. In other words, all marijuana activity in California is illegal and subject to federal prosecution.

During the process, The Partnership for a Drug Free America and the Community Rights Council government filed amicus curiae briefs with the court to support the government. Other briefs were filed in favor of the defendants by The Cato Institute, the Institute for Justice, NORML, libertarian organizations, and other groups opposed to the War on Drugs. The governments of

California, Maryland, and Washington also filed briefs supporting the defendants. The attorneys general of Alabama, Louisiana, and Mississippi filed a brief supporting the defendants on the grounds of states' rights.[9]

Oregon: Cynthia Willis

In 2012, the Supreme Court refused to hear a case revolving around the right of medical marijuana patients to own firearms. Cynthia Willis lived in a small town in Oregon, and held a concealed hand-gun permit for many years. As she was attempting to renew her permit, the sheriff discovered that Willis was also a medical marijuana patient. The Sheriff argued that issuing the renewed license would violate the Gun Control Act of 1968, which forbids anyone who uses or is addicted to a controlled substance from having a weapon.

The lower court found that the Sheriff had no precedent to deny Ms. Willis her gun permit simply because she was a medical marijuana patient. The sheriff appealed the decision, and Ms. Willis again prevailed. The sheriff then took the case to the Oregon Supreme Court, which agreed with the lower court rulings. The sheriff sought to take the case to the U.S. Supreme Court, but the justices there decided not to hear the case.[10] Thus, the ruling of the lower court stood.

San Diego County

The U.S. Supreme Court opted not to hear a case brought by San Diego County. In 1996, a new law was passed that required local governments to provide identification cards for those patients who were given permission to use medical marijuana by a doctor. The ID cards would be used as people entered marijuana shops, or to show to police officers who find patients who possessed marijuana. San Diego County argued that they were not required to provide ID cards to patients since the federal ban on marijuana trumps state law.

The suit was filed in 2006. Both the San Diego Superior Court and the Fourth District Court of Appeals rejected the argument made by San Diego County. The case went to the California Supreme Court, which, in 2008, refused to hear the case. The San Diego Board of Supervisors voted to appeal to the U.S. Supreme Court, but the justices chose not to hear the case.[11] This meant that ID cards would be distributed by local government officials.

Lower Federal Courts

Some legal cases have also been heard by lower federal courts. These cases involve violations of federal law, but do not contain questions of constitutionality and therefore were not heard in the U.S. Supreme Court.

Todd McCormick

Todd McCormick, who suffered from bone cancer, and Peter McWilliams, who was being treated for AIDs, faced federal drug charges in Los Angeles County when they were accused of illegally cultivating marijuana. During their trial on November 5, 1999, the judge in the U.S. District Court for the Southern District of California ruled that neither could use a medical necessity defense, and that their medical conditions were irrelevant to the criminal charges they faced.[12]

Kuromiya v. United States

This case addressed the right of patients to participate in the federal Compassionate Use Program. The argument was based on the fact that some defendants were not accepted into the program despite facing similar conditions as the eight people who were approved to receive marijuana from the federal government. The Kuromiya plaintiffs brought claims against the government using the Commerce Clause, Ninth and Tenth Amendments, the right to privacy, and the right to equal protections arguing that they should be allowed to participate in the program and receive marijuana from the government. All of these arguments were denied except for the equal protection claim. Federal officials argued that the program had ended and they were no longer accepting patients into the program, so the government was under no obligation to provide marijuana to these patients.

The case was heard in the Eastern District of Pennsylvania. The justices agreed with the plaintiffs' claim of a violation of their equal protection rights, based on the government's operation of its compassionate use program to provide medical marijuana for a small number of individuals, but not for others who were similarly situated. However, their claims were dismissed because the federal government had provided a rational argument to not supply marijuana to the plaintiffs through its program when it decided to terminate the program altogether.[13]

State Court Decisions

Legal issues surrounding medical marijuana have also been heard in state courts. Below is a description of some cases that have been heard in State supreme courts. These courts hear cases related to violations of state laws rather than federal statutes. These decisions can be appealed through the appellate process, even to the U.S. Supreme Court, if they contain a question of Constitutionality.

Michigan

In 2008, the voters in Michigan passed the Medical Marijuana Act (MMA). Since then, there have been many decisions regarding the new law. One was in August 2011, when a Court of Appeals in Michigan ruled that medical marijuana dispensaries are illegal under the law as written, a decision which basically shut down many shops across the state. In another decision in April 2012, a Court of Appeals panel ruled medical marijuana cannot be used as a defense for operating a motor vehicle while intoxicated.

In May 2012, the Michigan Supreme Court made its first major ruling about the MMA when they upheld a patients' right to use an affirmative defense to use medical marijuana even without a state-issued card. The justices unanimously chose to overturn a decision made by the Michigan Court of Appeals when they ruled that both registered and unregistered patients who use medical marijuana are entitled to a medical marijuana defense, as long as they meet the requirement of the law. That decision allowed those patients who had a doctor's approval to present a medical marijuana defense if arrested while possessing marijuana even if they did not have a medical marijuana card in their possession at the time, to be safe from prosecution if they could prove the marijuana was prescribed by a doctor.[14]

Also in May 2012, the Michigan Supreme Court decided to overturn a lower court decision in which a locked chain-link dog kennel was deemed to be an inappropriate facility in which to grow marijuana. Larry King had been charged with manufacturing marijuana after police found six cannabis plants in his outdoor kennel and six others inside his house. In the lower court, King claimed that he met the elements of an affirmative defense under the MMA, and the court agreed and dropped the charges upon an appeal from the state. The Michigan Court of Appeals reversed the decision and concluded that King could not use the affirmative action defense. But the Michigan Supreme Court again reversed the decision of the Court of Appeals, deciding that King's facility was legal and declared that the affirmative defense could be used.[15]

In June, 2012, a Court of Appeals decided that a medical marijuana patient could not be prosecuted for possession of marijuana even if he did not have proof of his registration at the time of his arrest. The court decided that police were correct to arrest the patient, James Nicholson, because he was not able to establish proof of registration upon his arrest. Prosecutors argued that Nicholson was not protected by the MMA because he did not possess a proper identification card. He told police that his registration card was in a car at his home. The court found that because Nicholson was a registered patient prior to his arrest, and that he possessed the registration card when he appeared in court, he was immune from prosecution.[16]

California

In 1997, the California Appeals Court heard *People v. Trippet* (66 Cal. Rptr. 2d 559 (1997); 56 Cal. App. 4th 1532), and reversed the defendant's conviction of possessing and transporting marijuana. Sudi Pebbles Trippet was arrested and charged with transporting marijuana and possessing of over 28.5 grams of the drug (she had approximately two pounds in her car at the time). At trial, the defendant was found guilty on both counts. Trippet argued that even though she suffered from migraine headaches, she was not able to present the medical necessity defense in her trial. Further, the convictions violated her right to exercise her religion, and Proposition 215 (enacted after her convictions) provided her a defense. Although the offense occurred in 1994, two years before the Compassionate Use Act was passed, the appellate court held the medical use defense could be used retroactively and allowed her to use it. The court held that the Compassionate Use Act may provide a legal defense for transporting marijuana if "the quantity transported and the method, timing and distance of the transportation are reasonably related to the patient's current medical needs."[17] The justices noted that there was no language in the Compassionate Use Act that expressly legalized the transportation of medical marijuana.[18] The case was remanded to the trial court for further proceedings.[19]

In another case, the California Court of Appeals held that even after the Compassionate Use Act was passed and implemented, the sale and possession for sale of marijuana was illegal, even if the sale is not for profit. In the case of *People v. Peron* (70 Cal. Rptr. 2d 20 (1997)), the court held that the Compassionate Use Act exempted only simple possession and cultivation of marijuana from prosecution. In addition, cannabis clubs were not authorized to exempt primary caregivers from charges of possession or cultivation of marijuana.[20]

In this case the court held that the Compassionate Use Act protects a defendant from only the possession and use of marijuana for medical purposes, but not the purchase or sale of marijuana. In other words, according to the Appellate court, if a defendant does not buy or sell marijuana but simply uses it or grows it for medical purposes, the criminal exemption may apply. However, once money changes hands, the conduct is not covered by the Compassionate Use Act.[21] The case was heard by the California Supreme Court in February, 1998. The Court let the ruling of the lower court stand, agreeing that the state's new medical marijuana law does not allow cannabis clubs to sell marijuana[22] (*People v. Peron*, Calif Ct App, 1stDist, No. A077630, 62 CrL 1267, (12/12/97)). The presiding Justice in the case, J. Clinton Peterson, stated that the only way a patient needing the drug can obtain it legally is to grow it themselves or obtain it from a primary caregiver who has grown it.[23]

Pack v. City of Long Beach

Some questions revolving around how local governments can regulate distribution of marijuana were addressed in *Pack v. City of Long Beach*. The number of marijuana collectives grew in California in 2009 and especially in LA county because of the high number of patients who held medical recommendations from their doctor.

After the Second Appellate District Court ruled that some provisions of the city's permitting process to regulate medical marijuana dispensaries was preempted by federal law (i.e. that the city's dispensary licensing process forced participants to violate federal law), the City Council members in Long Beach City passed a new ordinance that would ban all medical marijuana dispensaries. They granted a six month exemption to the ban for the eighteen groups that had already successfully applied through the city's permitting process. By granting the exemption, the State Supreme Court would have ample time to rule on an appeal by the city to clarify which provisions of the ordinance could be upheld and how they would regulate the collectives. In July, when the courts had not yet heard the appeal, the City Council members voted to deny a motion that would allow the eighteen medical marijuana clinics to operate past the date chosen to close their operations until the Supreme Court ruled in the case.[24] The officials in the City of Long Beach sought to appeal their case to the California Supreme Court. However, on June 29, 2012, the California Supreme Court declined to hear the case.

People v. Patrick Kelly

On May 22, 2008, the Second District Court of Appeals in California ruled 3–0 that possession and cultivation limits on medical marijuana set in state laws (SB 420) are unconstitutional in the case *People v. Patrick Kelly* ((2010) 47 Cal.4th 1008, 1014.)).

The justices overturned the defendant's conviction after he was arrested for possessing twelve ounces of dried marijuana plants. The Attorney General's office announced that it would appeal the decision.[25] On January 21, 2010, The California Supreme Court affirmed the ruling that possession limits are unconstitutional by a 7–0 decision.

People v. Solis

Three defendants, Juan Solis, Sinthia Martinez, and Rudy Lopez operated a medical marijuana collective in California that had approximately 1,700 members. The collective had a profit of about $80,000 per year, which was considered to be Solis' salary. But this made the operation illegal. Under the law in California, dispensaries are to operate on a not-for-profit basis. The collective was not registered as a nonprofit agency and they bought marijuana from outside "vendors."

Solis was convicted on three counts of possessing marijuana for sale, and a misdemeanor count of selling or transporting marijuana. Another defendant, Martinez, was found guilty on one count of possessing marijuana for sale. The third defendant, Lopez was convicted on one count each of possessing marijuana for sale and selling or transporting marijuana. They were each sentenced to three years of probation and ordered to serve time in jail. They defendants appealed, claiming that their collective was legal under the MMP.

When Solis was arrested, the police told him that the collective was illegal and he could not conduct business. But only nine days later, he was open for business and had put a sign in the window that said, "Yes We Are Open." During a search, the police verified that someone purchased marijuana from the collective. Solis said that he would reopen his business every time the police tried to close it.

The defendants argued that their convictions should be reversed because their activities were protected under the state's medical marijuana law. However, the court rejected that argument. The court concluded there was no evidence to raise a reasonable doubt whether the dispensary was operating on a nonprofit basis. The court explained that the California law directed that medical marijuana cooperatives and collectives must be nonprofit operations and must acquire marijuana only from their constituent members. The justices stated that the defendants did not provide evidence that the dispensary was nonprofit, but in fact was, beyond a reasonable doubt, for profit. In the end, the Court affirmed the judgment of the lower court.[26]

County of Los Angeles v. Alternative Medicinal Cannabis Collective (AMCC)

In July, 2012, the Second District Court of Appeal in California affirmed the legality of medical marijuana dispensaries under state law, and at the same time rejected the bans that had been imposed by cities and by Los Angeles County against them. In *County of Los Angeles v. Alternative Medicinal Cannabis Collective (AMCC)*, the justices decided that LA County's ban on medical marijuana was preempted by state law as well and therefore void. The decision provided support for the dispensaries that had been authorized by the new law, and affirmed that they are permitted to operate under the state law. Simply, this case affirmed the legality of dispensaries and rejected the bans that had been passed by municipal governments.[27]

On February 28, 2012, a federal judge dismissed a lawsuit against the federal government for its raids on medical marijuana clinics. After federal prosecutors in California announced a crackdown on medical marijuana dispensaries the previous year, the suppliers and their advocates claimed that the Obama administration broke a promise to leave them alone if they complied with state law. A federal judge in Sacramento dismissed the case, arguing that the Justice Department has the right to enforce federal drug laws. The judge also said that the Ogden memo was a statement of priorities, not a binding commitment, and "did not exempt dispensaries from the federal laws against marijuana cultivation and distribution."[28]

Florida

In 1991, the Florida First District Court of Appeals ruled on the application of a medical necessity defense in response to criminal prosecution in *Jenks v. State of Florida*. The justices decided that in the case of medical marijuana, the patient must be suffering from a medically recognized disease or illness, which is causing a symptom for which there is no effective treatment other than marijuana. Only then can a medical necessity defense be accepted.[29]

Colorado

Jason Beinor was a medical marijuana patient in Colorado. He was a custodian at a local mall, who was released from his job after he failed a random drug test. The company argued that they had a zero-tolerance policy when it came to illegal drugs to justify their actions. Beinor filed for unemployment benefits and was denied. This decision was reversed when a hearing officer ruled that Beinor should receive benefits because there was no evidence to show that he was not eligible for a medical marijuana license or that his job performance was affected because of his drug use. The employer appealed the decision and a judicial panel ruled in the company's favor. They relied on Article XVII of the Colorado Constitution which states that an employee who tests positive during working hours for drugs that are not "medically prescribed" is not eligible for benefits. Further, they noted that doctors in the state could not prescribe marijuana, just recommend it. The case went to the Colorado Court of Appeals, who agreed with the panel.[30] In 2011, marijuana activists appealed the case to the Colorado Supreme Court. The Supreme Court declined to review the case, so the appeals court ruling stands.

Washington

In 1996, a lawyer in Washington State, Ralph Seeley, appeared in front of the Washington Supreme Court to argue his case that the federal government's classification of marijuana as a Schedule I drug violated his equal protection rights under the Washington Constitution. Seeley had been diagnosed with a rare form of bone cancer while in law school, and he used marijuana during his chemotherapy treatments as a way to reduce the nausea and vomiting associated with the treatment. The court ruled against Seeley, arguing that the state constitution did not give citizens of the state any more right to use marijuana than they had under the United States Constitution, which was "none at all."[31]

Conclusion

To date, courts on all levels of government have made decisions regarding medical marijuana. The U.S. Supreme Court has ruled that the federal government has the right to regulate and criminalize cannabis, even for medical purposes. A person can therefore be prosecuted for a cannabis-related crime even if it is legal medical use according to state laws, because federal laws supersede state laws.

As more laws are passed by state legislatures or approved by voters, and more calls are made by the public to allow for medical marijuana use by ill patients, there is no doubt that many more cases will find their way into the court system as people seek to clarify what behaviors are legal or illegal. As more voters opt to enact laws allowing for medical marijuana, the courts will need to address the issues of federalism: can states allow a behavior when it is outlawed by the federal government?

Review/Discussion Questions

1. What is the role of the different types of courts?
2. What was the Supreme Court's decision in *United States v. Oakland Cannabis Buyer's Cooperative*?
3. How did the Court decide *Conant v. Walters*?
4. What was the significance of *Raich v. Ashcroft*?
5. Give some examples of lower court decisions regarding medical marijuana.

Key Terms

Dual Court System
Appellate Court
Trial Court
United States v. Oakland Buyer's Cooperative
Conant v. Walters
Raich v. Ashcroft

Chapter 8

Interest Groups

Overview: Interest groups play a vital role in the legislative process, representing the concerns of different segments of society. Many interest groups have developed around the issue of medical marijuana, and these are the topic of the following chapter.

Introduction

Interest groups are comprised of citizens who come together and, in some organized fashion, attempt to influence legislation so that it reflects their policy interests or goals. As a proposed law is winding its way through the legislative process, these groups put pressure on different officials to write or edit those proposals in such as way that it favors that group's interests. Put very succinctly, they want the laws to include provisions that benefit that group, or that turn their perspectives and ideas into law for all to follow. Thus, the term interest group refers to all organizations who actively seek to create, influence, or implement public policy in a particular way.[1]

Interest groups exist on the federal, state and local levels. Regardless of the level of government, all interest groups try to convince elected officials to vote for, or enact, policies in a way that benefits the group. One way groups do this is by lobbying officials. This means they meet directly, or face-to-face, with legislators (and/or their staff), the president, bureaucracies, or even members of the courts to discuss the issue at hand and present their arguments about why a policy should be passed and/or implemented in a particular way. Groups also use indirect methods to increase support for their proposals. They sometimes use litigation in the courts as a way to change policy. This way, the group can file different briefs and arguments to the justices, thus trying to shape their perceptions of the choices. In some cases, groups can reach out to citizens as a way to garner public support for one policy option. They can also use the media as a way to educate the public about issues. They can also use letter writing campaigns, organized phone calling, or even e-mails

When it comes to making policy, interest groups play many roles in the political process. Sometimes a group can make a legislator aware of an issue, and thus help put that issue on the agenda, or the list of problems to solve. Group members can also help formulate policy, which means they help write a proposal or have some kind of input into the initial formulation of the bill. Interest groups are sometimes asked to testify in front of a committee that is considering a bill as a way to inform the committee members about a problem. In some more public cases, group representatives testify in front of the entire Congress, sometimes receiving a great amount of media attention. Groups also play a role in implementing a policy, or carrying out the policy as enacted by a legislature.

People join interest groups as a way to have their voice heard in the legislature. As most people cannot travel to either their state capital or to the nation's capital to meet with legislators on a regular basis, they rely on an interest group to represent them instead. Members choose to pay money to join a group that they know will represent their perspectives about what a policy should include. In return for their membership dues, a person will not only be represented, but they may also receive literature from the group such as magazines or reports, calendars, or posters.

There are many interest groups that play a role in the political process and have as a goal the legalization of medical marijuana.[2] Some of these are described below.

Alabama Medical Marijuana Coalition

The Alabama Medical Marijuana Coalition (AMMC) was created in 2011 as a way to garner public support for the Medical Marijuana Patients Rights Act.[3] The AMMC's position was that excessive government regulations hinder a physician's ability to effectively treat a patient, as well as the patient's right to receive proper treatment. They supported a proposal that would authorize the medical use of marijuana for certain qualifying patients who have been diagnosed by a physician as having a serious medical condition.[4]

Alliance for Cannabis Therapeutics

The Alliance for Cannabis Therapeutics was founded in 1981 by Alice O'Leary and Robert Randall, who successfully used the medical necessity defense when charged with federal marijuana possession. The Alliance was the first non-profit organization that sought to change the laws that prohibited the use of, and access to, medical marijuana. Today the group provides information about legal and policy issues regarding medical marijuana to legislators and the public.[5]

American Alliance for Medical Cannabis

The members of the American Alliance for Medical Cannabis believes that there should be legal access to medical marijuana by patients, with the assistance of health professionals, members of the community, educators, patients, clergy and caregivers. They work to provide patients, caregivers and other volunteers with the information needed in order to make informed decisions about whether medical marijuana is the right treatment for each patient. They also provide information on the current laws pertaining to medicinal marijuana. For those who are interested in cooking with marijuana, the group provides recipes for edibles. There are also guides available to those who are interested in growing their own plants.

AAMC carries out many actions as they pursue their goal of educating the public about medical marijuana. They hold regular discussions with community leaders and other government representatives about how to promote safe access to marijuana. The members create and distribute educational materials on the topic, and post them on a website so the information is available to all who are interested. Members conduct "Medical Marijuana Schools" for members of the public, law enforcement, caregivers, health professionals, and patients to educate them on the current laws and other related issues. For those people who seek legal resources, the agency will provide this information as well. The agency constantly reviews medical and scientific literature and studies related to medical cannabis, and provide assistance to those patients and their caregivers who seek to create affordable home cannabis gardens.

American Medical Marijuana Association (Michigan)

Originally formed in 1999, the American Medical Marijuana Association is a grass-roots organization founded in Michigan to help patients with qualified, experienced and professionally trained licensed caregivers. They work to protect the rights of ill residents who choose to use marijuana as a treatment for their disease. To do this, they established Compassion Centers across Michigan to provide support to patients. The centers also provide research on issues pertaining to medical marijuana and help to increase the public's awareness of the medical benefits of marijuana. Their Learning Center and Orientation Program (LCOP) trains members to be safe and legal, ensuring that they are knowledgeable in all rules related to the Michigan Medical Marijuana Act and federal laws.

Some of the services provided by the AMMA include medication therapy consultations; affordable, pharmaceutical grade marijuana; a caregiver/patient network; physician certification services; legal protection services. They center provides counselors that can assist patients by answering their questions, and an on-call attorney who can assist with any legal problems.[6]

Americans for Safe Access

Americans for Safe Access (ASA) is the largest national organization that promotes safe and legal access to cannabis for therapeutic use. The membership includes patients, medical professionals, scientists and other concerned citizens who seek to create policies to improve access to medical cannabis for both patients and researchers.[7] They do this through public education, litigation, grassroots development and advocacy, media campaigns, and direct support services. Their motto is: Until there's safe access, we are Americans for Safe Access. ASA was founded in 2002 as a way to create a strong grassroots movement to protect medical marijuana patients and their right to have safe and legal access to the drug. The group provides legal help to patients so they understand the legal system, and also get involved in the legislative process as a way to influence new laws that provide for medical marijuana and that fairly and equally protect patients.

The ASA membership clearly understands the medical cannabis is not the best option for all patients, nor should it be the primary or sole option that a physician considers when treating patients. However, they believe that all patients and physicians should have as many effective options available to them as possible for treating severe pain or other symptoms of a serious or chronic illness. Further, the ASA membership agrees that patients diagnosed with these ailments should be legally permitted to consume their medicine in whatever form is most effective for treating their illness.

The ASA actively fights for medical marijuana by:

- using litigation and court battles to change the legal system;
- monitoring law enforcement activity and holding law enforcement agencies accountable for their actions;[8]
- supporting the push to reclassifying cannabis under the CSA as a way to expand scientific research on its use as for medical reasons;

- supporting expanded research into the effects of cannabis;
- giving patients the right to grow their own medical cannabis so that they have safe and affordable access to the drug;
- regulating dispensaries in a way that recognizes the legality of medical marijuana distribution in many states;
- Halting raids by the federal government against established medical cannabis distribution centers, leaving enforcement to local and state officials.

Table 8.1 indicates how successful the ASA has been in reaching their stated goals.

Arkansans for Compassionate Care

This organization worked to put the Arkansas Medical Marijuana Act on the ballot in November 2012. The initiative would permit those patients who are sick with serious, debilitating medical conditions the right to use medical marijuana, upon a doctor's recommendation. It would allow patients to purchase their medicine at tightly regulated not-for-profit dispensaries across the state.[9]

Coalition for Rescheduling Cannabis

In 2011, advocacy groups concerned with the rights of medical marijuana patients filed a suit in D.C. Circuit Court to compel the Obama Administration to respond to a nine-year-old petition to reclassify medical marijuana. One of the groups involved, the Coalition for Rescheduling Cannabis (CRC), originally petitioned the government for the reclassification in 2002, but never received a response. However, the Department of Health and Human Services made a formal recommendation in 2006 to the Drug Enforcement Administration, the final arbiter in the rescheduling process, about the petition. Other concerned groups include Americans for Safe Access (ASA), and Patients Out of Time.

The writ filed by the groups alleges that government officials have caused unreasonable delay in acting on the petition, which is in violation of the Administrative Procedures Act. Another petition to rescheduling marijuana that was filed in 1972 was not addressed for 22 years, at which point it was denied. In the writ, lawyers argued that marijuana is not a dangerous drug, and that there is sufficient scientific evidence that it has therapeutic value. In fact, the American Medical Association and the American College of Physicians have both asked government officials to review the Schedule I status for marijuana.

Table 8.1: ASA Accomplishments, 2011

Legal

- federal lawsuit challenging interference and intimidation in medical cannabis states; an effort to stop the Department of Justice from commandeering the law making authority of the states.
- lawsuit attacking the delay in a nine year old petition to reschedule marijuana.
- appealed the conviction of San Diego medical cannabis provider Jovan Jackson in a case that may establish that buying and selling medicine is legal under state law.
- authored many amicus ("friend of the court") briefs in support of patients' rights in civil and criminal proceedings.
- assisted more than 12,000 patients and caregivers with law enforcement encounters.

Legislative

- helped build support for federal bills that would protect medical cannabis patients and providers.
- introduced new legislation in California and Alabama, and adopted an affirmative defense bill in Maryland.
- rallied opposition to a bill in California that would place unreasonable restrictions on patients' associations.

Campaigns

- launched a "Stop the Attack Campaign" to put political pressure on the Department of Justice, refocus the national media debate on medical cannabis, and fight for patients rights in the courts.
- created the "Sick and Tired Campaign" as a way to put pressure on President Obama to fulfill his campaign promises for a more enlightened federal policy on medical cannabis.
- created a nationwide campaign to encourage state executives to stand up to federal pressure on medical cannabis.

Building the Movement

- helped facilitate statewide stakeholders meetings, strategy sessions, and skills trainings for advocates on the state-level.
- visited eleven cities in California in eleven days to hold stakeholders meetings and legal trainings.

New Programs

- created an Online Advocates Training Center to teach advocacy skills to the grassroots base of medical cannabis supporters.
- established a Medical Cannabis Policy Shop and Think Tank to provide professional support for patients and advocates working on local and state medical cannabis campaigns, legislation, and referendums.
- hosted Activist Boot Camps in twenty nine cities that serves as a crash course in medical cannabis.

Source: Americans for Safe Access, http://safeaccessnow.org/section.php?id=383; accessed 8/29/2012.

If the CRC petition is formally rejected, the advocacy groups would be able to challenge the government's assertion that marijuana has no medical value in court.[10]

Common Sense for Drug Policy

Common Sense for Drug Policy (CSDP) is a nonprofit organization that has a goal of reforming drug policy and expanding harm reduction. To do this, CSDP disseminates factual information on existing laws, policies and practices regarding marijuana. They also provide advice and assistance to individuals and organizations.

CSDP supports syringe exchanges, the expansion of Methadone programs for treating addictions, and other public health measures that can be used to reduce harm to users. CSDP supports regulating marijuana in a manner similar to alcohol and subject to local rules. CSDP also advocates clear federal guidelines for the practice of pain management so that physicians need not fear unwarranted law enforcement scrutiny of medical practices.

Drug Policy Alliance

The Drug Policy Alliance (DPA) is based in New York City. It was formed in 2000 when The Lindesmith Center, a think-tank, and the Drug Policy Foundation, a grant making organization, merged into one organization. DPA is headed by Ethan Nadelmann, a professor of politics at Princeton University.[11] The group has offices in several states that help to inform its members about current events regarding medical marijuana through its "Action Alerts." The group also sponsors annual conferences to help create a coherent drug policy reform movement.[12]

Law Enforcement Against Prohibition (LEAP)

LEAP is a nonprofit organization that was started in 2002 by former narcotics officers and other police who believe that drug legalization is the best policy for the country. They argue that the existing drug policies in the U.S. have failed to address the problems related to drug abuse, addiction, and crime caused by the black market in drugs. The "war on drugs" has actually made some of the problems worse, according to the group. About 10,000 former police have joined LEAP in the U.S. and ninety other countries,[13] but non-law enforcement can join as well. Their goal is to see a system of legalization and regulation that results in less violence, more protection for human rights, safer communities for children, a reduction in crime and disease, less addiction, and a greater respect and trust in law enforcement.[14]

Marijuana Policy Project

The Marijuana Policy Project was founded in 1995. It has 29,000 members, thirty-six staff members and an annual budget of about $6 million.[15] The organization is based on the premise that the federal policy of banning drugs has failed, and they seek to reform the U.S. marijuana laws. They do this by lobbying legislatures, organizing ballot initiatives that would allow for medical marijuana, and using the media to educate people about the issues. Members also become involved in campaigns to get medical marijuana proposals passed in different states. Their goal is to legalize federal medical marijuana legislation as well in states. This way, we can replace a policy of marijuana prohibition with a system of sensible regulation.

NORML

The National Organization for the Reform of Marijuana Laws (NORML) was founded in 1970 by Keith Stroup, who received $5,000 from the Hugh Hefner's Playboy Foundation for start-up funds. They chose not to promote marijuana use, but instead to attack the legislation governing its use.[16] Today, the members of NORML work to decriminalize (and ultimately legalize) cannabis on the federal and state levels. According to the organization, NORML "supports the removal of all criminal penalties for the private possession and responsible use of marijuana by adults, including the cultivation for personal use, and the casual nonprofit transfers of small amounts," and "supports the development of a legally controlled market for cannabis." NORML is a widely known and powerful organization, with 135 chapters and over 550 lawyers who support their cause. The organization has an annual budget of about $990,000, with six full-time employees.[17]

The members of NORML believe that marijuana use is not a behavior that is appropriate for children, but should be allowed by adults in a responsible manner. Marijuana use must never be an excuse for misconduct or other criminal or harmful behavior. For example, they have made it clear that driving an automobile or operating heavy equipment while impaired after using marijuana should be prohibited.

The NORML Foundation (a 501(d)(3) organization) was established in 1997 to sponsor educational and research activities pertaining to marijuana use.

They often publish reports and documents that describe drug use across the country and NORML's actions.

The members of NORML seek to educate the public on all issues involving marijuana. They do this in many ways, such as:

- working with the media to get their message out to the public;
- holding annual conferences and Continuing Legal Education (CLE) accredited seminars;
- lobbying members of Congress, state legislatures, and bureaucracies as a way to support more rational and fair marijuana laws;
- providing expert witnesses to legislative hearings to supports marijuana reform;
- defending individuals who have been charged with marijuana-related offenses through a legal committee of 350 criminal defense attorneys;
- using litigation to advance their goals;
- becoming involved in elections to provide electoral support candidates who will represent their interests once elected to government positions;
- providing support to local and state initiatives to legalize or decriminalize marijuana use;
- lobbying presidential administrations.[18]

When it comes to medical marijuana, members of NORML strongly support the right of sick patients to use the drug upon the recommendation of a physician as a way to relieve pain and suffering. NORML has advocated for the legal use of medicinal marijuana since 1972. That year, the organization filed a suit to remove marijuana from Schedule I to Schedule V of the CSA. The government did not hold hearings on the proposal, and NORML sued to force a rulemaking proceeding. After a lengthy battle, hearings were finally held in 1986 before Administrative Law Judge Francis Young, who declared that marijuana is a safe therapeutic substance and recommended it be categorized as a Schedule II drug. The recommendation was denied, and the question was finally resolved in 1994 favor of the DEA. The recommendation was to leave marijuana as a Schedule I drug.[19]

Ohio Medical Cannabis Association

The members of the Ohio Medical Cannabis Association believe that Americans should have the right to access to medical marijuana if they are seriously ill. They believe that medical marijuana can improve the quality of the lives of those who are ill and living in Ohio. The organization fought for passage of The Ohio Medical Cannabis Amendment of 2012, a citizen-initiated amendment to the state constitution. Not only does it provide rights to those seeking to use medical marijuana, but it also established the Ohio Commission of Cannabis Control that would support, uphold and defend the rights of these individuals, as well as regulate medical cannabis in Ohio.[20]

Pennsylvanians for Medical Marijuana

In 2006, those who supported legalizing compassionate cannabis in Pennsylvania organized a group called Pennsylvanians for Medical Marijuana. They were led by Barry Busch, who passed away in 2006. The group's members support medical marijuana in the state as well as for legal protections for all patients who opt to use medical marijuana. They also want to educate the public about the need to create medical marijuana policies in the state, as well as stop the arrest of residents who use marijuana as a therapy. Members believe that three concepts drive their work: states' rights, privacy (and freedom of treatment), and compassion.[21]

The group has actively sought to ensure passage of passage of a bill in the state legislature called the Raymond P. Shafer Compassionate Use Medical Marijuana Act (SB 1003/HB 1393). The bill was named after the former governor of the state who supported medical use of marijuana. The bill would authorize a state program for therapeutic cannabis in Pennsylvania.

People United for Medical Marijuana (Florida)

The members of the People United for Medical Marijuana seek to provide patients in Florida with safe, affordable, and effective medication for their illnesses and provide relied for seriously ill. The goal of their organization is to make medical marijuana legal in their state. They work for change with the legislators in the state as well as through ballot initiative process.

The organization is currently working to amend the state constitution in order to give patients the right to grow, obtain, purchase and possess medical marijuana under a doctor's supervision as a way to provide relief for those patients who are terminally or seriously ill. The amendment will provide patients with a safe place to obtain their medicine, allow patients to grow a limited supply for their medical needs, create a registry to help law enforcement distinguish between law abiding citizens and those who are violating the law, decrease health care costs through an inexpensive medication that provides lasting results, lower the crime rate and thereby save the state millions of dollars in prison costs, create thousands of new jobs, and create a new tax revenue for the state.[22]

Sensible Colorado

Sensible Colorado was established in 2004 as a way to convince legislators in Colorado to pass more sensible and effective drug laws. The mission of the organization is to educate the public about medical marijuana and to provide information and resources to marijuana patients. These group members recognize the need to change the law about medical marijuana in their state. They support legislation intended to prevent the arrest of those patients who use marijuana as a medical treatment. The members of Sensible Colorado seek to create a system in which drug use is considered to be a health issue, not a criminal issue and patients have access to effective treatment. At the same time, members also seek to reduce crime, drug use by underage people, and the number of people who are incarcerated for drug use in their state.[23]

Sensible Colorado has worked to establish the rights of medical marijuana patient rights. As early as 2005, the group was pivotal in getting a measure placed on the state ballot that removed all penalties for marijuana possession by adults. After this was passed, the organization did not stop there. In 2007, they won a lawsuit to overturn a law that placed limits on the number of patients a caregiver could help. This battle continued into 2009, when the group oversaw a campaign to defeat Colorado's attempts to re-establish the patient limit for caregivers and shut down marijuana dispensaries.

In 2010, Sensible Colorado members assisted in the implementation of a statewide, for-profit licensing plan for the distribution of medical marijuana and established a nationally-acclaimed distribution system for medical marijuana. When the U.S. attorneys in the state attacked licensed medical marijuana businesses in 2012, group members fought against them.[24]

Students for Sensible Drug Policy

Created in 1998, this organization has over a hundred chapters in 41 states and around the world.[25] The group is a student run organization that seeks to discover more sensible alternatives to the current federal policy of drug prohibition. As an international group, they seek to end the federal war on drugs by bringing young people together for conversations about drugs and drug policy. While they are concerned about the impact that drug abuse has had on communities, they believe that the War on Drugs is failing. The young people in the group seek to achieve a safer and more just future by changing the laws that directly harm students and youth. Some of their key values include shared power and authority; youth-controlled agenda; collaboration and partnership; constituent-specific strategies; learning; and diversity and inclusion.[26]

Other Organizations

There are many other groups that support legislation that allows for medical marijuana. Some are listed in Table 8.2.

Medical-Related Interest Groups

There are many medical groups support legislation written in such a way as to allow qualified physicians to discuss the medicinal benefits marijuana use with those patients who may benefit from it. This is the position taken by the American Medical Association and the American Society of Addictive Medicine. Other medical groups support more over-reaching laws that will allow for prescriptive access to medicinal marijuana. Groups supporting this perspective include the AIDS Action Council, American Public Health Association, and the American Academy of Family Physicians.[27] Below are some medical-related interest groups. Others are listed in Table 8.3.

Table 8.2: Other Interest Groups Working For Medical Marijuana

American Anthropological Association
American Bar Association
American Civil Liberties Union
American Medical Marijuana Association
American Medical Marijuana Society
Cannabis MD
Cannabis as Medicine
Cannabis Science
Drug Science.org
Green Cross
International Association for Cannabis as Medicine
Lawmen Protecting Patients
Medical Cannabis Network
Medical Marijuana Mission
Medical Marijuana of America
Medical MJ.org
Patients Out of Time
Union of Medical Marijuana Patients
Veterans for Medical Marijuana Access
Wo/Men's Alliance for Medical Marijuana

American Medical Association

Originally, the American Medical Association recommended that marijuana be retained in Schedule I of the Controlled Substances Act pending the outcome of further studies. However, in recent years the AMA has adopted a new policy in which they back continued scientific research into, and the development of, cannabionoid-based medicines. They adopted a new policy agenda in which they urge the federal government to review marijuana's status as a Schedule I substance. The group indicates that the limited number of rigorous scientific studies on the possible therapeutic use of cannabis to treat serious medical conditions is insufficient. At the same time, they expressed their view that they do not necessarily endorse state-based medical cannabis programs or the legalization of marijuana.

American College of Physicians

In a paper released on February 15, 2008, the American College of Physicians (ACP) described its support for the use of non-smoked forms of THC. They cited the research on the benefits of medical marijuana, supported a review of the federal scheduling of marijuana, and were in favor of an exemption from criminal prosecution for those who use medical marijuana within legal boundaries. The positions of the ACP are:

- Position 1: ACP supports programs and funding for rigorous scientific evaluation of the potential therapeutic benefits of medical marijuana and the publication of such findings.
- Position 1a: ACP supports increased research for conditions where the efficacy of marijuana has been established to determine optimal dosage and route of delivery.
- Position 1b: Medical marijuana research should not only focus on determining dug efficacy and safety but also on determining efficacy in comparison with other available treatment.
- Position 2: ACP encourages the use of non-smoked forms of THC that have proven therapeutic value.
- Position 3: ACP supports the current process for obtaining federal research-grade cannabis.
- Position 4: ACP urges review of marijuana's status as a Schedule I controlled substance and its reclassification into a more appropriate schedule, given the scientific evidence regarding marijuana's safety and efficacy in some clinical conditions.

- Position 5: ACP strongly exemption from federal criminal prosecution; civil liability; or professional sanctioning, such as loss of licensure or credentialing for physicians who prescribe or dispense medical marijuana in accordance with state law. Similarly, ACP strongly urges protection from criminal or civil penalties for patients who use medical marijuana as permitted under state laws.[28]

Table 8.3: Medical Associations Supporting Compassionate Use

The American Academy of Family Physicians

The American Academy of HIV Medicine

The American Alliance for Medical Cannabis

The American Association for Social Psychiatry

The American College of Physicians

The American Nurses Association

The American Public Health Association

The American Society of Addiction Medicine

Arthritis Research Campaign

Association of Medical Marijuana Caregivers

The British Medical Association

Lymphoma Foundation of America

The National Association for Public Health Policy

American Nurses Association

American Public Health Association

American Society of Addiction Medicine

Arthritis Research Campaign

Associated Medical Schools of New York

British Medical Association

The Lymphoma Foundation of America

The National Association for Public Health Policy

The National Nurses Society on Addiction

AIDS Care Ocean State

AIDS Foundation of Chicago

AIDS Project Rhode Island

Alaska Nurses Association

Associated Medical Schools of New York

California Academy of Family Physicians

California Medical Association

California Nurses Association

California Pharmacists Association

California Society of Addiction Medicine

Colorado Nurses Association

Florida Medical Association

Hawaii Nurses Association

Life Extension Foundation

Lymphoma Foundation of America

Medical Society of the State of New York

Medical Student Section of the AMA

Minnesota Nurses Association

Mississippi Nurses Association

Multiple Sclerosis California Action Network

New Jersey State Nurses Association

New Mexico Medical Society

New York AIDS Advisory Council

New Mexico Nurses Association

New York AIDS coalition

New York County Medical Society

New York State Nurses Association

North Carolina Nurses Association

People with HIV/AIDS Action
Committee (San Diego)

Physicians for Social Responsibility
(Oregon)

Rhode Island Medical Society

Rhode Island State Nurses
Association

San Francisco Medical Society

Texas Medical Association

Texas Nurses Association

United Nurses and Allied
Professionals (Rhode Island)

Virginia Nurses Association

Wisconsin Nurses Association

Wisconsin Public Health Association

Conclusion

Interest groups play a vital role in the policy process in the U.S., and that is no different when it comes to policy regarding medical marijuana. There are hundreds, of groups that have an interest in affecting new laws and policies to reflect their interests. While some are older than others, and some are larger than others, they all seek to have some say into the final policy that is passed and how that policy is then implemented or enacted, at the federal, state and local levels. As the issue of medical marijuana continues to grow, so will the number (and the power) of interest groups.

Review/Discussion Questions

1. What role do interest groups play in making legislation?
2. Name three groups and describe them: what are their goals, activities?
3. Design your own interest group for medical marijuana. With what issues would it be concerned?
4. What do these interest groups have in common? How are they different?

Key Terms

Interest Groups

Lobbying

Chapter 9

Bureaucracies

Overview: There are many agencies, or bureaucracies, in the federal government whose duty is to investigate violations of federal drug laws. The main agencies today are the DEA, the Office of National Drug Control Policy, and the Surgeon General. These are described in this chapter.

Introduction

Over the years, the federal government has created many bureaucracies that are responsible for enforcing federal laws that ban the use of illicit drugs, including medical marijuana. As the number of people using illicit substances has grown, and as new drugs have been developed or become popular amongst users, smaller agencies have been reorganized into one primary organization, the Drug Enforcement Administration (DEA), whose agents work to prevent the cultivating, trafficking, distribution, possession and use of all drugs, including marijuana. Another agency vital to today's federal policies regarding illicit drugs of all kinds, including medical cannabis, is the Office of National Drug Control Policy, which sets the general tone and direction of the nation's anti-drug strategy. The Surgeon General of the U.S. also makes recommendations about health-related issues. This chapter describes the agencies that are instrumental in the federal government's fight to keep marijuana away from those who wish to use it for either recreation or medical reasons, and how they became the agencies we know today.

Early History

In 1915, the Bureau of Internal Revenue was established within the Department of Treasury.[1] The agents were responsible for enforcing the drug tax imposed by the Harrison Narcotics Tax Act of 1914. In the 1920s, this responsibility was transferred to the Narcotics Division of the Bureau of Prohibition (still within the U.S. Department of the Treasury). The Prohibition Bureau was given the task of implementing the Volstead Act which declared alcohol sale and distribution illegal throughout the country.

Federal Bureau of Narcotics

In 1930, Congress created the Federal Bureau of Narcotics by consolidating the Narcotics Division in the Treasury Department and the Federal Narcotics Control Board. They chose to do this as a way to decrease the inefficiency resulting from two agencies that operated in the same arena.[2] There was also a significant amount of corruption within the previous narcotics agencies, and it was hoped that the restructuring would change that. The first commissioner of the FBN was Harry Anslinger, who worked under President Herbert Hoover.

With Anslinger as the leader, the primary focus of the FBN was to fight opium and heroin smuggling. To do this effectively, the FBN worked in conjunction with local drug enforcement agencies to gather intelligence, and opened overseas offices in places like France, Italy, Turkey, and Beirut to interrupt international drug trafficking. Anslinger fought for increased penalties for those who used drugs. Anslinger and the FBN are often credited for criminalizing drugs such as cannabis when the Marijuana Tax Act of 1937 was passed.[3] Anslinger also sought to strengthen the Harrison Narcotics Tax Act.[4]

As drug use increased dramatically during the 1960s, officials discovered that enforcing drug laws via tax enforcement was no longer effective. In 1966, a new agency, the Bureau of Drug Abuse Control (BDAC), was created within the Food & Drug Administration under the Department of Health, Education, and Welfare, to try and deal with the problem of drug addiction.[5] Then In 1968, President Johnson proposed combining this agency with the Federal Bureau of Narcotics to create a new agency that he believed would be better equipped to deal with the problem of drugs.[6] He decided to merge BDAC and FBN, and was placed in the U.S. Department of Justice as the newly created Bureau of Narcotics & Dangerous Drugs (BNDD).[7]

The BNDD became the primary drug law enforcement agency in the country. It concentrated its efforts on both international and interstate activities related to illicit drugs. By 1970, the BNDD had nine foreign offices — in Italy, Turkey, Panama, Hong Kong, Vietnam, Thailand, Mexico, France, and Colombia — to respond to the international drug trade. Domestically, the agency initiated a series of task forces comprised of federal, state, and local law enforcement. The first such task force was established in New York City.[8]

Table 9.1: Harry Anslinger

Harry Jacob Anslinger grew up in Altoona, Pennsylvania where his father worked on the Pennsylvania Railroad. When he was a boy about twelve years old, he heard a morphine addict screaming, which stopped only when a young boy returned from a pharmacist with more morphine. At the time, Anslinger was appalled that the drug had such a powerful effect on the man. When he was older, Anslinger was an investigator for the Pennsylvania Railroad. He enrolled at Pennsylvania State College where he studied business and engineering.

There was a lot of corruption in the Prohibition Unit during that time, and Anslinger was honest and incorruptible. He was appointed to serve as the Assistant Prohibition Commission in the Bureau of Prohibition, then at the age of 38 became the first commissioner of the Federal Bureau of Narcotics on August 12, 1930, and served for 32 years, until 1962. While Commissioner of the FBN, Anslinger declared war on drugs. He lobbied for more, and harsher, laws to fight drugs. Between 1930–1937, there were many laws about marijuana that passed by Congress with little public attention. He also put attention on stopping international drug trafficking.

Anslinger was able to shape many American's views about marijuana.[9] Anslinger supported a proposed legislation called the Uniform State Narcotic Act, which would require states spend their resources to enforce drug trafficking laws. When only nine states agreed to the plan, Anslinger began a nationwide media campaign against marijuana. He used the media to convince people that marijuana use caused temporary insanity. He wrote many articles about the dangers of marijuana. The media ads showed young people using, followed by scenes in which they committed crimes, committed murder, suicide, or otherwise died from using marijuana. In 1936, the propaganda film "Reefer Madness" was released as another attempt to scare young people from using marijuana. The film made it obviously clear that smoking marijuana causes people to go insane.[10]

Anslinger's propaganda campaign successfully convinced the American public that marijuana was a "killer drug." As a result, voters across the nation demanded government action even though there was no scientific research about the harms caused by marijuana.

After Anslinger left the FBN, he became the U.S. Representative to
the United Nations Narcotics Commission for two years.

Despite the reorganization, the BNDD was not the only organization that
enforced the federal drug laws. There were at least four other agencies responsible for dealing with the drug problem. One was the U.S. Customs Service Drug Investigation Unit found within the Department of Treasury. Another
was the Office of National Narcotics Intelligence (ONNI) and the Office of
Drug Abuse Law Enforcement (ODALE), both within the U.S. Department of
Justice. President Nixon had also created a new agency, the Narcotics Advance
Research Management Team, after realizing the pervasiveness of drug use at
the time. The Team was to coordinate all of the activities of the other federal
agencies dealing with the problems of drugs. Unfortunately, it quickly became
apparent that the team was not working and it was time to reorganize the various units so they could more easily cooperate with each other.[11]

Drug Enforcement Agency

In the Spring of 1973, President Nixon announced his Reorganization Plan
No. 2, calling for "an all-out global war on the drug menace."[12] He explained
the reorganization of the drug agencies as the following: "The federal government is fighting the war on drug abuse under a distinct handicap, for its efforts are those of a loosely confederated alliance facing a resourceful, elusive,
worldwide enemy. Certainly, the cold-blooded underworld networks that fun-
nel narcotics from suppliers all over the world are not respecters of the bu-
reaucratic dividing lines that now complicate our anti-drug efforts."[13]

On July 10, 1973, President Nixon issued Executive Order #11727, which
clarified some aspects of the reorganization plan. He stated "that all functions
of the Office for Drug Abuse Law Enforcement and the Office of National Narcotics Intelligence would, together with other related functions be merged into
the new Drug Enforcement Administration."[14] Thus, through the reorganization plan and the Executive Order, the U.S. Drug Enforcement Agency (DEA)
was officially created on July 1, 1973.

The benefits of this reorganization were debated by Congress, but eventually a report was issued in which the potential benefits of such a "super agency,"
would have. One benefit, as noted in the report, was that any rivalries that existed between the agency would disappear. It would also give the FBI a bigger
role in assisting the law enforcement community in the drug war. There was

hope that the reorganization would consolidate resources so the anti-drug policies would be more effective and accountable.

On October 4, 1973, John R. Bartels, Jr. became the first Administrator of the DEA. Bartels was a former federal prosecutor and was, at the time, Deputy Director of ODALE. He had two primary goals for the agency: 1) to integrate narcotics agents and U.S. Customs agents into one force, and 2) to restore public confidence in narcotics law enforcement.

In 1975, Bartels resigned and Peter S. Bensinger was appointed to replace him. Bensinger was Director of the Illinois Department of Corrections and was hired primarily to implement the White House White Paper on drug abuse in the United States that encouraged the DEA to shift its focus from low level marijuana and cocaine smuggling to focus more attention on major international drug dealing, especially that of heroin.

By this time, the Reagan and Bush Administrations were bringing much attention to the illegal drug trade, making it a centerpiece of their administrations.[15] Congress passed the Anti-Drug Abuse Act of 1988 that established the Office of National Drug Control Policy (ONDCP) allowing for one person, within the White House, to oversee all of the drug law enforcement in America.[16] This individual became known as the "Drug Czar."

Today, the Drug Enforcement Agency (DEA) is the lead agency for enforcing federal drug laws across the U.S., particularly the Controlled Substances Act. DEA agents investigate, disrupt and then dismantle any networks that attempt to grow, manufacture or traffic in illicit drugs. The DEA seeks to attack the drug organizations that use the profits from trafficking in illicit drugs to fund terrorism. Their hope is to dismantle the financial structures of these groups, and thereby weaken the organizations, both domestic and overseas.

Moreover, the DEA supports non-enforcement programs that are geared toward limiting or eliminating the availability of illicit substances on both the domestic and international markets. They support policies to reduce demand for drugs.[17]

As states have legalized marijuana for medicinal purposes, the DEA's enforcement of federal law have come into conflict with state laws. When the DEA made a number of raids on establishments selling the medical marijuana, it created much controversy particularly from those state that have passed laws allowing for cannabis use. Nonetheless, the federal government continues to enforce their laws, including carrying out raids on dispensaries, regardless of state regulations.

Table 9.2: Budget Authority for DEA (In Millions of Dollars)

2008 Actual	2,137
2010 Actual	2,356
2011 Estimate	2,271
2012 Estimate	2,294
2013 Estimate	2,302
2014 Estimate	2,306
2015 Estimate	2,331
2016 Estimate	2,388
2017 Estimate	2,449
2018 Estimate	2,513
2019 Estimate	2,579
2020 Estimate	2,648
2021 Estimate	2,720

Source: Office of Management and Budget, Fiscal Year 2012 Analytical Perspectives: Budget of the U.S. Government, Table 33-1. (http://www.gpo.gov/fdys/pkg/BUDGET-2012-PER/pdf/BUDGET-2012-PER-1-8-1.pdf)

Budget

In 2008, the DEA's budget was $2.1 billion, which increased slightly for FY 2010 to $2.3 billion. It is estimated that Congress will continue to fund the organization around that same amount for the future. These figures are described in Table 9.2.

Today, the DEA works to stop the spread of marijuana cultivation across the U.S. through their Domestic Cannabis Eradication/Suppression Program.[18] They also work with community leaders who serve as Demand Reduction Coordinators. They provide expertise and intelligence to individuals and community groups on drug prevention techniques.[19]

Office of National Drug Control Policy

The ONDCP was established through Anti-Drug Abuse Act of 1988. The agency is part of the Executive Office of the President and as such is responsible for advising the president on issues pertaining to drugs and drug use in the U.S. Headed by the "Drug Czar," it is also responsible for overseeing drug-control activities and funding across the federal government in within the states. Each year the office announces the National Drug Control Strategy which describes the Administration's plan to reduce illicit drug use, manufacturing and trafficking is announced to the public. The plan also illustrates the Administration's approach to reducing drug-related violence.

Under the Obama administration, the ONDCP is focusing on community-based drug use prevention programs, early intervention programs as a way to prevent illicit drug use, diverting non-violent drug offenders into treatment instead of jail, funding scientific research on drug use, and expanding access to substance abuse treatment for those who would benefit from such.[20] Specifically, their goals are:

- Preventing illicit drug use and addiction;
- Providing the appropriate level of treatment to those Americans who are in need;
- Protecting the safety of the public while at the same time providing that drug-involved offenders have the opportunity to rebuild their lives;
- Countering drug production and trafficking activities within the U.S.;
- Securing our borders against illicit drug importation;
- Working with governments from other countries to reduce drug production and trafficking.[21]

The current director of the ONDCP is R. Gil Kerlikoske, who became Director on May 7, 2009. Prior to this, he was in law enforcement, including nine years as the Chief of Police for the Seattle Police Department. A list of previous directors is noted in Table 9.3.

The ONDCP budget is about $25 billion each year. Most of the spending goes toward domestic law enforcement of anti-drug use laws. The specific breakdown of the agency's funds is listed in Table 9.4.

Table 9.3: Past Directors of National Drug Control Policy

Director	Term
William Bennett	1989-1991
Bob Maratinez	1991-1993
Lee P. Brown	1993-1995
Barry McCaffrey	1996-2001
John P. Walters	2001-2009
R. Gil Kerlikoske	2009-now

Source: http://www.allgovcom/departments/executive-office-of-the-president/office-of -national-drug.

Table 9.4: Federal Drug Control Spending by Function (in millions)

Function	FY 2012 Final	FY 2014 Request
Treatment	7.848.3/ 32.0%	9,261.1/36.5%
Prevention	1,339.2/5.5%	1,408.7/5.5%
Domestic Law Enforcement	9,439.5/38.5%	9,562.9%/37.7%
Interdiction	4,036.5/16.5%	3,705.0/14.6%
International	1,833.7/7.5%	1,455.0/5.7%

Source: Office of National Drug Control Policy, April 2013, "National Drug Control Budget."

Under President Obama, the ONDCP is putting a focus on the health threat of drug addiction, especially for youth. In the 2010 National Drug Control Strategy, the Federal Interagency task Force on Drug Endangered Children (DEC) was established as a way to determine the best practices related to preventing youth drug use. It was a response to the growing number of children living in drug-infested environments. The DEC is an attempt to identify and rescue children who are in poor environments and provide them with appropriate attention and care. The Interagency task Force on Drug Endangered Children was formed as a way to coordinate the government's response.[22]

The Obama White House drug abuse policy also includes multiple substance abuse prevention programs for youth, such as the National Youth Anti-Drug Media Campaign and Above the Influence. The ONDCP also provide funding to support community-based anti-drug programs to prevent youth drug abuse.[23]

Another important part of the ONDCP is the Drug Free Communities Support Program. This is a federal grant program that provides funding the community-based organizations that work to prevent youth drug use. Part of this is the Drug Free Communities Mentoring Program, and the Drug-Free Communities Support Program Grants. They also provide funding operating in areas that have been categorized as "High Intensity Drug Trafficking Areas." The grant money is to reduce drug trafficking by facilitating cooperation among federal, state, and local law enforcement groups, providing intelligence to law enforcement agencies, and supporting strategies that are meant to reduce the supply of illicit drugs in the U.S.

One topic that continues to receive attention by the ONDCP is drugged driving and the dangers of driving with distractions. They have developed a teen drugged driving guide to help educate parents and others about drugged driving. They also sponsor the "Over the Limit. Under Arrest" program that is an effort to crack down on impaired driving.

Finally, the Obama administration has made it clear that they want to give attention to science and research as a way to drive their policy decisions regarding drugs. The National Institute on Drug Abuse (NIDA) funds research on drug abuse as a way to create new ways of developing and tracking drug problems and treatments.[24]

Surgeon Generals

The U.S. Surgeon General is the head of the U.S. Public Health Service Commissioned Corps and is responsible for overseeing the general public's overall health for the federal government. The Surgeon General answers to the Assistant Secretary for Health, who in turn is a principal advisor to the Secretary of Health and Human Services. It is the responsibility of the Surgeon General to educate the public about better lifestyle choices, and to issue warnings about products that could be dangerous to consumers. Some of the past Surgeon Generals have held positions about medical marijuana.[25]

For example, the Surgeon General from 1982–89 was C. Everett Koop, who was appointed by President Reagan. He said, "Based on scientific evidence published to date, it is the opinion of the Department of Health and Human Services that marijuana has a broad range of psychological and biological effects, many of which are dangerous and harmful to health ... Marijuana is not a benign drug. As Surgeon General, I urge other physicians and professionals to advise parents and patients about the harmful effects of using marijuana and to urge discontinuation of its use."[26]

The surgeon general from 1993 to 1994 was M. Joycelyn Elders, appointed by President Clinton. She was in favor of medical marijuana. She said, "The evidence is overwhelming that marijuana can relieve certain types of pain, nausea, vomiting and other symptoms caused by such illnesses as multiple sclerosis, cancer and AIDS — or by the harsh drugs sometimes used to treat them. And it can do so with remarkable safety. Indeed, marijuana is less toxic than many of the drugs that physicians prescribe every day."[27]

The surgeon general from 1998–2002 was David Satcher, appointed by President Clinton. He was opposed to the use of medical marijuana. " ... The Department of Health and Human Services recommends that marijuana continue to be subject to control under Schedule I ... marijuana has a high potential for abuse, has no currently accepted medical use in treatment in the United States, and has a lack of accepted safety for use under medical supervision."[28]

The surgeon general from 2002–2006 was Richard H. Carmona, who was appointed by George W. Bush. He was not for or against medical marijuana. He said, "Right now, we can't answer all those questions (about risks and benefits) for marijuana ... I've had some of my own patients over the years tell me that, yeah, I felt better after I smoked that joint and they had pain or they had discomfort, so on. Those are anecdotal responses. We don't really know if it's a placebo effect, that is would they have had the same effect if they smoked a regular cigarette as opposed to marijuana? ... How often should (a patient) smoke this marijuana? Two times a day? Five times a day? That hasn't been studied. What are the possible deleterious effects? What is the risk benefit analysis (doctors are) obligated to discuss with the patient?"[29]

The current surgeon general, Regina M. Benjamin (appointed by President Obama), does not seem to be either openly for or against medical cannabis. She has said, "There's evidence that shows that it's useful for medicine, but we need to investigate how to avoid the adverse effects of smoking marijuana."[30]

Conclusion

Because medical marijuana remains illegal under federal law, many federal organizations exist to enforce those laws against anyone who possesses uses or distributes cannabis. Others exist to help educate the public about health concerns, which, for the most part, do not support changes in the medical marijuana laws. These agencies have all evolved over time, changing as needs develop and progress, or as administrations change. Regardless of these factors, it is clear that these agencies will continue to exist and operate for many years to come, and have an impact on the policies regarding medical cannabis.

Review/Discussion Questions

1. Describe the history of today's drug enforcement agencies.
2. What are the responsibilities of the Drug Czar?
3. How and why did President Nixon create the DEA?
4. What is the nation's drug policy under the Obama administration?
5. What role does the Surgeon General play in drug policy, and what have past Surgeons General said about medical marijuana?

Key Terms

Drug Enforcement Administration
Office of National Drug Control Policy
Drug Czar
Harry Anslinger
Bureau of Drug Abuse Control
Bureau of Narcotics and Dangerous Drugs
Surgeon General

Chapter 10

Campaigns and Elections

Overview: This chapter begins with a discussion of how public opinion about medical marijuana has changed over time, but basically supports the use of cannabis for medical reasons. The chapter then discusses how the issues regarding medical marijuana have been used in campaign rhetoric.

Introduction

When a candidate runs for public office, they make statements about what they will do if elected to serve. They discuss issues relevant to the concerns of the voters as a way to gain the trust of their constituents and garner support for their candidacy. These statements are, in effect, setting an agenda for their term in office.[1] This means that candidates are making policy decisions for their potential administrations.[2]

To some extent, the issues that are discussed and debated among candidates are dependent upon the public's opinions about current problems in their communities. The issues with which is the public is concerned, or discussing on a regular basis, often appear in the campaign. Obviously, candidates must let the voters know that they understand the issues that are important, and have plans to address those concerns.

The approaches that candidates will have to solving problems will, in part, be dependent upon their political ideology. The "best" resolution to the issue of drugs differs between the Republican and Democratic parties. In general terms, candidates belonging to the Republican party tend to support anti-drug policies that reflect more conservative ideas, such as harsh (longer) punishments for wrongdoing, with a focus on law enforcement powers to detect those who traffic, cultivate, use or possess illicit drugs. Under this perspective, drug use is a choice made by the offender, who must then be punished for their ac-

185

tions. On the other hand, those belonging to the Democratic Party are more likely to support anti-drug policies that reflect a liberal perspective of criminal justice, including a focus on due process with policies that revolve around increased treatment or rehabilitation of offenders and societal change,[3] since crime (and drug use) is often a result of larger societal problems such as poverty, unemployment and discrimination.[4]

The policy position that Republicans have about medical marijuana also differs from that of Democrats. In general, Republican office holders will take a much more conservative approach toward drug use and punishment for drug-related offenses. They are more likely to support laws that prohibit medical use of the drug, along with cultivation, distribution, and possession. They tend to also support harsher punishments for those convicted of drug-related offenses. Moreover, Republicans are more likely to support increased law enforcement resources for upholding the laws. On the other hand, members of the Democratic Party will more than likely be in favor of more reasonable medical marijuana laws and opposed to high spending levels for enforcement purposes. They would like to see policies that favor less harsh punishment with more treatment for those offenders with addiction problems, easy access to medical cannabis through dispensaries or compassion centers, and the medical necessity defense.

Medical marijuana is not an issue that has been discussed often by candidates for public office on the federal, state, or local levels. This implies that the issue is not a primary concern for the public. It also implies that the issue is not being placed high on the agenda of the office-seekers. This chapter will demonstrate how the public thinks about the issue of medical marijuana, and consequently how candidates and others use the issues surrounding medical marijuana as campaign issues in campaigns on the federal and state levels.

Public Opinion

On the whole, public opinion polls show that the American public overwhelmingly supports medical marijuana.[5] This trend has been apparent for many years, as shown below.

2010

In 2010, eight out of ten Americans (81 percent) supported the legalization of medical marijuana, according to a national ABC News/Washington Post telephone poll, which was an increase from 69 percent in 1997. Moreover, about 56 percent of respondents reported that if medical marijuana was made legal, doctors should be able to prescribe it to anyone they think might benefit. Overall, 56 percent thought there should be no restrictions on who could use it, while 21 percent reported it should be limited to terminally ill patients and an additional 21 percent said it should be limited to those with serious but not necessarily terminal illnesses. Further, according to the results, liberals were 23 points more likely than conservatives, and Democrats 20 points more likely than Republicans, to oppose restrictions on medical marijuana. There's also a difference between the sexes, with men 10 points more likely than women to say the doctor should decide.[6]

2011

A 60 Minutes/Vanity Fair Poll taken in January, 2011, asked respondents, "If a loved one had an illness for which medical marijuana might be prescribed, would you support or oppose that use?" The response showed that 77 percent supported it, 18 percent would be opposed; and 5 percent had another answer or didn't know.[7] The following charts separate the results by different factors. Overall, young people (between the ages of 18–29) showed the most support for medical cannabis (86 percent), and others over the age of 65 the least. Respondents with some college education were more likely to support use of the drug for medical reasons. Interestingly, men and women had an equal number of people showing support. When it comes to income, people making between $30,000 to $49,000 showed more support. As expected, more support came from liberals (82 percent) then conservatives (72 percent), and by Democrats (84 percent) than Republicans (69 percent).

1. By Age

	18-29	30-44	45-64	65 and over	Total
Support	86%	74%	82%	63%	77%
Oppose	10%	22%	15%	31%	18%
DK/NA	4%	5%	3%	6%	4%
Total	100%	100%	100%	100%	100%

2. By Education

	LT HS Grad	HS Grad	Some College	College Plus	Total
Support		77%	82%	74%	78%
Oppose		19%	14%	20%	18%
DK/NA		3%	4%	6%	4%
Total	100%	100%	100%	100%	100%

3. By Gender

	Male	Female	Total
Support	77%	77%	77%
Oppose	18%	19%	18%
DK/NA	4%	4%	4%
Total	100%	100%	100%

4. By Ideology

	Liberal	Moderate	Conservative	Total
Support	82%	82%	72%	78%
Oppose	17%	15%	24%	18%
DK/NA	1%	3%	4%	3%
Total	100%	100%	100%	100%

5. By Income

	< 30,000	30,000-49,999	50,000-74,999	>75,000	Total
Support	78%	83%	75%	76%	78%
Oppose	15%	13%	22%	23%	19%
DK/NA	6%	4%	3%	2%	4%
Total	100%	100%	100%	100%	100%

6. By Party ID

	Repub	Dem	Ind	Total
Support	69%	84%	78%	77%
Oppose	28%	11%	19%	19%
DK/NA	3%	5%	3%	4%
Total	100%	100%	100%	100%

7. By Region

	Northeast	North Central	South	West	Total
Support	83%	81%	76%	71%	77%
Oppose	15%	13%	20%	24%	18%
DK/NA	3%	6%	3%	5%	4%
Total	100%	100%	100%	100%	100%

2012

In 2012, polls showed that 83 percent of Americans favored allowing doctors to prescribe small amounts of marijuana for patients suffering from serious illnesses. This was true regardless of age and political party.[8] When asked if most marijuana was prescribed for serious illness or other reasons, respondents agreed that it was often for other reasons. The majority also believed that the decision to legalize cannabis for medical use should be made on the state level as opposed to by the federal government. These results are outlined below.
Q1: Should Doctors be Allowed to Prescribe Marijuana for Medical Use?[9]

Allowed	83%
Not Allowed	13%

Q2: Most Marijuana Prescribed by Doctors is ... [10]

For serious medical illnesses	29%
For other reasons	53%

Q3: Who Should Determine Whether Marijuana is Legal?[11]

State Governments	59%
Federal Governments	34%

2013

By 2013, polls indicated that 77 percent of respondents believed that marijuana has legitimate medical uses in certain circumstances. The results showed that there were small differences between members of different political parties: 82 percent of independents, 76 percent of Democrats and 72 percent of Republicans agree that marijuana has medical uses.[12] In this survey, those most likely to be in favor of medical cannabis were those in the 18–29-year-old category. More information on these polls is given in the chart below.

Q: Does Marijuana have Legitimate Medical use:

	Does	Does Not	Don't Know
Total	77%	16%	7%
18-29	84%	12%	4%
30-49	81%	14%	5%
50-64	77%	17%	6%
65+	60%	23%	16%
Republican	72%	20%	8%
Democrat	76%	16%	8%
Independent	82%	13%	5%

Source: Pew Research Center, March 13-17, 2013, Q 88.

Medical Marijuana in Campaigns and Elections

As noted earlier, the issues that are important to the public should appear during campaigns, as political parties and candidates address the public's concerns. The remainder of this chapter demonstrates how medical marijuana is used in campaigns, and how that reflects the public's ideas and thoughts. It will show how the issue of medical marijuana is an issue for political parties and candidates running for federal and state offices.

Political Parties

A party platform is an indication of the topics that political party membership deems to be the top priority for the upcoming years. These are statements written by the political party officials during the convention and prior to the election. When party officials choose to include a particular issue in the platform, they are informing the public that that issue is one of importance to not only the party, but to candidates in that party. The discussion below shows how marijuana has become an issue relevant to the different political parties.

Republican Party

Over the years, the Republicans have not chosen to place the issue of medical marijuana on their party platforms. However, the Republican Platforms have included the issue of recreational marijuana. This was first done in 1964, in which was stated that the country needed a "vigorous nation-wide drive against trafficking in narcotics and dangerous drugs, including special emphasis on the first steps toward addiction the use of marijuana and such drugs as LSD." Marijuana was not mentioned again in Republican party platforms until 1972, when it said, "We found many more were abusing other drugs, such as amphetamines and barbiturates. Marijuana had become commonplace." Additionally, in the platform it was stated that "We firmly oppose efforts to make drugs easily available. We equally oppose the legalization of marijuana. We intend to solve problems, not create bigger ones by legalizing drugs of unknown physical impact."

It was twelve years later, in 1984, when the subject of marijuana was again part of the Republican platform. This time, the Republicans indicated: "We set up an aggressive Marijuana Eradication and Suppression Program, gave the FBI authority to investigate drugs, and coordinated FBI and DEA efforts. We reaffirm that the eradication of illegal drug traffic is a top national priority." Then in 1996, the Republican platform used marijuana to attack the incumbent President, Bill Clinton. In that platform, the Republicans said, "The verdict is in on Bill Clinton's moral leadership: after 11 years of steady decline, the use of marijuana among teens doubled in the two years after 1992.... Hundreds of suspected drug smugglers have been allowed to go free at the border. Simultaneously, the use of marijuana, cocaine, and heroin has increased, especially among young people."

The last year that the topic of marijuana appeared in a Republican party platform was 2000, in which the party officials indicated the growth of young people who use the drug. They wrote, "Since 1992, among 10th graders, overall drug use has gone up 92 percent, marijuana and hashish use has risen 91 percent...."[13]

Oddly enough, despite the lack of action by the national Republican Party on medical cannabis, the Montana GOP members chose to include it in their 2012 platform. The platform supports a workable medical marijuana law for the state. A preliminary platform from party members says, "We recognize that a significant problem exists with Montana's current laws regarding the medical use of marijuana and we support action by the next legislature to create a workable and realistic regulatory structure."[14]

Democratic Party

The topic of marijuana has appeared less frequently in Democratic party platforms than in Republican platforms. It first appeared for the Democrats in 1984. This year, it the platform read: "As a result, drug trafficking and abuse have risen to crisis proportions in the United States. In 1983, an estimated 60 tons of cocaine, 15,000 tons of marijuana, and 10 tons of heroin entered the United States, clear evidence that we are losing the effort overseas to control the production and transshipment of these and other dangerous drugs. Domestically, the illicit trafficking in drugs is a $100 billion per year business; the economic and social costs to our society are far higher. Today, in our country, there are 25 million regular abusers of marijuana, close to twelve million abusers of cocaine, and half a million heroin addicts. Since 1979, hospital emergency room incidents — including deaths — related to cocaine have soared 300 percent' incidents related to heroin have climbed 80 percent. According to the 1983 National High School Survey on Drug Abuse, 63 percent of high school seniors have tried an illicit drug, and 40 percent have tried a drug other than marijuana. Alcohol abuse is also a serious problem which must be faced."

Grassroots Party: Minnesota

The Grassroots Party was created in 1986 by four men who had the goal of legalizing drugs. The standing platform for the party is the U.S. Bill of Rights, and all candidates representing this party would support ending the prohibition on marijuana. The Party first had a candidate in 1986 when one of the founders, Derrick Grimmer, ran for the office of Attorney General in Minnesota. The party has since run candidates for Attorney General in 1990, 1992 and 1994, a candidate for U.S. Senate in 2000, and president in 2000.[15]

Grassroots Party: Vermont

The Vermont Grassroots Party (VGP) formed in 1994. That year, the representatives of VGP ran for multiple offices, including governor, U.S. Senate, U.S. Representative, auditor of accounts, and attorney general. In 1996 VGP ran another slate of candidates including governor, lieutenant governor, U.S. representative, attorney general, auditor of accounts, state treasurer, and secretary of state. The candidates actually received enough votes to achieve "major party" status in the state.

In 1998 VGP candidates received between 1.5 percent and 8.8 percent of the votes cast. The percentage increased to 14.7 percent of the votes in 2000, when Sandy "Wells" Ward ran for the state's Attorney General as a member of the VGP. The party ran a full statewide ticket in 2002 again. Even though the VGP was not successful in these campaigns, the party membership nominated candidates for state office. The VGP dissolved in 2004.

Marijuana Party

The Marijuana Party was formed in 2002 by Loretta Nall in Alabama after she was arrested for misdemeanor possession of marijuana. Nall served as the party chairperson until she resigned in 2006 to run for Governor under the Libertarian Party. The primary goal of the Marijuana Party is to end the war on drugs and legalize marijuana use.[16] There are currently local chapters of the Marijuana Party in eight states: Colorado, Kentucky, Illinois, Maryland, Pennsylvania, Oregon, Idaho and Texas. In the 2012 election, the Marijuana party endorsed former New Mexico Governor Gary Johnson and former federal judge James Gray for president and vice president of the U.S. Another member of the Marijuana Party, Edward Forchhion, has run for many offices. The goals of the Marijuana Party are listed in Table 10.1.

Table 10.1: Marijuana Party Goals

- We seek to remove all penalties for adults 18 and over who choose to consume cannabis in a responsible manner.
- We demand an end to the war on productive and otherwise law abiding citizens by the powers that be who claim to protect us.
- We demand the right to use any medication our healthcare providers and we deem fit without government interference.
- We demand the release of all people imprisoned on marijuana charges and that their criminal records be expunged.

- We demand that all property seized in marijuana raids be returned to the rightful owners at once.
- We demand that our law enforcement officers make more efficient use of our tax dollars and use the resources they have at their disposal to go after violent criminals and crimes that actually have victims.
- We demand the right to grow marijuana for personal consumption, just as alcohol can be brewed at home legally so long as it is not sold untaxed.
- We demand that you stop treating us like second-class citizens for consuming something that is less dangerous than alcohol and tobacco, both of which are legal and cause numerous deaths each year. Cannabis has never been reported to have caused one.

Marijuana Reform Party

The Marijuana Reform Party of New York is a progressive minor party whose members seek to legalize cannabis. Founded in 1997, the Marijuana Reform Party ran candidates for Governor of the state and other statewide offices in 1998 and 2002. In 2004, a federal judge held that, by running candidates in 1998 and 2002 statewide elections, the Marijuana Reform Party demonstrated a "modicum of support" sufficient to compel the New York State Board of Elections to recognize the party as legitimate and allow voters to enroll in it. The organization remains the only political party in the United States that is recognized on a statewide level and dedicated to the advocacy of marijuana law reform, except for the Libertarian Party, which advocates legalization of all drugs.

In 1998, Tom Leighton, a gubernatorial candidate, accused the Green Party of attempting to have him removed from the ballot by challenging the validity of the signatures on his petition. The Board of Elections rejected the claim. During the election, neither the Green party candidate nor the Marijuana Reform Candidate party received enough votes to obtain a place on local and statewide ballots.[17]

Federal Campaigns

Not only do political parties make statements about issues during campaigns, so do candidates. Candidate's statements often reflect the public's attitudes about subjects that may cause alarm or distress. It is interesting to see how candidates for political office discuss medical marijuana.

Barack Obama

During the 2008 Democratic National Convention, candidate Barack Obama (D) said he would not interfere with access to legal medical cannabis.[18] Then in the 2008 campaign for the presidency, Obama announced a hands-off policy toward cannabis dispensaries that followed state laws, despite being illegal under federal law. Further, he held that his administration would not pursue raids against medical marijuana dispensaries in California and elsewhere.[19] However, Federal prosecutors sent letters to landlords and owners of dispensaries across California that warned them to stop selling marijuana or face property seizures and other legal backlash. U.S. Attorneys in California announced they would begin prosecuting operations across California, going much further than the Bush administration in cracking down on legal medical marijuana. Some of Obama's statements about medical marijuana are listed in Table 10.2.

Herman Cain

2008 Republican presidential candidate Herman Cain said that regulating medical marijuana dispensaries should be left to the states rather than the federal government. He said that when a policy is enacted at the federal level, "you try to force one-size-fits-all."[20] Earlier in the campaign process, Cain was asked about legalizing cannabis, and he refused to answer and instead walked away.

John McCain

Presidential Candidate John McCain (R) was flatly opposed to medical marijuana. On September 30, 2007, McCain stated in a Town Hall meeting in Derry, New Hampshire: "Every medical expert I know if, including the AMA, says that there are much more effective and much better treatments for pain than medical marijuana … I still would not support medical marijuana because I don't think that the preponderance of medical opinion in America agrees with (the) assertion that it's the most effective way of treating pain."[21] This makes his position rather clear.

Gary Johnson

Republican presidential candidate Gary Johnson supported legalizing marijuana, explaining that he felt the drug would eventually be legalized.[22]

Table 10.2: Obama's Quotes from the campaign trail

"My attitude is if the science and the doctors suggest that the best palliative care and the way to relieve pain and suffering is medical marijuana then that's something I'm open to because there's no difference between that and morphine when it comes to just giving people relief from pain. But I want to do it under strict guidelines. I want it prescribed in the same way that other painkillers or palliative drugs are prescribed."—November 24, 2007 town hall meeting in Iowa

"I would not have the Justice Department prosecuting and raiding medical marijuana users. It's not a good use of our resources."—August 21, 2007, event in Nashua, New Hampshire

"I don't think that should be a top priority of us, raiding people who are using ... medical marijuana. With all the things we've got to worry about, and our Justice Department should be doing, that probably shouldn't be a high priority."—June 2, 2007, town hall meeting in Laconia, New Hampshire

"You know, it's really not a good use of Justice Department resources."—responding to whether the federal government should stop medical marijuana raids, August 13, 2007, town hall meeting in Nashua, New Hampshire

"The Justice Department going after sick individuals using [marijuana] as a palliative instead of going after serious criminals makes no sense."—July 21, 2007, town hall meeting in Manchester, New Hampshire

Source: Wayne Laugesen, Obama Promised to Respect medical marijuana; May 5, 2011, Colorado Springs Gazette; http://www.gazette.com/articles/promises-117589-campaign-marijuana.html; accessed 7/25/12; see also http://www.gazette.com/articles/promises-117589-campaign-marijuana.html#ixzz21f1sTn4r.

Mitt Romney

Presidential candidate Mitt Romney (R), the former Governor of Massachusetts, stated the following in a Town Hall meeting on July 25, 2007, in Bedford, New Hampshire:

People talk about medicinal marijuana. And you know, you hear that story that people who are sick need medicinal marijuana. But marijuana is the entry drug for people trying to get kids hooked on drugs.

I don't want medicinal marijuana; there are synthetic forms of marijuana that are available for people who need it for prescription. Don't
open the doorway to medicinal marijuana.[23]

Michelle Bachman

Michele Bachman (R-MN) had no public statements about medical
cannabis. However, she voted against the Hinchey Amendment (H. Amdt 674)
in July, 2007, that would prohibit the Justice Department from using funds to
enforce federal, anti-medical marijuana laws in states where the use, distribution, possession, or cultivation of medical marijuana has been legalized.

John Kerry

Democratic presidential candidate John Kerry (D-MA) reported that he
supported the medical use of marijuana. He stated that, as president, he would
put a stop the DEA raids on seriously ill medical marijuana patients. Kerry
also stated that he favors federal legislation to allow people with cancer, AIDS,
and other serious illnesses to have medical marijuana upon the recommendation of their doctor.[24]

Rick Perry

Republican presidential candidate and Texas Governor Rick Perry supported
a states' rights approach to medical marijuana.[25] In his book, *Fed Up!*, Perry
wrote that he did not believe marijuana should be legal, but he supported the
right of states to legalize it if the citizens desired.

Ron Paul

Representative Ron Paul (R-TX) noted that the war on drugs should end
and that marijuana laws should be created and enforced by individual states.
In fact, Paul co-sponsored a bill with Representative Barney Frank (D-MA) to
remove marijuana from the list of federally regulated substances. Paul made
the argument for state authority on drug laws a regular part of his campaign
for the presidency. "I think the federal war on drugs is a total failure," Paul said
in one of the Republican presidential debates.[26]

Hillary Clinton

Hillary Clinton, the former U.S. Secretary of State and former U.S. Senator, stated the following during an October 11, 2007 town hall meeting at Plymouth State College:

> With respect to medical marijuana, you know I think that we have had a lot of rhetoric and the federal government has been very intent upon trying to prevent states from being able to offer that as an option for people who are in pain. I think we should be doing medical research on this. We ought to find what are the elements that claim to be existing in marijuana that might help people who are suffering from cancer and nausea-related treatments. We ought to find that out. I don't think we should decriminalize it, but we ought to do research into what, if any, medical benefits it has.[27]

Dennis Kucinich

Dennis Kucinich, U.S. Representative (D-OH) and 2008 Democratic Candidate for U.S. President, stated the following in an August 8, 2007, Democratic presidential forum:

> It's a matter between doctors and patients, and if doctors want to prescribe medical marijuana to relieve pain, compassion requires that the government support that. And so as president of the U.S., I would make sure that our Justice Department was mindful that we should be taking a compassionate approach. I want to go one step further, because this whole issue of drugs in our society is misplaced. Drugs have infected the society, but I think we need to look at it more as a medical and a health issue than as a criminal justice issue.[28]

Rudy Giuliani

The former mayor of New York City, Mr. Giuliani was a candidate for the Republican nomination for the presidency in 2008. During a town hall meeting on Oct 3, 2007 in Windham, New Hampshire, he said:

> I checked with the FDA. The FDA says marijuana has no additive medical benefit of any kind, that the illegal trafficking of marijuana is so great that it makes much more sense to keep it illegal. I will keep it illegal.[29]

Jill Stein

Jill Stein, a physician and former Professor of Medicine at Harvard Medical School, ran for Governor as a member of the Green Party in 2010. During the campaign she said,

> Our current approach to the regulation of marijuana is a failure. It has resulted in a massive black market that is creating violence in our communities and pouring hundreds of millions of dollars each year into the pockets of criminal supply networks. Taxpayers are footing the bill for ineffective law enforcement efforts and unnecessary judicial expenses. And the most that can be achieved is to keep a few people from purchasing an herb that appears to be much less harmful than alcohol or tobacco.... One option to be examined would permit limited marijuana sales through existing liquor stores. The use of marijuana for medical purposes would be expedited under separate provisions in which a doctor's prescription would be required.... As a physician I believe in caution and moderation with regard to any substance we take into our bodies. And I would apply that same caution to marijuana. But evidence suggests that the effects of marijuana on health are far less harmful than those of tobacco and alcohol.[30]

Newt Gingrich

Newt Gingrich (R-GA) was the Speaker of the House of Representatives and later ran for president. He said, "There is no medical marijuana. Marijuana is a drug. There is nothing in the Food and Drug Administration that supports the idea that it's medical. There's nothing in the Institute of Medicine that supports the idea it's medical. The American Medical Association has not said it's medical. This is a clever ad for a terrible idea. And the fact is it is a drug, it is currently illegal, it should remain illegal, that's better for our children, and it's better for Florida, and it's better for America."[31]

However, Mr. Gingrich also said, "We believe licensed physicians are competent to employ marijuana, and patients have a right to obtain marijuana legally, under medical supervision, from a regulated source. The medical prohibition does not prevent seriously ill patients from employing marijuana; it simply deprives them of medical supervision and denies them access to a regulated medical substance. Physicians are often forced to choose between their ethical responsibilities to the patient and their legal liabilities to federal bureaucrats.... Federal policies do not reflect a factual or balanced assessment of marijuana's use as a medicant. The Council, by thoroughly investigating the available materials, might well discover that its own assessment of marijuana's therapeutic value has, in the past, been more than slightly shaded by federal policies that are less than neutral."[32]

Conclusion

Medical marijuana is evolving as a concern to the American public and, as a result, for candidates who choose to run for public office. As candidates for elected offices, these men and women must respond to the wishes of the voters. In this way, they show the public that they know about, and understand, the voters' concerns, and will be able to represent them in the legislative process. As they give campaign speeches, candidates are informing the voters about their intended agenda: what issues will receive attention if that person is elected. To date, the candidates for federal office have opted to speak only rarely about medical marijuana, indicating that it will not be a primary issue on the agenda. But as the issue becomes more accepted by the American public, and more demands are made on federal officials to change the laws regarding medical marijuana, candidates will speak more frequently about medical cannabis.

Review/Discussion Questions

1. Why would candidates for political office discuss medical marijuana in a campaign?
2. How do Republicans and Democrats differ on their approaches to medical marijuana?
3. Describe public opinion towards medical marijuana. How does it differ based on education? Age?
4. How has marijuana been discussed in political party platforms?
5. What have presidential candidates said about medical marijuana?

Key Terms

Public Opinion
Platforms
Republican
Democrat
Grassroots party

Marijuana Party
Green Party

Chapter 11

The Cannabis Industry

Overview: As more states pass medical marijuana laws, businesses have emerged to cater to those who use marijuana or who are caretakers for patients, and for dispensaries as well. The new industry that has emerged is rapidly changing but expected to grow as more states pass similar laws.

Introduction

The medical marijuana business is no small industry, and it continues to grow as more states choose to legalize it. The demand for medical cannabis and related products has increased steadily over many years and continues to grow. In fact, it is estimated that the market for such products is worth about 5 billion dollars. A research study completed in 2011 determined that medical cannabis was a $1.3 billion market, with a projection of $8.9 billion by 2016. At this time, cannabis is thought to be the top agricultural crop in California, representing a $14 billion marketplace as reported by the *New York Times*, *Washington Post*, and Bloomberg.[1] Table 11.1 lists potential cannabis and hemp-based pharmaceutical opportunities. This illustrates the potential medical aspects of cannabis and hemp.

Many companies provide consulting, cannabinoid-based pharmaceuticals, specialty equipment, financing, and/or other industry-specific services to the medical cannabis community. Some of the biggest companies are: BG Medical Technologies, Cannabis Science, Cannavest Corp., GW Pharmaceuticals, and Medical Marijuana Inc.

Table 11.1: Cannabis Pharmaceutical Opportunities

Condition	Potential Market
AIDs	$12.6 billion
Alzheimer's	$8.3 billion
Anti-aging	$50 billion
Asthma	$25 billion
Arthritis	$35 billion
Autism	$22 billion
Cancer	$75 billion
Chronic Pain Management	$22 billion
Diabetes	$25 billion
Digestive Diseases	$6 billion
Glaucoma	$14 billion
High Blood Pressure	$25 billion
Influenza	$28 billion
Multiple Sclerosis	$8 billion
PTSD	$72 billion

Source: PRNewswire, Dec 23, 2011, "Medical Marijuana Inc., Update." http://www.prnewswire.com/news-releases/medical-marijuana-inc-update-136136573.html.

BG Medical Technologies

BG Medical Technologies, Inc. analyzes scientific data on software solutions, patients and medical professionals and then develops technology systems and media content for the medical cannabis industry. BG medical is best known for BudGenius.com, an Internet portal and research laboratory that serves the medical cannabis industry. Because each strain of medical cannabis has different genetic potential, the cultivation of the plant can have an impact on whether the plant reaches this potential. Every crop is often slightly different because of differences in the environment such as sunlight, rainfall amount, and soil. Moreover, when dispensaries obtain cannabis from many independent growers, there is not a consistent inventory of strains that have a consistent effect for patients. BG Medical's laboratory and research software, BudGenius.com, tries to test every harvest of cannabis and then rates each of the crops for their potency and potential medical effects. They use a rating scale that indicates the plant's effectiveness at relieving pain, mood modification, relief of anxiety, helping the patient sleep, relieving nausea, and stimulating the appetite. At the same time, BudGenius also tests for pathogens such as mold, pesticides and insect problems. BG's Medical's BudGenius.com helps address the consistency through their testing service.

Cannabis Science, Inc.

Cannabis Science, Inc. is a biotech company based in Colorado Springs, Colorado, that was incorporated in 2009. They are at the heart of cannabinoid research for yet unmet medical needs. They are involved in the research and development of medical marijuana and seek to use whole cannabis extracts that contain THC and cannabidol to develop prescription medicines. They work with leading experts in drug development. The group concentrates on phytocannabinoid science, spotlighting the development and production of commercial phytocannabinoid-based pharmaceutical products. Currently, their attention is on medicines for skin cancer, PTSD and HIV. Their ultimate goal is to get cannabis-based medicines approved by the FDA. The company is aiming to develop two product groups: over the counter products for skin care and prescription products for serious illness, including over the counter skin products including lip balm, sun screen, lotions for eczema and psoriasis, and a moisturizing lotion.

Cannavest Corp

CannaVest Corp develops, produces, markets and sells consumer products containing hemp-based compounds with a focus on Cannabidol. A legal substance, CBD is derived from hemp stalk and seed that can be used with foods and other nutritional supplements for health and wellness benefits, as well as in the pharmaceutical industry. In March, 2013, Cannavest Corp acquired assets of PhytoSPHERE Systems, including the license to the name PhytoSPHERE and PhytoSPHERE systems for use in the development and commercialization of different hemp-based products.

GWPharmaceuticals

GWPharmaceuticals was founded in 1998 in the United Kingdom. In the beginning, the company obtained the only cultivation license in the UK that permitted them to cultivate marijuana from seeds and then to conduct scientific research on those medicinal uses of Cannabis plant. They partnered with Hortapharm B.V., a cannabis research and development business based in the Netherlands. This company was growing medicinal strains of cannabis for the Dutch government.

The company currently pursues the research, development, and commercialization of a variety of cannabinoid prescription medicines that are designed to meet the needs of patients who suffer from many different medical conditions. They are involved in all aspects of cannabinoid product development, from extraction technology to drug delivery theology, and clinical trials of new drugs, at a Metabolic Research Laboratory at the University of Buckingham. They are developing a series of prescription medicines, including their main product, Sativex, a cannabinoid mouth spray used for patients who suffer from multiple sclerosis to relieve symptoms of pain, spasticity, overactive bladder, and other problems. In 2011, GWPharmaceuticals concluded a partnership with Bayer for the distribution of Sativex in North America.

Medical Marijuana Inc.

Medical Marijuana Inc. (OTC: MJNA) is the first publicly held company active in the medical marijuana and industrial hemp industries. In the beginning, the company concentrated on providing educational seminars on medical marijuana and supporting the industry with technology and was made up of small, local dispensaries. Over the past few years, the company has grown and gone through many changes, and today has numerous hemp and cannabis based businesses and have invested in medical marijuana research studies and future experiments as well as technology.[2]

The company has been described as a "leading hemp innovator." Its mission is "to be the premier cannabis and hemp industry innovators, leveraging our team of professionals to source, evaluate and purchase value-added companies and products, while allowing them to keep their integrity and entrepreneurial spirit. We strive to create awareness within our industry, develop environmentally friendly, economically sustainable businesses, while increasing shareholder value."[3] The company does not grow, sell or distribute any substances that violate United States Law or the controlled substance act. Medical Marijuana, Inc. currently has the following divisions and subsidiaries:

The Hemp Network ("THN") sells hemp products directly to thousands of hemp network distributors. The company has five proprietary products. THN also serve as a platform from which other products from other companies can be launched.

HEMP Compounds ("HC") is focused on the pharmaceutical market and nutraceutical raw materials market. It focuses on hemp strains that range from those with little or no Tetrahydrocannabinol (THC) properties, to strains with high levels of Cannabidiol (CBD). They are working with genetically altered varieties of hemp. In agricultural production facilities, HC materials can be added to existing products that are sold to or through THN, or directly to pharmaceutical and nutraceutical companies.

MMI Technology ("MMIT") is working with others to develop the most comprehensive information source focusing on hemp and cannabis strain usage, crop cost, crop cycles, history of genetics, origins of genetics, efficacy, strain stability, climate and yields.

MMI Biotechnology ("MMIB") deals in biotechnology and equipment that are required by those in the hemp agricultural and medicinal technology industry. This includes technology and equipment to assist with hemp extraction methods, processes techniques, technology as well as equipment.

Wellness Managed Services ("WMS") acquires management services contracts for medical clinics. Once a clinic is acquired, WMS will oversee its supply, technology, accounting, marketing, advertising and its purchasing power. Because of this, WMS stores will have a significant advantage over non-WMS stores. They were recently in negotiations for additional facilities in California, Colorado and Arizona.[4] Wellness Managed Services manages and develops Health and Wellness facilities throughout North America. [5]

CannaFuel researches hemp bio-fuel as an alternative to coal burning biomass opportunities. The waste produce of other businesses, such as HEMP compounds or products developed for THN, is a high-value bio-mass, which yields when converted to bio-fuel nearly three times as much per acre as conventional corn based ethanol. This is a great alternative to the coal fire energy plants. Coal can thus be replaced with a renewable, sustainable, eco-friendly and even in some cases carbon negative, hemp.

The Pet Hemp Emporium ("TPHE") has developed everyday pet products, from hemp leashes to hemp beds.

Featured Companies of Medical Marijuana Inc include:

1. CanChew Biotechnologies seeks to bring cannabinoid-based chewing gum to market. In the U.S., the CanChew Advantage Chewing gum will be available on an over the counter basis and online, without prescription or the need for a medical marijuana card. Each piece will contain approximately 7 mg of CBD to provide health and wellness benefits to consumers. The product was launched in December of last year with a free product trial.[6] CanChew is a unique, socially acceptable, patient friendly, and convenient delivery format for delivery of cannabinoid-based pharmaceuticals. The delivery of these medications via gum provides for rapid and near complete absorption directly into the system.[7]

2. Canipa Holdings was created in 2012 to oversee the marketing, sales and distribution of medical Marijuana Inc's portfolio of products throughout Europe and the European Union Trade Zone participant counties. The new company, based in Bucharest, Romania, will oversee the European product launch and distribution in addition to obtaining European product and marketing approvals for Medical Marijuana Inc.'s products. The

products will be sold under distribution partnerships throughout the European Union Member Countries: Austria, Belgium, Bulgaria, Cyprus, Czech Republic, Denmark, Estonia, Finland, France, Germany, Greece, Hungary, Ireland, Italy, Latvia, Lithuania, Luxembourg, Malta, Netherlands, Poland, Portugal, Romania, Slovakia, Slovenia, Spain, Sweden, and the United Kingdom. Other target countries include Albania, Andorra, Armenia, Azerbaijan, Belarus, Bosnia & Herzegovina, Georgia, Liechtenstein, Moldova, Monaco, Norway, Russia, San Marino, Switzerland, Ukraine, and the Vatican City State.[8]

3. Hemp Meds was established as a way to develop online platforms for the marketing and sales of cannabis/hemp based consumer products. The company has been in development of its platform and actively acquiring additional online properties.

4. KannaLife Sciences helps to develop standardized packaging for cannabis based products that are used as transport carriers. They develop natural, phyto-medical products that are used in health and wellness regimens.[9]

5. PhytoSPHERE identified the plants that contain the highest levels of Cannabidiol, then are analyzing them for future development and production. PhytoSPHERE Systems is capable of producing plants with a high level of genetic purity issues surrounding seed-based inconsistency. PhytoSPHERE produces Hemp Oil Products, distributing them in many International markets. It has been producing Hemp oils and extracts since January, 2012. The high-quality, CBD-enriched hemp oil may fight aggressive forms of cancer, and provide other patients with pain and anxiety relief without the euphoric effects associated with THC.[10]

   PhytoSphere Systems, LLC is the world's leading cannabinoid based bio-technology Company. They entered into an agreement with CannaVest Corp for the rights to use its brand name, PhytoSphere Systems, along with the outsourcing to CannaVest its hemp facility cultivation, management and processing. The majority of the company (80 percent) is still owned by Medical Marijuana, Inc.

6. Dixie Elixirs and Edibles, Inc. was bought in April, 2012, by Medical Marijuana, Inc. Company officials paid $1.45 million to the Colorado-based company that manufactures and distributes THC-infused products. The company has line of over 40 infused products including medicated beverages and tonics, cannabis capsules, medicated lozenges and edibles as well as a full line of topicals and salves as part of the Dixie Botanicals line of products. Dixie Elixirs serves over 400 of Colorado's medical marijuana centers.[11,12]

Dixie Elixirs & Edibles provides patients with different methods to ingest medical marijuana. Known for their THC-laced sparkling beverages, they also manufacture medicated chocolate truffles, ice cream, crispy rice treats, fruit lozenges, capsules and droplets. They also make topical applications, capsules, energy shots, and tinctures with medicine. Their products are made for those patients who, for health or social reasons, would prefer to ingest the drug by not smoking. These THC-infused edible products make up about 38 percent of total sales at marijuana dispensaries in Colorado, up from twelve percent only two years ago.

7. Red Dice Holdings was created when Medical Marijuana, Inc. and Dixie Elixirs formed a third company, a marketing and licensing company, which will manage and license the assets of the Dixie Elixirs & Edibles brand and product.[13] They will market products in other states, especially in Arizona, California and Washington, D.C. Red Dice Holdings will launch on-line sales of the CBD based Dixie X and CanChew products in the U.S. through licensed distribution companies. They will also start to market their products in selected international distribution. Red Dice Holdings owns the formulas, equipment, brands, and intellectual property of the Dixie brand of products, which includes Dixie, Dixie Botanicals, Dixie Elixir's Dixie Edibles. They help to distribute the Dixie Botanical brand of CBD-infused products.[14]

In September, 2012, Red Dice Holdings began a Customer Care Program as a way to support their valued customers who have made Dixie X products part of their daily health and wellness regime. Thousands of customers have purchased the non-THC, Hemp-derived products. The company will allow customers to sign up for auto shipments of products on a customer-controlled timeframe of no less than monthly shipments. By committing to a one-year shipment plan, they will also receive 30 percent off of each purchase automatically billed to their credit card.[15] The program will ensure that those customers who need the products will receive them easily, quickly and affordably and on a timely basis. The program offers customers convenience, cost savings, and an unlimited supply of the products.[16]

Others

Rapid Fire Marketing Inc.: Incorporated in July, 1989, Rapid Fire Marketing is a holding company for several businesses, but the core business is the Vapro Inhaler, which is the technology found in CANNAcig, which allows for vaporizing dried plant material. A new version allows for an oil option as well as dried herbs. The company offers inbound marketing, social media marketing, email and internet marketing services to its client companies such as the medical cannabis industry in California.

Hemp, Inc.: Hemp, Inc. supplies services, products, and information related to the medical marijuana industry. Their products include nutraceutical products that are designed to improve concentration and joint flexibility, increase awareness and energy, and improve overall patient wellness. They are not involved in growing, transporting, or marketing of medical marijuana, but instead create an infrastructure to do this if the drug is legalized federally or in all states.

Conclusion

The medical cannabis industry is a new but maturing industry. As the number of older patients with medical conditions continues to rise, so will the demand for all kinds of products related to medical marijuana. There could be significant growth opportunities for businesses dealing in product safety controls, tracking, commerce software, digital marketing, social media, data mining, and patient education, among other areas. It is thought by many in the business field that the medical marijuana industry presents many opportunities for investment. Those who have analyzed delivery of medical marijuana by means of edible and drinkable products are likely to increase in coming years, as it is an easy delivery mechanism for patients.[17] The trend will more than likely continue, especially as more states opt for legalizing medical cannabis and more patients and caregivers seek ways to obtain and use the drug.

Review/Discussion Questions

1. Describe some of the companies that have emerged in the medical marijuana market.
2. Develop a company related to the medical marijuana field. What types of services/products would it provide?

Key Terms

BG Medical Technologies
Cannabis Science

Cannavest Corp
GW Pharmaceuticals
Medical Marijuana Inc.
Rapid Fire Marketing Inc.
Hemp, Inc.

Chapter 12

Conclusion

Despite a long history of marijuana use for medicinal reasons throughout the world, the U.S. federal government has made marijuana illegal to grow, distribute, possess and/or use through the Comprehensive Drug Abuse and Prevention and Control Act of 1970, which categorizes marijuana as a drug with no medical benefits but a high potential for abuse. Regardless, many states are making the use of medical cannabis legal for patients who have debilitating medical conditions. The voters or legislators in these states believe that there is at least enough evidence, be it anecdotal or scientific, that marijuana helps to alleviate serious medical symptoms in some patients. An increasing number of doctors are prescribing the drug for a variety of medical conditions. Both doctors and patients believe that the drug is more effective in treating some types of medical conditions, and a more natural approach to treating ailments than many of the drugs currently available.

Because cannabis remains illegal by the federal government, those who use marijuana, dispense it, or prescribe it (recommend it) to patients face legal action by the federal law enforcement. Federal law enforcement agents continue to carry out raids on dispensaries and homes, arresting employees, patients and caregivers and confiscating marijuana plants and paraphernalia. Some patients have been charged with marijuana use and/or possession or even drug trafficking and face serious punishments. Other patients have faced losing their jobs as a result of random drug testing that take place in the workplace. In some places, physicians feel intimated or threatened for recommending marijuana to their patients.

Advocates of medical marijuana agree that the time has come to make changes in the federal medical marijuana policies and allow states to regulate such choices. They argue that traditionally in the U.S., health and criminal activity are responsibilities of state government officials rather than federal. Marijuana advocates also argue that federal policymakers have lost sight of the idea that the needs of the patient are central to medical treatment.[1] They argue that most people support medical marijuana, so the federal government should leave enforcement to the states and allow states to implement their laws as passed.

However, the division of roles between the federal and state governments is always changing. What responsibilities belong to each level of government is constantly being altered. When it comes to medical marijuana, there are many questions about who can make laws and who should enforce the law. As these questions become more apparent, the court system, and the Supreme Court in particular, will have to review cases to ensure the federal government has not reached too far into states' rights.[2]

One option is to delay federal enforcement of drug laws and permit the states to experiment with different legalization policies. In this way, the best practices can be determined and then possibly adopted on a national scale.[3] States could determine what patients would receive the drug, distribution methods, the role of caregivers, and the role of physicians, among other things. U.S. Supreme Court Justice Brandeis supported this type of approach, as he recognized the importance of states experimenting with policies. He said, "the importance of maintaining the states as laboratories of democracy—the ability of fifty separate communities to test fifty methods of dealing with a problem, the most effective of which may be adopted by the federal government."[4]

Congress may also choose to revise the law as it now exists. Most advocates agree that there is more than sufficient evidence to call for a thorough investigation into reclassifying marijuana from a Schedule I to a Schedule II drug. If the DEA would do this, the drug could be used as for medical purposes. Federal officials could also regulate the use of marijuana so that physicians and pharmacies could provide patients with standardized and doses of marijuana that are not tainted with chemicals. It would also reduce the possibility that patients would be forced to use marijuana from the black-market, risking legal prosecution.

The exact effects of marijuana and cannabinoids on patients are still unknown. Because there are only a limited number of research studies that support medical marijuana, there are many challenges for doctors and patients who would like to at least consider it as an option. Currently, it is not known if marijuana will work for a patient, or if it will be more or less effective than traditional drugs. Unlike prescription drugs that have been approved by the FDA, marijuana has no accepted dosing regimen.

More research is needed to understand the possible medical uses of the plant. The effects of different types or strains of cannabis on different symptoms could be established to link a particular strain with a disease.[5] This could be done via the same process that is required for any other new drug seeking to be put on the market. The possible medical benefits of marijuana would need to be determined in the manner as other drugs that are proposed for medical purposes.[6]

There should be no doubt that federal efforts to circumvent state medical marijuana laws will continue. But to what extent remains unknown. As more states pass medical cannabis laws, the federal government may rethink the Schedules that now exist and modify them. Congress may come under pressure from voters to take another look at the issue.

Endnotes

Endnotes for Chapter 1

1. "Cannabis history." Retrieved online at http://www.cannabissearch.com/history/.

2. Booth, Martin (2003). *Cannabis: A History.* New York: St. Martin's Press.

3. Abel, Ernest L. (1984). *A Dictionary of Drug Abuse Terms and Terminology.* Westport, CT: Greenwood Press.

4. "Medical Marijuana: An Overview" Retrieved online at http://criminal.findlaw.com/criminal-charges/medical-marijuana-an-overview.html.

5. Martinez, Martin (2000). *The New Prescription: Marijuana as Medicine.* Oakland: Quick American Archives.

6. Ibid.

7. Ibid.

8. Rofman, Roger A. (1982). *Marijuana as Medicine.* Seattle: Madrona Publishers.

9. Booth, Martin (2003). *Cannabis: A History.* New York: St. Martin's Press.

10. Ibid.

11. Mack, Alison and Janet Joy (2001). *Marijuana as Medicine? The Science Beyond the Controversy.* Washington, D.C.: National Academy Press.

12. "10 Little Known Facts in the Medical Marijuana Debate" Retrieved online at //medicalmarijuana.procon.org/view.resource.php?resourceID=004289.

13. Caulkins, Jonathan P.; Angela Hawken, Beau Kilmer and Mark A. R. Kleiman (2012). *Marijuana Legalization: What Everyone Needs to Know.* New York: Oxford University Press.

14. Dusek, Dorothy E. and Daniel A. Gidano (1993). *Drugs: A Factual Account.* New York: McGraw Hill.

15. Earlywine, Mitch (2007). "Values and the Marijuana Debate" in Mitch Earlywine, ed. *Pot Politics: Marijana and the Costs of Prohibition.* New York: Oxford University Press, pp. 355-359; Earlywine, Mitch (2002). *Understanding Marijuana: A New Look at the Scientific Evidence New York.* New York: Oxford University Press.

16. Martinez, Martin (2000). *The New Prescription: Marijuana as Medicine.* Oakland: Quick American Archives; Mack, Alison and Janet Joy (2001). *Marijuana as Medicine? The Science Beyond the Controversy.* Washington, D.C.: National Academy Press.

17. Caulkins, Jonathan P. Angela Hawken, Beau Kilmer and Mark A. R. Kleiman (2012). *Marijuana Legalization: What Everyone Needs to Know.* New York: Oxford University Press.

18. "Deaths from Marijuana v. 17 FDA Approved Drugs" Retrieved online at http://medicalmarijuana.procon.org/view.resource.php?resourceID=000145.

19. FDSA Office of Pharmacoepidemiology and Statistical Science (2005). "Adverse Event Reporting System (AERS) Brief Description with Caveats of System" Retrieved online at http://medicalmarijuana.procon.org/sourcefiles/fdaaers.pdf.

20. "Medical Marijuana: Pharmaceutical drugs Based on Cannabis" Retrieved online at http://medicalmarijuana.procon.org/view.resource.php?resourceID=000883.

21. "10 Little Known Facts in the Medical Marijuana Debate" Retrieved online at // medicalmarijuana.procon.org/view.resource.php?resourceID=004289.

22. Matthews, Anna Wilde (January 19, 2010). "Is Marijuana a Medicine?" *Wall Street Journal.* Retrieved online at http://online.wsj.com/article/SB10001424052748703626604575011223512854284.html.

23. Mathews, Anna Wilde (January 19, 2010). "Is Marijuana a Medicine? *Wall Street Journal.* Retrieved online at http://online.wsj.com/article/SB10001424052748703626604575011223512854284.html.

24. "10 Little Known Facts in the Medical Marijuana Debate" Retrieved online at // medicalmarijuana.procon.org/view.resource.php?resourceID=004289.

25. Armentano, Paul (July 29, 2012), "Five Scientific Conclusions About Cannabis that the mainstream media doesn't want you to know"; Retrieved online at http://www.alternet.org/drugs/five-scientific-conclusions-about-cannabis-mainstream-media-doesnt-want-you-know.

26. "Reefer Madness" (April 27, 2006). *The Economist* Retrieved online at http://www.economist.com/science/displaystory.cfm?story_id=6849915.

27. Mack, Alison and Janet Joy (2001). *Marijuana as Medicine? The Science Beyond the Controversy.* Washington, D.C.: National Academy Press.

28. "US Government Reports on Medical Marijuana" Retrieved online at http://medicalmarijuana.procon.org/view.resource.php?resourceID=000155; Caulkins, Jonathan P., Angela Hawken, Beau Kilmer and Mark A. R. Kleiman (2012). *Marijuana Legalization: What Everyone Needs to Know.* New York: Oxford University Press; Martinez Martin (2000). *The New Prescription: Marijuana as Medicine.* Oakland: Quick American Archives.

29. Paul Armentano (July 29, 2012). "Five Scientific Conclusions About Cannabis that the mainstream media doesn't want you to know"; Retrieved online at http://www.alternet.org/drugs/five-scientific-conclusions-about-cannabis-mainstream-media-doesnt-want-you-know.

30. Mack, Alison and Janet Joy (2011). *Marijuana as Medicine? The Science Beyond the Controversy.* Washington, D.C.: National Academy Press.

31. Earlywine, Mitch (2007). "Values and the Marijuana Debate" in Mitch Earlywine, ed. *Pot Politics: Marijana and the Costs of Prohibition.* New York: Oxford University Press, pp. 355-359.

32. "Cannabis Oil and Cancer Treatment" Retrieved online at http://www.medicalmarijuanablog.com/benefits/cannabis-oil-and-cancer-treatment.html.

33. "Medical Marijuana Chewing Gum for Pain Relief" Retrieved online at http://www.medicalmarijuanablog.com/benefits/medical-marijuana-chewing-gum-for-pain.html.

34. Grinspoon, Lester (1971). *Marijuana Reconsidered.* Cambridge: Harvard University Press; Caulkins, Jonathan P. Angela Hawken, Beau Kilmer and Mark A. R. Kleiman (2012). *Marijuana Leaglization: What Everyone Needs to Know.* New York: Oxford Univer-

sity Press, 2012.

35. Mathews, Anna Wilde (January 19, 2010). "Is Marijuana a Medicine? *Wall Street Journal*. Retrieved online at http://online.wsj.com/article/SB100014240527487036266045 75011223512854284.html.

Martinez, Martin (2000). *The New Prescription: Marijuana as Medicine*. Oakland: Quick American Archives; Mack, Alison and Janet Joy (2001), *Marijuana as Medicine? The Science Beyond the Controversy*. Washington, D.C.: National Academy Press.

36. Grinspoon, Lester (1971). *Marijuana Reconsidered*. Cambridge: Harvard University Press.

37. Iuvone, T., G. Esposito, R. Esposito, R. Santamaria, M. DiRosa, and A.A. Izzo (2004). "Neuroprotective effect of cannabidiol, a non-psychoactive component from Cannabis sativa, on beta-amyloid-induced toxicity in PC12 cells" *Journal of Neurochemistry*, pp. 134-41. Retrieved online at http://www.ncbi.nlm.nig.gov/pubmed/15030397; Martin-Moreno, A., D. Reigada, BG Ramirez, R. Mechoulam, N. Innamorato, A. Cuadrado, and ML deCeballos (2011). "Cannabidiol and other cannabinoids reduce microglial activation in vitro and in vivo: relevance to Alzheimer's disease" *Molecular Pharmacology*, pp. 964-73, Retrieved online at http://www.ncbi.nlm.nig.gov/pubmed/21350020; Campbell, V.A. and A. Gowran (2007). "Alzheimer's disease: taking the edge off with cannabinoids?" *British Journal of Pharmacology*, 152 (5): 655-662 available online at http://www.ncbi.nlm.nih.gov/pmc/articles/PMC2190031/.

Mack, Alison and Janet Joy (2001). *Marijuana as Medicine? The Science Beyond the Controversy*. Washington, D.C.: National Academy Press.

38. Earlywine, Mitch (2002). *Understanding Marijuana: A New Look at the Scientific Evidence*. New York: Oxford University Press.

39. Grinspoon, Lester (1971) *Marijuana Reconsidered*. Cambridge: Harvard University Press; Martinez, Martin (2000). *The New Prescription: Marijuana as Medicine*. Oakland: Quick American Archives; Rofman, Roger A. (1982). *Marijuana as Medicine*. Seattle: Madrona Publishers.

40. PRNewswire (September 21, 2012). "Can Cannabidiol (CBD) Fight Metastatic Cancer? According to the latest research the answer is yes" Retrieved online at http://www.prnewswire.com/news-releases/can-cannabidiol-cbd-fight-metastatic-cancer-according-to-the-latest-research-the-answer-is-yes-170681736.html; Zuardi, A.W. (2008). "Cannabidiol: from an inactive cannabinoid to a drug with wide spectrum of action" *Revista Brasileira de Psiquiatria* (Brazilian Association of Psychiatry) Retrieved online at http://www.ncbi.nlm.nig.gov/pubmed/18833429.

41. Marcu, Jahan P., Rigel T. Christian; Darrul Lau; Anne J. Zielinski; Maxx P. Horowitz; Jasmine Lee; Arash Pakdel, Juanita Allison; Chandani Limbad; Dan H. Moore; Garret L. Yount; Peirre-Yves Desprez and Sean D. McAllister (January 6, 2010). "Cannabidiol enhances the inhibitory effects of Delta-9-tetrahydrocannabinol on human glioblastoma cell proliferation and survival" NIH Public Access, Retrieved online at http://www.ncbi.nlm.nih.gov/pmc/aricles/PMC2806496/; Marcu, JP, RT Christian; D. Lau; AJ Zielinski; MP Horowitz; J. Lee; A. Pakdel; J. Allison; C. Limbad; DH Moore; GL Yount; PY Desprez; and SD MacAllister (January 2010) "Cannabidiol enhances the inhibitory effects of delta9-tetrahydrocannabinol on human glioblastoma cell proliferation and survival" *Cancer Therapy*, 9:1, pp. 180-189, Retrieved online at http://www.ncbi.nlm.nih.gov/pubmed/20053780.

42. Ligresti, A., AS Moriello, K. Starowicz, I. Matias; S. Pisanti; L. DePetrocellis; C.

Laezza, G. Portella; M. Bifulco; and V. DiMarzo (September 2006). "Antitumor activity of plant cannabinoids with emphasis on the effect of cannabidiol on human breast carcinoma" *Journal of Pharmacology and Experimental Therapeutics*; 18:3, pp. 1375-87, Retrieved online at http://www.ncbi.nlm.nih.gov/pubmed/16728591.

43. Shrivastava, A., PM Kuzontkoski; JE Groopman, and A. Prasad (July 2011). "Cannabidiol induces programmed cell death in breast cancer cells by coordinating the cross-talk between apoptosis and autophaby" *Molecular Cancer Therapy.* 10(7):1161-72; Retrieved online at http://www.ncbi.nlm.nih.gov/pubmed/21566064.

44. Munson, A.E., L.S. Harris, M.A. Friedman, W.L. Dewey and R.A. Carchman (September 1975). "Antineoplastic activity of cannabinoids" *Journal of the National Cancer Institute,* 55:3, pp. 597-602, Retrieved online at http://www.ukcia.org/research/AntineoplasticActivityOfCannabinoids/index.php.

45. Martinez, Martin (2000). *The New Prescription: Marijuana as Medicine.* Oakland: Quick American Archives; Rofman, Roger A. (1982). *Marijuana as Medicine.* Seattle: Madrona Publishers; Mack, Alison and Janet Joy (2001). *Marijuana as Medicine? The Science Beyond the Controversy.* Washington, D.C.: National Academy Press.

46. Capasso, R., F. Borrelli, G. Aviello, B. Romano, C. Scalisi, F. Capasso, and A. A. Izzo (2008). "Cannabidiol extracted from Cannabis sativa, selectively inhibits inflammatory hypermotility in mice" *British Journal of Pharmacology* 154 (5), pp 1001-1008, Retrieved online at http://www.ncbi.nlm.nig.gov/pmc/articles/PMC2451037; Borrelli, F., G. Aviello, B. Romano, P. Orlando, R. Capasso, F. Maiello, F. Guadagno, S. Petrosino, F. Capasso, V. DiMarzo, A.A. Izzo (2009). "Cannabidiol, a safe and non-psychotropic ingredient of the marijuana plant Cannabis sativa, is protective in a murine model of colitis" *Journal of Molecular Medicine* 87(11): 1111-1121, Retrieved online at http://www.ncbi.nlm.nig.gov/pubmed/19690825.

47. Zanelati, T.V., C. Biojone, F.A. Moreira, F.S. Guimaraes, S.R. Joca (2010). "Antidepressant-like effects of cannabidiol in mice: possible involvement of 5-HT1A receptors" *British Journal of Pharmacology,* 159 (1); 122-128; Retrieved online at http://www.ncbi.nlm.nig.gov/pubmed/20002102.

48. El-Remessy, A.B., Y. Khalifa, S Ola, A.S. Ibrahim and G.I. Liou (2010). "Cannabidiol protects retinal neurons by preserving glutamine synthetase activity in diabetes" *Molecular Vision,* 16: 1487-1495, Retrieved online at http://www.ncbi.nlm.nig.gov/pmc/articles/PMC2925907/; Raiesh, Mohanraj, Partha Mukhopadhyay, Sandor Batkai, Gyorgy Hasko, Lucas Liaudet, Viktor R. Drei, Irina G. Obrosova, and Pal Pacher (2007). "Cannabidiol attenuates high glucose-induced endothellal cell inflammatory response and barrier disruption" *American Journal of Physiology- Heart and Circulatory Physiology* 293 (1) H610-H619, retrieved online at http://www.ncbi.nlm.nig.gov/pmc/articles/PMC2228254; Weiss, Lola, Michael Zeira, Shoshana Reich, Shimon Stavin, Itamar Raz, Raphael Mechoulam, and Ruth Gallily (2007). "Cannabidiol Arrests Onset of Autoimmune Diabetes in NOD Mice" *Neuropharmacology,* 54 (1) 244-249, Retrieved online at http://www.ncbi.nlm.nig.gov/PCM2270485/; Rog, D.J., T.J. Nurmikko, C.A. Young (2007). "Oromucosal delta9-tetrahydrocannabinol/cannabidiol for neuropathic pain associated with multiple sclerosis: an uncontrolled, open-label, 2-year extension trial" *Clinical Therapy,* 29 (9): 2068-2079, Retrieved online at http://www.ncbi.nlm.nig.gov/pubmed/18035205.

49. Caulkins, Jonathan P., Angela Hawken, Beau Kilmer and Mark A. R. Kleiman (2012). *Marijuana Leaglization: What Everyone Needs to Know.* New York: Oxford University Press; Earlywine, Mitch (2002). *Understanding Marijuana: A New Look at the Scientific Evidence.*

New York: Oxford University Press; Martinez, Martin (2000). *The New Prescription: Marijuana as Medicine.* Oakland: Quick American Archives; Rofman, Roger A. (1982). *Marijuana as Medicine.* Seattle: Madrona Publishers; Mack, Alison and Janet Joy (2001). *Marijuana as Medicine? The Science Beyond the Controversy.* Washington, D.C.: National Academy Press.

50. Grinspoon, Lester (1971). *Marijuana Reconsidered.* Cambridge: Harvard University Press.

51. Grinspoon, Lester (1971). *Marijuana Reconsidered.* Cambridge: Harvard University Press; Martinez, Martin (2000). *The New Prescription: Marijuana as Medicine.* Oakland: Quick American Archives.

52. Rog, D.J., T.J. Nurmikko, C.A. Young (2007). "Oromucosal delta9-tetrahydrocannabinol/cannabidiol for neuropathic pain associated with multiple sclerosis: an uncontrolled, open-label, 2-year extension trial" *Clinical Therapy*, 29 (9): 2068-2079, Retrieved online at http://www.ncbi.nlm.nig.gov/pubmed/18035205; Kozela, E., N. Lev, N. Kaushansky, R. Eilam, N. Rimmerman, R. Levy, A. Ben-Nun; A. Juknat; and Z. Vogel (2011). "Cannabidiol inhibits pathogenic T cells, decreases spinal microglial activation and ameliorates multiple sclerosis-like disease in C57BL/6 mice" *British Journal of Pharmacology*, 163 (7): 1507-19, Retrieved online at http://www.ncbi.nlm.nig.gov/pubmed/21449980; Lakhari, Shaheen E. and Marie Rowland, (2009). "Whole plant cannabis extracts in the treatment of spasticity in multiple sclerosis: a systematic review" *BMC Neurology* 9:59, Retrieved online at http://www.ncbi.nlm.nig.gov/pmc/articles/PMC2793241.

53. Parker, Linda A. Raphael Mechoulam, and Coralynne Schlievert (2002), "Cannabidiol, a non-psychoactive component of cannabis and its synthetic dimethylheptyl homolog suppress nausea in an experimental model with rats" *Neuroreport*; 13 (5): 567-570, Retrieved online at http://journals.lww.com/neuroreport/Abstract/2002/04160/Cannabidiol,_a_non_psychoactive.

54. PRNewswire (Aug 1, 2012). "Medical Marijuana Inc. and Canipa Holdings Drive Dixie X and CanChew Gum Toward EU Marketing Approval And Clinical Development" Retrieved online at http://www.prnewswire.com/news-releases/medical-marijuana-inc-and-canipa-holdings-drive-dixie-x-and-canchew-gum-toward-eu-marketing-approval-and-clinical-development-164569876.html.

55. "Opiate Treatments Improved with Medical Marijuana" Retrieved online at http://www.medicalmarijuanablog.com/benefits/opiate-treatments-improved-with-medical-marijuana.html; Martinez, Martin (2000). *The New Prescription: Marijuana as Medicine.* Oakland: Quick American Archives; Mack, Alison and Janet Joy (2001). *Marijuana as Medicine? The Science Beyond the Controversy.* Washington, D.C.: National Academy Press.

56. Mathews, Anna Wilde (January 19, 2010). "Is Marijuana a Medicine?" *Wall Street Journal.* Retrieved online at http://online.wsj.com/article/SB10001424052748703626604575011223512854284.html.

57. Rofman, Roger A. (1982). *Marijuana as Medicine.* Seattle: Madrona Publishers; Mack, Alison and Janet Joy (2001). *Marijuana as Medicine? The Science Beyond the Controversy.* Washington, D.C.: National Academy Press.

58. http://articles.timesofindia.indiatimes.com/2012-11-19/india/35204451_1_cultivation-marijuana-uruguayan-president-jose-mujica; http://abcnews.go.com/ABC_Univision/News/uruguayan-president-time-ripe-marijuana-legalization/story?id=18029022; http://www.tokeofthetown.com/2012/09/guatemalas_president_lets_legalize_drugs.php.

59. "Medical Marijuana: An Overview" Retrieved online at http://criminal.findlaw.com/criminal-charges/medical-marijuana-an-overview.html.

60. "Can the First Dispensary in New Jersey Handle it?" Retrieved online at http://www.medicalmarijuanablog.com/dispensaries/greenleaf-compassion-center.html.

61. Shactman, Brian (November 7, 2012). "Marijuana and Money: State by State—Colorado" Retrieved online at http://www.cnbc.com/id/49729596.

62. Mathews, Anna Wilde (January 19, 2010). "Is Marijuana a Medicine?" *Wall Street Journal*. Retrieved online at http://online.wsj.com/article/SB10001424052748703626 604575011223512854284.html.

Endnotes for Chapter 2

1. Martinez, Martin (2003). *The New Prescription: Marijuana as Medicine*. Oakland: Quick American Archives; Booth, Martin (2003). *Cannabis: A History*. New York: St. Martin's Press.

2. "Marijuana History and Timeline" Retrieved online at http://www.concept420.com/information/marijuana-timeline-history/; Martinez, Martin (2000). *The New Prescription: Marijuana as Medicine*. Oakland: Quick American Archives.

3. National Institute on Drug Abuse (NIDA), 1977 "Marijuana Research Findings: 1976, 1977," Retrieved online at http://archives.drugabuse.gov/pdf/monographs/14.pdf; Earlywine, Mitch (2002). *Understanding Marijuana: A New Look at the Scientific Evidence*. New York: Oxford University Press; Martinez, Martin (2000). *The New Prescription: Marijuana as Medicine*. Oakland: Quick American Archives; Rofman,Roger A. (1982). *Marijuana as Medicine*. Seattle: Madrona Publishers; Mack, Alison and Janet Joy (2001). *Marijuana as Medicine? The Science Beyond the Controversy*. Washington, D.C.: National Academy Press.

4. Dusek, Dorothy E. and Daniel A. Gidano (2001). *Drugs: A Factual Account*. New York: McGraw Hill.

5. Joy, Janet and Alison Mack (2001). *Marijuana as Medicine: Beyond the Controversy*.

6. Abel, Ernest L. (1980). *Marihuana, the First Twelve Thousand Years*. New York: Plenum Press; Booth, Martin (2003). *Cannabis: A History*. New York: St. Martin's Press.

7. Booth, Martin (2003). *Cannabis: A History*. New York: St. Martin's Press.

8. U.S. National Commission on Marijuana and Drug Abuse (1972). "Marijuana, A Signal of Misunderstanding" Retrieved online at druglibrary.org.

9. "Cannabis History" Retrieved online at http://www.cannabissearch.com/history/.

10. "History of Marijuana" Retrieved online at http://www.narconon.org/drug--information/marijuana-history.html.

11. Mack, Alison and Janet Joy (2001). *Marijuana as Medicine? The Science Beyond the Controversy*. Washington, D.C.: National Academy Press.

12. "Christopher Columbus, Discoverer of the New World: Avid Cannabis User" Retrieved online at http://www.cannabissearch.com/history/christopher-columbus-discoverer-of-the-new-world-avid-cannabis-user/.

13. Segal, Bernard (1986). *Perspectives on Drug Use in the United States*. New York: Haworth Press; Rofman, Roger A. (1982). *Marijuana as Medicine*. Seattle: Madrona Publishers.

14. Deitch, Robert (2003). *Hemp: American History Revisited: The Plant with a Divided History*. New York: Algora; Booth, Martin (2003). *Cannabis: A History*. New York: St. Martin's Press.

15. Thomas Jefferson Foundation (2003). "Spurious Quotations" Retrieved online at Monticello.org; Booth, Martin (2003). *Cannabis: A History*. New York: St. Martin's Press.

16. Grinspoon, Lester (1971). *Marijuana Reconsidered.* Cambridge: Harvard University Press; Earlywine, Mitch (2002). *Understanding Marijuana: A New Look at the Scientific Evidence.* New York: Oxford University Press; Martinez, Martin (2000). *The New Prescription: Marijuana as Medicine.* Oakland: Quick American Archives; Rofman, Roger A. (1982). *Marijuana as Medicine.* Seattle: Madrona Publishers; Mack, Alison and Janet Joy (2001). *Marijuana as Medicine? The Science Beyond the Controversy.* Washington, D.C.: National Academy Press; Booth, Martin (2003). *Cannabis: A History.* New York: St. Martin's Press.

17. "42.0 Milestones in the History of Marijuana" Retrieved online at http://brainz.org/ 420-milestones-history-marijuana/.

18. "Marijuana History and Timeline" Retrieved online at http://www.concept420.com/ information/marijuana-timeline-history/.

19. Grinspoon, Grinspoon (1971). *Marijuana Reconsidered.* Cambridge: Harvard University Press; Reinerman, Craig (2011). "Cannabis in Cultural and Legal Limbo" in Suzanne Fraser and David Moore, eds. *The Drug Effect.* Sydney: Cambridge University Press, pp. 171-188; Earlywine, Mitch (2002). *Understanding Marijuana: A New Look at the Scientific Evidence.* New York: Oxford University Press.

20. Whitebread, Charles (1995). "The History of the Non-Medical Use of Drugs in the United States" Retrieved online at http://www.druglibrary.org/schaffer/History/whiteb1.htm; Booth, Martin (2003). *Cannabis: A History.* New York: St. Martin's Press.

21. U.S. Food and Drug Administration (FDA) "FDA History—Part I" Retrieved online at http://www.fda.gov/AboutFDA/WhatWeDo/History/Origin/ucm054819.htm.

22. Bonnie, Richard J. and Charles H. Whitebread II (1999). *The Marijuana Conviction: A History of Marijuana Prohibition in the United States.* New York: The Lindesmith Center.

23. Gieringer, http://medicalmarijuana.procon.org: Dale H. (1999). "The Forgotten Origins of Cannabis Prohibition in California," *Contemporary Drug Problems,* 26 (2), 237-289.

24. Bonnie, Richard J. and Charles H. Whitebread II (1999). *The Marijuana Conviction: A History of Marijuana Prohibition in the United States.* New York: The Lindesmith Center.

25. Whitebread, Charles (1995). "The History of the Non-Medical Use of Drugs in the United States" Retrieved online at http://www.druglibrary.org/schaffer/History/whiteb1.htm.

26. Inciardi, James A. (1992). *The War on Drugs II.* Mountain View, CA: Mayfield.

27. London, Jeffrey Matthew (2009). How the Use of Marijuana was Criminalized and Medicalized Lewiston: Edwin Mellen: 56; Padwa, Howard and Jacob A. Cunningham, (2010) "Harrison Narcotics Act," in *Addiction: A Reference Encyclopedia.* Santa Barbara, CA: ABC-CLIO, *ABC-CLIO eBook Collection.*

28. Booth, Martin (2003). *Cannabis: A History.* New York: St. Martin's Press.

29. "History of Marijuana" Retrieved online at http://www.narconon.org/drug--information/marijuana-history.html.

30. Schaller, Michael (1970). "The Federal Prohibition of Marihuana," *Journal of Social History.* 4 (1), 61-74.

31. Whitebread, Charles (1995). "The History of the Non-Medical Use of Drugs in the United States" Retrieved online at http://www.druglibrary.org/schaffer/History/whiteb1.htm.

32. Reinarman, Craig (2011). "Cannabis in Cultural and Legal Limbo" in Suzanne Fraser and David Moore, eds. *The Drug Effect.* Sydney: Cambridge University Press, pp. 171-188.

33. Sloman, Larry (1979). *Reefer Madness: The History of Marijuana in America.* Indianapolis: Bobbs-Merrill.

34. Booth, Martin (2003). *Cannabis: A History.* New York: St. Martin's Press.

35. Pacula, Rosalie Liccardo, J.F. Chriqui, D.A. Reichmann, and Y.M Terry-McElrath, (2002). "State Medical Marijuana Laws: Understanding the Laws and Their Limitations," *Journal of Public Health Policy,* 23 (4), pp. 413-39.

36. Dusek, Dorothy E. and Daniel A. Gidano (1993). *Drugs: A Factual Account.* New York: McGraw Hill.

37. Eddy, Mark (April 2, 2010). "Medical Marijuana: Review and Analysis of Federal and State Policies" CRS Report for Congress, Retrieved online at http://www.fas.org/sgp/crs/misc/RL33211.pdf.

38. London, Jeffrey Matthew (2009). *How the Use of Marijuana was Criminalized and Medicalized.* Lewiston: Edwin Mellen: 65; Padwa, Howard and Jacob A. Cunningham, "Marihuana Tax Act," *Addiction: A Reference Encyclopedia.* Santa Barbara, CA: ABC-CLIO, 2010, *ABD-CLIO eBook Collection.*

39. Mack, Alison and Janet Joy (2001). *Marijuana as Medicine? The Science Beyond the Controversy.* Washington, D.C.: National Academy Press.

40. London, Jeffrey Matthew (2009). *How the Use of Marijuana was Criminalized and Medicalized.* Lewiston: Edwin Mellen: 73, citing H.J. Anslinger and W.F. Tompkins (1953). *The Traffic in Narcotics.* (United States: Funk and Wagnalls): 18-26; Padwa, Howard and Jacob A. Cunningham (2010). "Boggs Act," *Addiction: A Reference Encyclopedia.* Santa Barbara, CA: ABC-CLIO, *ABD-CLIO eBook Collection.*

41. Bonnie, Richard J. and Charles H. Whitebread II (1999). *The Marijuana Conviction: A History of Marijuana Prohibition in the United States.* New York: The Lindesmith Center.

42. London, Jeffrey Matthew (2009). *How the Use of Marijuana was Criminalized and Medicalized.* Lewiston: Edwin Mellen: 74; Padwa, Howard and Jacob A. Cunningham (2010). "Narcotic Control Act," *Addiction: A Reference Encyclopedia.* Santa Barbara, CA: ABC-CLIO, *ABD-CLIO eBook Collection.*

43. "History of Marijuana" Retreived online at http://www.narconon.org/drug--information/marijuana-history.html.

44. United Nations Office on Drugs and Crime, "U.N. Single Convention on Narcotic Drugs, 1961". Retrieved online at http://www.unodc.org/unodc/en/treaties/single-convention.html; National Research Council of the National Academy of Sciences, (1982) "An Analysis of Marijuana Policy" Retrieved online at http://www.nap.edu/openbook.php?record_id=662.

45. London, Jeffrey Matthew (2009). *How the Use of Marijuana was Criminalized and Medicalized.* Lewiston: Edwin Mellen, 2009: 81; Rofman, Roger A.(1982). *Marijuana as Medicine.* Seattle: Madrona Publishers.

46. U.S. Drug Enforcement Administration (DEA) "A Tradition of Excellence: The History of the DEA from 1973-2003" Retrieved online at http://www.deamuseum.org/dea_history_book/index.html; U.S. Drug Enforcement Administration (DEA) "Marijuana," Retrieved online at http://www.justice.gov/dea/pr/multimedia-library/image-gallery/images_marijuana.shtml.

47. Richard Nixon, "The President's News Conference," May 1, 1971. Online by Gerhard Peters and John T. Woolley, *The American Presidency Project.* http://www.presidency.ucsb.edu/ws/?pid=2995.

48. Richard Nixon, "Remarks About an Intensified Program for Drug Abuse Preven-

tion and Control: The President's News Conference," June 17, 1971. Online by Gerhard Peters and John T. Woolley, *The American Presidency Project.* http://www.presidency.ucsb.edu/ws/?pid=3047.

49. Nancy E. Marion (1994). *A History of Federal Crime Control Initiatives* Westport, CT: Praeger.

50. National Institute on Drug Abuse (NIDA) (1998). "Provision of Marijuana and Other Compounds For Scientific Research—Recommendations of The National Institute on Drug Abuse National Advisory Council," Retrieved online at http://archives.drugabuse.gov/about/organization/nacda/MarijuanaStatement.html.

51. Russo, Ethan, Mary Lynn Mathre, Al Byrne, Robert Velin, Paul J. Bach, Juan Sanchez-Ramos, Kristin A. Kirlin (2002). "Chronic Cannabis Use in the Compassionate IND Program," *Journal of Cannabis Therapeutics*, (2)1: 3-57.

52. U.S. Drug Enforcement Administration (DEA) "A History of the DEA: 2003-2008," Retrieved online at deamuseum.org; Romney, Lee (March 18, 2006)"12 Accused of Making Marijuana-Laced Candy, Soda," *Los Angeles Times.* Retrieved online at latimes.com.

53. Johnson, Alex (February 27, 2009) "DEA to Halt Medical Marijuana Raids," Retrieved online at http://www.nbcnews.com/id/29433708/ns/health-health_care/t/dea-halt-medical-marijuana-raids/.

54. U.S. Department of Justice "Memorandum for Selected United States Attorneys" Retrieved online at http://blogs.justice.gov/main/archives/192.

55. U.S. Drug Enforcement Administration (DEA) (March 1, 2011) "Schedules of Controlled Substances: Temporary Placement of Five Synthetic Cannabinoids Into Schedule I" Retrieved online at DEA.gov.

56. Cooper, Michael (November 30, 2011). "2 Governors Asking U.S. to Ease Rules on Marijuana to Allow for Its Medical Use" *New York Times*, Retrieved online at http://www.nytimes.com/2011/12/01/us/federal-marijuana-classification-should-change-gregoire-and-chafee-say.html?_r=0.

57. Americans for Safe Access (ASA), (November 4, 2011). "ASA Sues Feds To Halt Anti-Pot Surge," Retrieved online at http://safeaccessnow.org/.

58. Miller, Mark (October 18, 2012). "U.S. Court of Appeals Hears Arguments to Reschedule Cannabis" *High Times Magazine*, Retrieved online at hightimes.com.

Endnotes for Chapter 3

1. Thompson, Cadie (April 20, 2010). "The East Coast Stumble In Legalizing Medical Marijuana," Retrieved online at http://www.cnbc.com/id/36179752.

2. "Alaska Medical Marijuana: Alaska Ballot Measure 8" Retrieved online at http://www.mmj-guide.com/Alaska-Medical-Marijuana.html.

3. Lee, Michelle Ye Hee (November 13, 2010). "Arizona Voters Have Approved Medical Marijuana Measure," *Arizona Republic,* Retrieved online at http://www.azcentral.com/news/election/azelections/articles/2010/11/13/20101113arizona-medical-marijuana-approved.html.

4. Riverside County District Attorney's Office (September 2006). "White Paper Medical Marijuana: History and Current Complications" Retrieved online at http://

www.rivcoda.org/News/Articles/Medical%20Marijuana%20-%20White%20Paper.pdf.

5. "Guidelines for the Security and Non-diversion of Marijuana Grown for Medical Use" (August 8, 2008), Retrieved online at http://ag.ca.gov/cms_attachments/press/pdfs/n1601_medicalmarijuanaguidelines.pdf.

6. Linthicum, Kate (July 24, 2012). "L.A. City Council Votes 14-0 to Ban Medical Marijuana Shops," *Los Angeles Times*, Retrieved online at http://latimesblogs.latimes.com/lanow/2012/07/la-council-votes-on-pot-shops.html; Risling, Greg, (July 25, 2012)."Los Angeles Officials Vote to Ban Marijuana Shops," Retrieved online at http://news.yahoo.com/los-angeles-officials-vote-ban-marijuana-shops-071533665.html.

7. "Colorado Medical Marijuana: A Detailed Review of the Colorado Medical Marijuana Laws" Retrieved online at http://www.mmj-guide.com/Colorado-Medical-Marijuana. html.

8. "Press Release: Strengthens Medical Marijuana Oversight," Office of Governor Bill Ritter, Jr., June 7, 2010; Retrieved online at http://www.colorado.gov/cs/Satellite%3Fc%3DPage%26cid%3D1251574630880%26p%3D1251574630880%26pagename%3DGovRitter%252FGOVRLayout.

9. Ingold, John (February 28, 2013), "Colorado pot task force recommends special sales and excise taxes" *Denver Post*, Retrieved online at http://www.denverpost.com/breakingnews/ci_22689447/tax-legal-issues-tap-at-last-colorado-marijuana.

10. O'Keefe, Karen (June 1, 2012), "Gov. Malloy Signs Connecticut Medical Marijuana Bill" Marijuana Policy Project, Retrieved online at http://blog.mpp.org/medical-marijuana/gov-malloy-signs-connecticut-medical-marijuana-bill/06012012/.

11. "Gov. Malloy Signs Legislation Providing Relief to Some Patients with Chronic, Debilitating Medical Conditions," June 1, 2012, Retrieved online at http://www.governor.ct.gov/malloy/cwp/view.asp?Q=505366&A=4010; "Bill Status H.B. No. 5389," Retrieved online at http://www.cga.ct.gov/asp/cgabillstatus/cgabillstatus.asp?selBillType=Bill&bill_num=HB05389&which_year=2012.

12. "Connecticut now has legal medical marijuana" June 18, 2012, Retrieved online at http://www.medicalmarijuanablog.com/state-laws/connecticut-185.html; "Connecticut is the 17th State to allow medical marijuana" June 2, 2012, *The Columbus Dispatch*, Retrieved online at http://www.dispatch.com/content/stories/national_world/2012/06/02/connecticut-is-17th-state-to-allow-medical-marijuana.html.

13. "Connecticut Medical Marijuana: House Bill 5389" Retrieved online at http://www.mmj-guide.com/Connecticut-Medical-Marijuana.html.

14. Denison, Doug (May 13, 2011). "Gov. Jack Markell Signs Medical Marijuana Bill," *Dover Post*, Retrieved online at http://www.doverpost.com/article/20130612/CCH/130619917.

15. Smith, Phillip (February 13, 2012). "Delaware Suspends Medical Marijuana Program" Stop the Drug War.com, Retrieved online at http://stopthedrugwar.org/chronicle/2012/feb/13/delaware_suspends_medical_mariju.

16. "Hawaii Medical Marijuana: A Detailed Review of the Hawaii Medical Marijuana Laws" Retrieved online at http://www.mmj-guide.com/Hawaii-Medical-Marijuana.html.

17. "Maine's Medical Marijuana Law," Retrieved Online at http://www.maine.gov/legis/lawlib/medmarij.html.

18. "Program Bulletin," (September 28, 2011), Retrieved online at http://www.maine.gov/dhhs/dlrs/mmm/index.shtml.

19. "Medical Marijuana Bill in Massachusetts General Election" Retrieved online at

http://www.squidoo.com/medical-marijuana-bill-in-massachusetts-general-election.

20. Duke, Alan (November 7, 2012). "2 States Legalize Pot, but Don't 'Break Out the Cheetos' Yet," Retrieved online at CNN.com.

21. Jacobi, Sara (July 19, 2012). "November Election Ballot Questions: Medical Marijuana, Death with Dignity, Right to Repair" *Wakefield Patch*, Retrieved online at http://wakefield.patch.com/articles/november-election-ballot-questions-medical-marijuana-death-with-dignity-right-to-repair.

22. Quinn, Colleen (April 10, 2012). "Medical Marijuana Debated at hearing, headed for November Ballot" *Wicked Local Foxborough*, http://www.metrowestdailynews.com/archive/x1047088759/Medical-marijuana-debated-at-hearing-headed-for-November-ballot#ixzz20kb7IDXk.

23. Loyd, Dan (2013). "House bill would allow medical marijuana dispensaries" Retrieved online at http://thenewsherald.com/aricles/2013/03/10/news/doc5136160362f5a557382580.txt.

24. Associated Press (July 1, 2011). "Medical Marijuana Changes Cause Confusion," *Billings Gazette*, Retrieved online at http://billingsgazette.com/news/state-and-regional/montana/medical-marijuana-changes-cause-confusion/article_e1bde7e0-a41b-11e0-9dde-001cc4c002e0.html.

25. Kocieniewski, David (January 11, 2011). "New Jersey Vote Backs Marijuana for Severely Ill," *New York Times*, Retrieved online at http://community.nytimes.com/comments/www.nytimes.com/2010/01/12/nyregion/12marijuana.html?sort=newest.

26. "New Mexico Medical Marijuana: A Detailed Review of the New Mexico Medical Marijuana Laws" Retrieved online at http://www.mmj-guide.com/New-Mexico-Medical-Marijuana.html.

27. "Oregon Medical Marijuana: A Detailed Review of the Oregon Medical Marijuana Laws: the Oregon Medical Marijuana Act" Retrieved online at http://www.mmj-guide.com/oregon-medical-marijuana.html.

28. "Rhode Island Medical Marijuana: A Detailed Review of the Rhode Island Medical Marijuana Laws" Retrieved online at http://www.mmj-guide.com/Rhode-Island-Medical-Marijuana.html.

29. "Vermont Medical Marijuana: A Detailed Review of the Vermont Medical Marijuana Laws" Retrieved online at http://www.mmj-guide.com/Vermont-Medical-Marijuana.html.

30. "Washington Medical Marijuana: A Detailed Review of the Washington Medical Marijuana Laws" Retrieved online at http://www.mmj-guide.com/washington-medical-marijuana.html.

31. Associated Press "WA Governor Allows More to OK Medical Marijuana," *Seattle Times*, April 1, 2010; Retrived online at http://seattletimes.com/html/localnews/2011503825_apwaxgrmedicalmarijuana.html.

32. Craig, Tim (July 27, 2010). "Medical Marijuana Now Legal," *Washington Post*, Retrieved online at http://voices.washingtonpost.com/dc/2010/07/medical_marijuana_now_legal.html.

Endnotes for Chapter 4

1. "Alabama: Medical Marijuana Bill Introduced In Alabama Legislature" Retrieved

online at *Hemp News* http://www.hemp.org/news/content/alabama-medical-marijuana-bill-introduced-alabama-legislature.

2. Smith, Phillip (April 9, 2010). "Medical Marijuana: Alabama Bill Wins House Committee Vote, but unlikely to Pass this year" Retrieved online at http://stopthedrugwar.org/chronicle/2010/apr/09/medical_marijuana_alabama_bill_w.

3. "Alabama: Medical Marijuana Bill Introduced In Alabama Legislature" Retrieved online at *Hemp News* http://www.hemp.org/news/content/alabama-medical-marijuana-bill-introduced-alabama-legislature.

4. "Medical marijuana proposals die in 2012, renewed effort planned for 2013" (July 13, 2012). Retrieved online at Marijuana Policy Project http://www.mpp.org/states/alabama/.

5. Nall, Loretta (April 9, 2010). "Cannabis Culture, Reflections on Alabama Medical Marijuana Hearing" Retrieved online at http://www.cannabisculture.com/content/2010/04/09/Reflections-Alabama-Medical-Marijuana-Hearing.

6. Smoker, Jay (August 30, 2011). "Alabama Medical Marijuana Coalition Kicks off 'Write Your Legislator' Campaign" Retrieved online at http://www.theweedblog.com/alabama-medical-marijuana-coalition-kicks-off-write-your-legislator-campaign/.

7. Americans for Safe Access (March 19, 2012). "Two Medical Marijuana Bills Introduced in Alabama in 2012" Retrieved online at http://asanational.org/two-medical-marijuana-bills-introduced-in-alabama-for-2012/.

8. "Medical marijuana stalls in Boise" April 30, 2012, *Marijuana Policy Project,* Retrieved online at http://www.mpp.org/states/idaho/; "Should Idaho Legalize medical marijuana?" April 22, 2010, *Idaho Press Tribune,* Retrieved online at http://www.idahopress.com/opinion/editorial/article_33f3f42e-4da0-11df-964d-001cc4c002e0.html.

9. Lang, Lou (April 21, 2009). "TV Ad Campaign boosts Illinois Medical Marijuana Bill" Retrieved online at http://reploulang.wordpress.com/2009/04/21/tv-ad-campaign-boosts-illinois-medical-marijuana-bill/.

10. Ormsby, David (November 30, 2010). "Illinois Medical Marijuana Bill Fails 53-59," *The Illinois Observer,* Retrieved online at http://illinoisobserver.org/2010/11/30/illinois-medical-marijuana-bill-fails-53-59/.

11. McDermott, Kevin (November 30, 2010). "Medical Marijuana Bill stalls in the Illinois House" *St. Louis Dispatch,* Retrieved online at http://www.stltoday.com/news/local/govt-and-politics/political-fix/article_5d4284c4-fcac-11df-9328-0017a4a78c22.html.

12. Ormsby, David (March 9, 2011). "House Panel Approves Illinois Medical Marijuana Legislation," *The Illinois Observer,* Retrieved online at http://illinoisobserver.org/2011/03/09/house-panel-approves-illinois-medical-marijuana-legislation/.

13. Hancock, Jason, (March 9, 2009). "Iowa Senate to Consider medical marijuana law" *The Iowa Independent,* Retrieved online at http://iowaindependent.com/12442/iowa-senate-to-consider-medical-marijuana-law.

14. "Iowa encourages serious talk on medical marijuana" (July 24, 2009). *The Quad City Times,* Retrieved online at http://qctimes.com/news/opinion/editorial/article_c92a4a30-7898-11de-a0e0-001cc4c03286.html.

15. Kellett, Claire (November 13, 2009). "Iowans already turn to marijuana for health problems" *The Gazette,* Retrieved online at http://thegazette.com/2009/11/13/iowans-already-turn-to-marijuana-for-health-problems.

16. Davis, Charles (November 3, 2010). "Iowa Activist Pledges to Sue for Medical Marijuana." Retrieved online at http://news.change.org/stories/iowa-activist-pledges-to-sue-for-medical-marijuana.

17. Iowa Department of Public Health (February 17, 2010). "Iowa Board of Pharmacy Issues Recommendation" Retrieved online at http://medicalmarijuana.procon.org/sourcefiles/IowaPharmacyMJ2010.pdf.

18. Buhrman, Matt (November 26, 2010). "Medical Marijuana in Iowa?" *Heartland Connection* Retrieved online at http://www.heartlandconnection.com/news/story.aspx?id =546576.

19. Medical Marijuna: One Step Closer in Iowa (February27, 2010) Available online at http://5250702-medical-marijuana-one-step-closer-in-iowa.

20. Hughes, Mike (January 28, 2011). "Iowa State Rep Breaks California Law to show disdain for medical pot" *High Times*; Retrieved online at http://hightimes.com/news/mike_hughes/6941.

21. Marijuana Policy Project, "Marijuana's medical efficacy both championed and questioned in Des Moines during 2011-12 Session" (July 6, 2012), Retrieved online at http://www.mpp.org/states/iowa.

22. Marijuana Policy Project, "Marijuana's medical efficacy both championed and questioned in Des Moines during 2011-12 Session" (July 6, 2012), Retrieved online at http://www.mpp.org/states/iowa.

23. "Kansas Legislature to Consider Medical Marijuana Bill," Retrieved online at http://www.csdp.org/news/news/medmj_013108.htm.

24. "Bill proposes legalizing medical marijuana in KS" (February 5, 2010), Retrieved online at http://www.marijuana.com/threads/ks-bill-proposes-legalizing-medical-marijuana-in-kansas.257777/.

25. Elliott, Steve (February 18, 2011). "Medical Marijuana Bill Introduced in Kansas" Retrieved online at http://www.tokeofthetown.com/2011/02/medical_marijuana_bill_introduced_in_kansas.php.

26. Bender, Jonathan (January 23, 2012). "Medical marijuana bill slated for Kansas House Committee hearing tomorrow," *Pitch News,* Retrieved online at http://www.pitch.com/plog/archives/2012/01/23/medical-marijuana-bill-slated-for-kansas-house-committee-hearing-tomorrow.

27. Wistrom, Brent, (January 27, 2012). "Group Drafts Bill to Legalize medical Marijuana in Texas", originally from *The Wichitah Eagle* Retrieved online at http://www.cannabisculture.com/content/2012/01/26/Group-Drafts-Bill-Legalize-Medical-Marijuana-Kansas.

28. Clarke, Thomas H. (March 14, 2012). "Kentucky Medical Marijuana Bill Stalled In Committee," *The Daily Chronic*; Retrieved online at http://www.thedailychronic.net/2012/9818/kentucky-medical-marijuana-bill-stalled-in-committee/; Elliott, Steve (July 5, 2012), "Lawmaker: Kentucky Could Legalize Medical Marijuana in 2013" Retrieved online at http://www.tokeofthetown.com/2012/07/lawmaker_kentucky_could_legalize_medical_marijuana.php.

29. "Maryland Grassroots Medical Marijuana Campaign Kicks Off" (January 31, 2008), Retrieved online at http://safeaccessnow.org/blog/?p=58.

30. Marijuana Policy Project (October 4, 2011). Campaign Event for Medical Marijuana Sponsor Del. Dan Morhaim, M.D. Retrieved online at http://www.mpp.org/states/maryland/alerts/md-campaign-event-for.html.

31. "Another Small Step: Protecting Patients From Arrest in Maryland" (March 20, 2012) Retrieved online at http://safeaccessnow.org/blog/?p=2429#more-2429.

32. Marijuana Policy Project, "The irony continues: Mississippi continues growing medical marijuana, but fails to protect patients" Retrieved online at http://www.mpp.org/states/mississippi/.

33. Marijuana Policy Project, "New Hampshire Committee Overwhelmingly Approves Medical Marijuana Bill" Retrieved online at K"http://blog.mpp.org/medical-marijuana/medical-marijuana-moves-forward-in-new-hampshire"http://blog.mpp.org/medical-marijuana/medical-marijuana-moves-forward-in-new-hampshire; Marijuana Policy Project, "Medical Marijuana Moves Forward in New Hampshire" Retrieved online at http://www.mpp.org/media/press-releases/medical-marijuana-moves.

34. "New York: Medical Marijuana on the Move in Albany and NYC" (2/27/04). Retrieved online at http://stopthedrugwar.org/chronicle-old/326/nymedmj.shtml.

35. "Medical Marijuana in New York State: Current Situation" (November 2010), Retrieved online at http://www.medicalmarijuanablog.com/state-laws/new-york-180.html.

36. Brou, Jonathan (February 18, 2010). "Medical Marijuana Day brings legalization fight to Capitol" Retrieved online at http://oudaily.com/news/2010/feb/18/medical-marijuana-day-brings-fight-capitol/.

37. "Legalization of Medical Marijuana in Oklahoma" Retrieved online at http://www.medicalmarijuanablog.com/state-laws/oklahoma-158.html/comment-page-1 Oct 20, 2010.

38. Pickens, Jeff (January 26, 2011). "Medical Marijuana Bill (sb573) still alive!" Retrieved online at http://paynecountydemocrats.org/blog/2011/01/oklahoma-medical-marijuana-bill-introduced/.

39. "To Medical Marijuana Patients and Supporters" Retrieved online at http://okmedicalmarijuana.org.

40. Baker, David (March 30, 2009). "Pennsylvania Ponders Legalizing Medical Marijuana" Retrieved online at http://www.campaignforliberty.com/blog.php?view=14933; Rosenzweig, Derek (October 1, 2009). "Medical Marijuana to be introduced in PA: Cohen will push for medical marijuana" Retrieved online at http://phillynorml.org/pages/news/63.

41. McDonnell, Sean (May 26, 2009). "The Push for Medical Marijuana in Pennsylvania," Retrieved online at http://www.marijuana.com/threads/pa-the-push-for-medical-marijuana-in-pennsylvania.242299/.

42. Manganaro, John (May 12, 2010), "Medical Marijuana bill introduced in Pa. Senate," The Pitt News Retrieved online at http://pittnews.com/newsstory/medical-marijuana-bill-introduced-in-pa-senate/.

43. Philly NORML (April 28, 2011)."Medical Marijuana Bill Reintroduced in Pennsylvania" Retrieved online at http://www.cannabisculture.com/content/2011/04/28/Medical-Marijuana-Bill-Re-Introduced-Pennsylvania.

44. Miller, Mark (July 28, 2011). "Pennsylvania Medical Marijuana Update," High Times, Retrieved online at http://hightimes.com/news/mmiller/7215; Philly NORML (April 28, 2011). "Medical Marijuana Bill Reintroduced in Pennsylvania" Retrieved online at http://www.cannabisculture.com/content/2011/04/28/Medical-Marijuana-Bill-Re-Introduced-Pennsylvania.

45. Miller, Mark (July 28, 2011), "Pennsylvania Medical Marijuana Update," Retrieved online at http://hightimes.com/news/mmiller/7215.

46. "Medical Marijuana Push in Pennsylvania" (March 14, 2010). Retrieved online at http://asanational.org/medical-marijuana-push-in-pennsylvania.

47. Rick, Lynn Taylor (November 3, 2010). "South Dakota Voters Say No to Medical Marijuana," Rapid City Journal, Retrieved online at http://rapidcityjournal.com/news/south-dakota-voters-say-no-to-medical-marijuana/article_1ae826c6-e6f2-11df-8018-001cc4c002e0.html.

48. Clarke, Thomas H. (April 5, 2012), "Tennessee Medical Marijuana Bill Dies After

Hearing" *The Daily Chronic* Retrieved online at http://www.thedailychronic.net/2012/10946/tennessee-medical-marijuana-bill-dies-after-hearing/.

49. "Patients' Request for public hearing rejected; sponsors offer study resolution" (July 5, 2012). *Marijuana Policy Project*; Retrieved online at http://www.mpp.org/states/west-virginia/.

50. Smith, Phillip (October 16, 2009). "Medical Marijuana: Wisconsin Bill to Be Filed" StoptheDrugWar.com, Retrieved online at http://stopthedrugwar.org/chronicle/2009/oct/16/medical_marijuana_wisconsin_bill/.

Endnotes for Chapter 5

1. Teten, Ryan Lee (2007). "We the People" The "Modern" Rhetorical Popular Address of the Presidents during the Founding Period" *Political Research Quarterly*, 60 (4): 669-682.

2. Marion, Nancy E., Colleen M. Smith and Willard M. Oliver, Gubernatorial Crime Control Rhetoric; *Criminal Justice Policy Review.*

3. Cohen, Jeffrey E. (1995). "Presidential Rhetoric and the Public Agenda" *American Journal of Political Science* 39 (1): 87-107; Kingdon, John (1995). *Agendas, Alternatives and Public Policies.* Boston: Little Brown; Young, Garry and William B. Perkins (2005). "Presidential Rhetoric, the Public Agenda and the End of Presidential Television's "Golden Age"" *Journal of Politics*, 67 (4): 1190-1205.

4. Marion, Nancy E. and Willard M. Oliver (2012) *The Public Policy of Crime and Criminal Justice.* Boston: Prentice Hall; DiClerico, Robert E. (1995). *The American President,* 4th ed. Englewood Cliffs, N,J.: Prentice Hall; Thomas, Norma C. and Joseph A. Pika (1996). *The Politics of the Presidency,* 4th ed. Washington, D.C.: Congressional Quarterly Press.

5. Fairchild, Erika and Vince Webb (1985). *Crime, Justice and Politics in the United States Today.* In E.S. Fairchild and V.J. Webb (eds), *The Politics of Crime and Criminal Justice.* Beverly Hills, CA: Sage, pp. 1-21; Cohen, Jeffrey E. (1995). "Presidential Rhetoric and the Public Agenda" *American Journal of Political Science.* 39 (1): 87-107; Whitford, Andrew B. and Jeff Yates (2003). "Policy Signals and Executive Governance: Presidential Rhetoric in the War on Drugs," *The Journal of Politics* 65 (4): 995-1012.

6. Marion, Nancy E. (1994). *A History of Federal Crime Control Initiatives, 1960-1993.* Westport, CT: Praeger.

7. Marion, Nancy E. (1992) Presidential agenda setting in Crime control. *Criminal Justice Policy Review* 6 (2): 159-184; Shull, S.A. and A.C. Ringlestein (1989). "Presidential attention, support and symbolism in civil Rights, 1953-1984," *The Social Science Journal* 26; 45-54; Shull, S. and A.C. Ringelstein (1995). "Presidential Rhetoric in Civil Rights Policymaking, 1953-1992". In J.W. Riddlesperger, Jr. and D.W. Jackson (eds), *Presidential leadership and Civil Rights Policy.* Westport, CT: Greenwood Press, pp. 15-28.

8. Edelman, Murray (1964). *Symbolic Uses of Politics.* University of Illinois Press, Urbana.

9. Mack, Alison and Janet Joy (2001). *Marijuana as Medicine? The Science Beyond the Controversy.* Washington, D.C.: National Academy Press.

10. Johnson, Lyndon B. (March 1, 1968). "Remarks at a Testimonial Dinner in Beaumont, Texas, for Representative Jack Brooks." Online by Gerhard Peters and John T. Woolley, *The American Presidency Project,* Retrieved online at http://www.presidency.ucsb.edu/

ws/?pid=28704.

11. Martinez, Martin (2000). *The New Prescription: Marijuana as Medicine.* Oakland: Quick American Archives.

12. Nixon, Richard M. (March 10. 1973). "Radio Address About the State of the Union Message on Law Enforcement and Drug Abuse Prevention," Online by Gerhard Peters and John T. Woolley, *The American Presidency Project.* Retrieved online at http://www.presidency.ucsb.edu/ws/?pid=4135.

13. Nixon, Richard M. (March 14, 1973). "State of the Union Message to the Congress on Law Enforcement and Drug Abuse Prevention," Online by Gerhard Peters and John T. Woolley, *The American Presidency Project.* Retrieved online at http://www.presidency.ucsb.edu/ws/?pid=4140.

14. Nixon, Richard M. (March 15, 1973). "The President's News Conference," Online by Gerhard Peters and John T. Woolley, *The American Presidency Project.* Retrieved online at http://www.presidency.ucsb.edu/ws/?pid=4142.

15. Nixon, Richard M. (March 15, 1973). "The President's News Conference," Online by Gerhard Peters and John T. Woolley, *The American Presidency Project.* Retrieved online at http://www.presidency.ucsb.edu/ws/?pid=4142.

16. Nixon, Richard M. (August 21, 1970). "Joint Statement Following Discussions With President Diaz Ordaz of Mexico," Online by Gerhard Peters and John T. Woolley, *The American Presidency Project.* Retrieved online at http://www.presidency.ucsb.edu/ws/?pid=2640.

17. Nixon, Richard M. (March 14, 1973). "State of the Union Message to the Congress on Law Enforcement and Drug Abuse Prevention," Online by Gerhard Peters and John T. Woolley, *The American Presidency Project.* Retrieved online at http://www.presidency.ucsb.edu/ws/?pid=4140.

18. Ford, Gerald R. (September 16, 1975). "The President's News Conference" Online by Gerhard Peters and John T. Woolley, *The American Presidency Project.* Retrieved online at http://www.presidency.ucsb.edu/ws/?pid=5255.

19. Ford, Gerald R. (October 7, 1975). "Interview With Reporters in Knoxville, Tennessee," Online by Gerhard Peters and John T. Woolley, *The American Presidency Project.* Retrieved online at http://www.presidency.ucsb.edu/ws/?pid=5311.

20. Booth, Martin (2003). *Cannabis: A History.* New York: St. Martin's Press.

21. Martinez, Martin (2000). *The New Prescription: Marijuana as Medicine.* Oakland: Quick American Archives.

22. Booth, Martin (2003). *Cannabis: A History.* New York: St. Martin's Press.

23. Reagan, Ronald R. (June 24, 1982). "Remarks on Signing Executive Order 12368, Concerning Federal Drug Abuse Policy Functions," Online by Gerhard Peters and John T. Woolley, *The American Presidency Project.* Retrieved online at http://www.presidency.ucsb.edu/ws/?pid=42671.

24. Reagan, Ronald R. (June 30, 1984). "Radio Address to the Nation on Drug Abuse," Online by Gerhard Peters and John T. Woolley, *The American Presidency Project.* Retrieved online at http://www.presidency.ucsb.edu/ws/?pid=40117.

25. Reagan, Ronald R. (October 2, 1982). "Radio Address to the Nation on Federal Drug Policy," Online by Gerhard Peters and John T. Woolley, *The American Presidency Project.* Retrieved online at http://www.presidency.ucsb.edu/ws/?pid=43085.

26. Reagan, Ronald R. (March 16, 1983). "Message to the Congress Transmitting Proposed Crime Control Legislation," Online by Gerhard Peters and John T. Woolley, *The American Presidency Project.* Retrieved online at http://www.presidency.ucsb.edu/ws/?pid=41058.

27. Reagan, Ronald R. (November 30, 1982)."Responses to Questions Submitted by Latin American Newspapers," Online by Gerhard Peters and John T. Woolley, *The American Presidency Project*. Retrieved online at http://www.presidency.ucsb.edu/ws/?pid=42046; Reagan, Ronald R. (October 6, 1984)."Radio Address to the Nation on Drug Abuse," Online by Gerhard Peters and John T. Woolley, *The American Presidency Project*. Retrieved online at http://www.presidency.ucsb.edu/ws/?pid=39198.

28. Reagan, Ronald R. (May 12, 1983). "Remarks of the President and Prime Minister George Cadle Price of Belize Following Their Meetings," Online by Gerhard Peters and John T. Woolley, *The American Presidency Project*. Retrieved online at http://www.presidency.ucsb.edu/ws/?pid=41314.

29. Booth, Martin (2003). *Cannabis: A History*. New York: St. Martin's Press.

30. Reagan, Ronald R. (August 6, 1986). "Remarks at the National Conference on Alcohol and Drug Abuse Prevention in Arlington, Virginia," Online by Gerhard Peters and John T. Woolley, *The American Presidency Project*. Retrieved online at http://www.presidency.ucsb.edu/ws/?pid=37710.

31. Gerber, Rudy (2004). *Legalizing Marijuana: Drug Policy Reform and Prohibition Politics*. Westport, CT: Praeger: 133.

32. Booth, Martin (2003). *Cannabis: A History*. New York: St. Martin's Press.

33. Clark, Peter A. (2000). "The Ethics of Medical Marijuana: Government Restrictions vs. Medical Necessity" *Journal of Public Health Policy* 21 (1): 40-60: 41.

34. Claiborne, William (January 1, 1997). "Federal Warning on Medical Marijuana Leaves Physicians Feeling Intimidated." *Washington Post*, p. A6.

35. Claiborne, William and Roberto Suro, "Medicinal Marijuana Brings Legal Headache" *Washington Post*, December 5, 1996, p. A1.

36. Newbern, Alistair E. (2000), "Good Cop, Bad Cop: Federal Prosecution of State-Legalized Medical Marijuana Use after United States V. Lopez" *California Law Review*, 88 (5): 1575-1634: 1577.

37. Gerber, Rudy (2004). *Legalizing Marijuana: Drug Policy Reform and Prohibition Politics*. Westport, CT: Praeger: 121.

38. Ibid., 98.

39. Clark, Peter A. (2000). "The Ethics of Medical Marijuana: Government Restrictions vs. Medical Necessity" *Journal of Public Health Policy* 21 (1): 40-60: 53.

40. Kreit, Alex (2003). "The Future of Medical Marijuana: Should the States Grow their Own?" *University of Pennsylvania Law Review* 151 (5): 1787-1826.

41. Kreit, Alex (2003). "The Future of Medical Marijuana: Should the States Grow their Own?" *University of Pennsylvania Law Review* 151 (5): 1787-1826: 1789-1790.

42. Barack Obama, "Exclusive Mail Tribune Interview with Obama" March 22, 2008; Retrieved online at http://www.mailtribune.com/apps/pbcs.dll/article?AID=/20080322/MEDIA03/80322004/-1/NEWS0802.

43. Obama, Barack (September 26, 2011). "Remarks at a Democratic National Committee Fundraiser in West Hollywood, California," Online by Gerhard Peters and John T. Woolley, *The American Presidency Project*. Retrieved online at http://www.presidency.ucsb.edu/ws/?pid=96812.

44. Obama, Barack (August 15, 2011). "Remarks at a Town Hall Meeting and a Question-and-Answer Session in Cannon Falls, Minnesota," Online by Gerhard Peters and John T. Woolley, *The American Presidency Project*. Retrieved online at http://www.presidency.ucsb.edu/ws/?pid=90721.

45. Strohm, Mitch (June 12, 2013). "More States Look to Pass Medical Marijuana Laws" Retrieved online at http://www.foxreno.com/news/news/crime-law/more-states-look-pass-medical-marijuana-laws/nYJmw/#sthash.PVOP3HiA.dpuf.

46. Reuteman, Rob (April 20, 2010). "The Confused State of Pot Law Enforcement" Retrieved online at http://www.cnbc.com/id/36179498.

47. Sherer, Step (July 23, 2012). "Wake Up, Obama: Medical Marijuana Patients are Voters" *Huff Post Politics*. Retrieved online at http://www.huffingtonpost.com/steph-sherer/obama-medical-marijuana_b_1695358.html.

48. Kain, Erik (October 7, 2011)."Obama Administration Shatters Campaign promise, escalates Crackdown on Medical Marijuana" *Forbes* Retrieved online at http://www.forbes.com/sites/erikkain/2011/10/07/obama-administration-shatters-campaign-promise-escalates-crackdown-on-medical-marijuana/.

49. Elliott, Steve (May 23, 2011). "Marijuana Advocates Sue Fed Govt over Rescheduling Delay" Retrieved online at http://pa4mmj.org/.

50. Roman, Roger A. and Anne Nicoll, (2007)."Disseminating Accurate and Balanced Marijuana Education: An Opportunity for the Policy Reform Movement" in Mitch Earleywine, ed. *Pot Politics: Marijana and the Costs of Prohibition.* New York: Oxford University Press, pp. 159-75; Martinez, Martin (2000). *The New Prescription: Marijuana as Medicine.* Oakland: Quick American Archives.

51. Gerber, Rudy (2004). *Legalizing Marijuana: Drug Policy Reform and Prohibition Politics.* Westport, CT: Praeger: 91; Liccardo Pacula, Rosalie, Jamie F. Chriqui, Deborah A. Reichmann, and Yvonne M. Terry-McElrath (2002). "State Medical Marijuana Laws: Understanding the Laws and their Limitations" *The Journal of Public Health Policy*, 23 (4), pp. 413-439: 417; Martinez, Martin, (2000). *The New Prescription: Marijuana as Medicine.* Oakland: Quick American Archives.

52. Clark, Peter A. (2000). "The Ethics of Medical Marijuana: Government Restrictions vs. Medical Necessity" *Journal of Public Health Policy* 21 (1): 40-60: 45.

53. Gerber, Rudy (2004). *Legalizing Marijuana: Drug Policy Reform and Prohibition Politics.* Westport, CT: Praeger: 92.

54. Liccardo Pacula, Rosalie, Jamie F. Chriqui, Deborah A. Reichmann, and Yvonne M. Terry-McElrath (2002). "State Medical Marijuana Laws: Understanding the Laws and their Limitations" *The Journal of Public Health Policy*, 23 (4): 413-439: 436-437; Kreit, Alex (2003). "The Future of Medical Marijuana: Should the States Grow their Own?" *University of Pennsylvania Law Review,* 151 (5): 1787-1826: 1795.

55. Stolberg, Sheryl Gay (March 19,1999). "For a Very Few Patients, U.S. Provides Free Marijuana" *The New York Times*, A-10.

56. Stolberg, Sheryl Gay (March 18, 1999) "Government Study on Marijuana Sees Medical Benefits," *The New York Times*, A-1.

57. Joy, Janet E., Stanley J. Watson, Jr., and John A. Benson (1999). *Marijuana And Medicine: Assessing the Science Base.* Washington, D.C.: Institute of Medicine: 99; Clark, Peter A. (2000). "The Ethics of Medical Marijuana: Government Restrictions vs. Medical Necessity" *Journal of Public Health Policy* 21 (1): 40-60.

58. Clark, Peter A. (2000) "The Ethics of Medical Marijuana: Government Restrictions vs. Medical Necessity" *Journal of Public Health Policy* 21 (1): 40-60: 46.

59. Marion, Nancy E., Colleen M. Smith and Willard M. Oliver (2009). "Gubernatorial Crime Control Rhetoric," *Criminal Justice Policy Review.* 20: 457-474.

60. Associated Press (August 6, 2012). "Gov. Jan Brewer: 'no change' on medical mar-

ijuana program" Retrieved online at http://azcapitoltimes.com/wp-content/plugins/tdc-sociable-toolbar/wp-print.php?p=49010; accessed 10/21/2012.

61. Culp-Ressler, Tara (July 31, 2012)."Arizona Governor Defends Medical Marijuana Program" *Cannabis Culture*. Retrieved online at http://www.cannabisculture.com/content/2012/07/31/Arizona-Governor-Defends.

62. Governor Bill Ritter (January 14, 2010). "Colorado State of the State Address" Retrieved online at http://www.stateofthestate.com/content.aspx?state=CO&date=01/14/2010.

63. Pazniokas, Mark (June 20, 2007). "Rell Vetoes Marijana Bill" *Courant,* Retrieved online at http://articlels.courant.com/2007-06-20/news/0706200978_1_medical-marijuana.

64. Associated Press (June 1, 2012). "Connecticut Governor signs medical marijuana law" Retrieved online at http://www.wishtv.com/dpps/health/healthy_living/conn-governor-signs-medical-marijuana.

65. Smith, Phillip (February 13, 2012). "Delaware Suspends Medical Marijuana Program" *Stop The Drug War,* Retrieved online at http://stopthedrugwar.org/print/28881; accessed 10/22/2012.

66. "Maine's Governor Signs Law Expanding Medical Marijuana Privacy" (June 29, 2011) Retrieved online at http://the420times.com/2011/06/maines-governor-sgns-law-expanding-medical-marijuana.

67. Walker, Andrea K. (March 9, 2012). "O'Malley would veto medical marijuana bill" Retrieved online at http://articles.baltimoresun.com/2012-03-09/health/b-hs-medical-marijuana-20120308.

68. "New Hampshire Governor Vetoes Medical Marijuana Bill Despite Strong Bipartisan Support" June 22, 2012, Retrieved online at http://www.enewspf.com/latest-news/health-and-fitness/34481-new-hampshire-governor.

69. McLure, Jason (June 21, 2012). "New Hampshire Medical Marijuana Legalization Bill Vetoed by John Lynch" *Reuters,* Retrieved online at http://www.huffingtonpost.com/2012/06/21/new-hampshire-medical-marijuana_n_16170 ; Boozer, Chelsea (July 15, 2012). "Medical marijuana moving toward more state ballots" *Kentucky Post,* Retrieved online at http://www.kypost.com/dpps/news/state/medical-marijuana-moving-toward-more-state-ballots_7660242.

70. Corzine, Jon, (January 12, 2010). "New Jersey State of the State 2010" Retrieved online at http://www.stateofthestate.com/content.aspx?state=NJ&date=01/12/2010.

71. Bond, Anastasia (May 28, 2010). "Governor Christie Expresses support for medical marijuana, contrary to campaign stance" Retrieved online at http://www.examiner.com/article/governor-christie-expresses-support-for-medical-marijuana-contrary-to-campaign-stance.

72. Hester, Tom, Sr. (July 19, 2011) "N.J. medical marijuana gets green light by Gov. Christie" *NewJerseyNewsroom*, Retrieved online at http://www.newjerseynewsroom.com/healthquest/nj-medical-marijuana-gets-green-light-by-gov-christie; Livio, Susan K. (July 19, 2011). "Governor Christie gives green light for N.J. medical marijuana" Retrieved online at http:/blog.nj.com/ledgerupdates_impact/print.html?entry=/2011/07/gov_christie_ is_expected.

73. "Governor Christie: I won't force N.J. towns to allow medical marijuana facilities" (January 12, 2012), retrieved online at http://blog.nj.com/ledgerupdates_impact/print.html?entry=/2012/01/gov_christie_i_wont.

74. "Cuomo: Medical Marijuana Won't Pass This Year" (April 9, 2012), Retrieved online at http://www.nbcnewyork.com/news/local/New-York-Medical-Marijuana-Legalization-Cuomo-146712615.html.

75. "Medical Marijuana in New York" (April 12, 2012) Retrieved online at http://

blog.whitesidemanor.com/; "New York Gov. Andrew Cuomo is reconsidering his stance on medical marijuana" (July 20, 2011) Retrieved online at http://www.syracuse.com/have-you-heard/index.ssf/2011/07/new_york_gov_andrew_cuomo_is_r.html.

76. Hughes, Mike (April 11, 2012). "Gov Nixes Potential Medical Pot Bill in New York" Medical marijuana.org, Retrieved online at http://medical-marijuana.org/gov-nixes-potential-medical-pot-bill-in-new-york.

77. Howard, Zach (September 30, 2011). "Governor Scraps medical Marijuana plan for Rhode Island" *Reuters*. Retrieved online at http://www.reuters.com/assets/print?aid=USTRE78T5LU20110930.

78. Graves, Lucia (June 29, 2011). "Chris Gregoire, Washington Governor, Vetoes Critical Parts of Medical Marijuana Bill" *Huffington Post*, Retrieved online at http://huffingtonpost.com/2011/04/29/washington-marijuana-bill-veto.

79. "Governors Gregoire and Chafee file Petition to Reclassify Marijuana on Federal Level" (November 30, 2011) Salem-News.com, Retrieved online at http://salem-news.com/print/21188; "United States Governors ban together to ask Federal Government to reclassify Marijuana to Schedule II" Retrieved online at http://www.nytimes.com/2011/12/01/us/federal-marijuana-classification-should-change-gregoire-and-chafee-say.html

80. Gerber, Rudy (2004). *Legalizing Marijuana: Drug Policy Reform and Prohibition Politics*. Westport, CT: Praeger: 92.

81. Ibid.

82. Ibid., 93.

83. Potter, Phillip (April 11, 2012). "San Francisco Mayor Speaks About Recent Federal Dispensary Closures" *Marijuana*, Retrieved online at http://www.marijuana.com/news/2012/04/san-francisco-mayor-speaks-about-recent-federal.; Roberts, Chris (April 12, 2012). "Ed Lee on Medical Marijuana: San Francisco Mayor Finally Breaks His Silence" *The Huffington Post*, Retrieved online at http://www.cannabisculture.com/content/2012/04/12/Ed-Lee-Medical-Marijuana-San Francisco.

84. "Villaraigosa Supports ban on Marijuana Dispensaries in L.A." (July 24, 2012). *Los Angeles Times*, Retrieved online at http://latimesblogs.latimes.com/lanow/2012/07/villaraigosa-ban-marijuana-dispensaries.html.

85. Legum, Judd (May 24, 2012). "Newark Mayor Cory Booker Declares War "A Failure," Endorses Medical Marijuana" Retrieved online at http://thinkprogress.org/politics/2012/05/24/489912/newark-mayor-cory-booker-declares"; Jeltsen, Melissa (May 23, 2012). "Cory Booker Calls Drug War "National Nightmare," Supports Medical Marijuana" *The Huffington Post*; Retrieved online at http://www.huffingtonpost.com/2012/05/23/cory-booker-drug-war_n_1541082.html.

86. McIntire, Nathan (June 21, 2012). "Mayor: Medical Marijuana Should Be Sold at Pharmacies" *Monrovia Patch*, Retrieved online at http://Monrovia.patch.com/articlels/mayor-medical-marijuana-should-be-sold-at-pharmacies.

87. Bell, Deborah (August 27, 2012). "Mayor Says Medical Marijuana Warehouse is 'Welcome in Woodbridge'" *Woodbridge Patch*, Retrieved online at http://woodbridge.patch.com/articlels/mayor-says-medical-marijuana-warehouse-is-welcome.

88. Bell, Deborah (September 5, 2012). "Mayor Says Pot Shop is Just Another 'Retail Store'" *Woodbridge Patch*, http://woodbridge.patch.com/articlels/mayor-says-pot-shop-is-just-another-retail-store.

89. Linthicum, Kate (July 25, 2012). "L.A. City Council bans medical marijuana dispensaries" *Los Angeles Times*, Retrieved online at http://articles.latimes.com/2012/jul/25/

local/la-me-0725-pot-ban-20120725.

90. Orlov, Rick (October 2, 2012). "City Council Rescinds ban on medical marijuana dispensaries in Los Angeles" *Daily News,* Retrieved online at http://cpf.cleanprint.net/cpf/ cpf?action=print&type=filePrint&key=LA-Daily_News.

Endnotes for Chapter 6

1. Newbern, Alistair E. (2000). "Good Cop, Bad Cop: Federal Prosecution of State-Legalized Medical Marijuana Use after United States. V Lopez" *California Law Review,* 88 (5): 1575-1634: 1576.

2. Newbern, Alistair E. (2000). "Good Cop, Bad Cop: Federal Prosecution of State-Legalized Medical Marijuana Use after United States. V Lopez" *California Law Review,* 88 (5): 1575-1634: 1585.

3. Gerber, Rudy (2004). *Legalizing Marijuana: Drug Policy Reform and Prohibition Politics.* Westport, CT: Praeger: 101.

4. Ibid., 103.

5. Ibid., 133.

6. "FDA Overhaul, 2007" *Congress and the Nation,* 2005-2008, 12: 563-69. Washington, DC: CQ Press. Retrieved online at http://library.cqpress.com/catn/catn05-1184-60877-2262340.

7. "H.R. 2306 (112th): Ending Federal Marijuana Prohibition Act of 2011" Retrieved online at http://www.govtrack.us/congress/bill.xpd?bill=h112-2306.

8. "Medical Marijuana Inc Reviews State of the Industry and Prospects for Future Growth" (February 27, 2013). Retrieved online at http://www.prnewswire.com/news--releases/medical-marijuana-inc-reviews-state-of-the-industry-and-prospects-for-future-growth-193700301.html; "Federal Bill introduced to reschedule marijuana," Retrieved online at http://www.govtrack.us/congress/bill.xpd?bill=h112-2306.

9. Smith, Phillip (July 12, 2012). "Pelosi: Dems May Take Up Medical Marijuana Reform After the Election" Retrieved online at http://www.theweedblog.com/pelosi-feds-may-take-up-medical-marijuana-reform-after-the-election/ accessed 7/23/12; Smith, Phillip (July 11 2012). "Pelosi Suggests Movement Post-Election on Medical Marijuana" Retrieved online at http://stopthedrugwar.org/chronicle/2012/jul/11/pelosi_suggests_movement_postele.

Endnotes for Chapter 7

1. Newbern, Alistair E. (2000). "Good Cop, Bad Cop: Federal Prosecution of State-Legalized Marijuana Use after United States v. Lopez" *California Law Review,* 88 (5): 1575-1634.

2. Clark, Peter A. (2000). "The Ethics of Medical Marijuana: Government Restrictions vs. Medical Necessity" *Journal of Public Health Policy* 21 (1): 40-60: 55.

3. London, Jeffrey Matthew (2009). *How the Use of Marijuana was Criminalized and Medicalized.* Lewiston: Edwin Mellen: 109-111; Gerber, Rudy (2004). *Legalizing Marijuana: Drug Policy Reform and Prohibition Politics.* Westport, CT: Praeger: 127-8.

4. "The Supreme Court, 2001-2004 Overview" (2006). In *Congress and the Nation,*

2001-2004, Vol. 11. Washington, DC: CQ Press, Retrieved online at http://library.cqpress.com/catn/catn01-426-18124-974624; "Criminal Law and Procedure, Supreme Court Decisions, 2000-2004" (2006). In *Congress and the Nation, 2001-2004*, vol. 11. Washington, DC: CQ Press. http://library.cqpress.com/catn/catn01-426-18124-974715.

    5. Newbern, Alistair E. (2000). "Good Cop, Bad Cop: Federal Prosecution of State-Legalized Medical Marijuana Use after United States v. Lopez" *California Law Review*, 88 (5): 1575-1634: 1589.

    6. London, Jeffrey Matthew (2009). *How the Use of Marijuana was Criminalized and Medicalized*. Lewiston: Edwin Mellen; Newbern, Alistair E. (2000). "Good Cop, Bad Cop: Federal Prosecution of State-Legalized Medical Marijuana Use after United States v. Lopez" *California Law Review*, 88 (5): pp. 1575-1634: 1586; Gerber, Rudy (2004), *Legalizing Marijuana: Drug Policy Reform and Prohibition Politics*. Westport, CT: Praeger: 126, 130; Kreit, Alex (2003). "The Future of Medical Marijuana: Should the States Grow their Own?" *University of Pennsylvania Law Review* 151 (5): 1787-1826: 1799.

    7. "State and Local Governments, Supreme Court Decisions, 2004-2008." In *Congress and the Nation, 2005-2008*, vol. 12, 774-76. Washington, DC: CQ Press, Retrieved online at http://library.cqpress.com/catn/catn05-1184-60881-2263125.

    8. "Introduction to the U.S. Supreme Court, 2005-2008." In *Congress and the Nation, 2005-2008*, vol. 12, 727-37, Washington, DC: CQ Press, Retrieved online at http://library.cqpress.com/catn/catn05-1184-60881-2262710.

    9. Kreit, Alex (2003). "The Future of Medical Marijuana: Should the States Grow their Own?" *University of Pennsylvania Law Review* (151): 5: 1787-1826: 1809; Cohen, Peter J. (2006). "Medical Marijuana, Compassionate Use, and Public Policy: Expert Opinion or Vox Populi?" The Hastings Center Report, 36 (3): 19-22.

    10. NORML (January 10, 2012). "Supreme Court Rejects Medical Marijuana Gun Rights Case" Retrieved online at http://www.opposingviews.com/i/society/drug-law/us-supreme-court-rejects-appeal-medical-marijuana-patients%E2%80%99-gun-rights-case.

    11. Grim, Ryan (June 18, 2012). "Supreme Court Hands Medical Marijuana Major Victory" *Huff Post Politics*, Retrieved online at http://www.huffingtonpost.com/2009/05/18/supreme-court-hands-medic_n_204681.html.

    12. Newbern, Alistair E. (2000). "Good Cop, Bad Cop: Federal Prosecution of State-Legalized Medical Marijuana Use after United States v. Lopez" *California Law Review*, 88 (5), 1575-1634: 1598.

    13. Newbern, Alistair E. (2000). "Good Cop, Bad Cop: Federal Prosecution of State-Legalized Medical Marijuana Use after United States v. Lopez" *California Law Review*, 88 (5): 1575-1634: 1595-1596; Kuromiya v. U.S. 37 F. Supp 2d 717 (1999).

    14. "Court Decision Upholds Voters' Intent of Medical Marijuana Law" (June 14, 2012). *Huffpost Detroit, Retrieved online at* http://www.huffingtonpost.com/michael-komorn/unanimous-michigan-suprem_b_1598051; Karoub, Jeff (May 31, 2012). "Michigan Supreme Court makes first medical pot rulings" *The Republic*, http://www.therepublic.com/view/story/ac45957f55e44124abc76b14cc3543b0/MI—medical; "Michigan Supreme Court issues 1st medical pot rulings" Retrieved online at http://www.theoaklandpress.com/articles/2012/06/01/news/state/doc4fc80611951cb; "Michigan Supreme Court Protects Medical Marijuana Affirmative Defense" Retrieved online at http://www.onmedical marijuana.com/2012/05/31/michigan-supreme-court-protects-medical-marihuana-affirmative-defense/; Bell, Dawson (May 31, 2012). "Michigan Supreme Court: Medical

Marijuana patients safe from prosecution" *Detroit Free Press*, Retrieved online at http://www.freep.com/article/20120531/NEWS06/120531054/.

15. Zaniewski, Ann (June 13, 2012). "After Supreme Court decision, Auburn Hills medical marijuana user withdraws plea" *The Oakland Press*, Retrieved online at http://www.theoaklandpress.com/articles/2012/06/13/news/local_news/doc4fd8fd09900d6383 643938.txt?viewmode=fullstory.

16. Bell, Dawson (June 27, 2012). "Michigan Court of Appeals rules in favor of medical marijuana patient" *Detroit Free Press*, Retrieved online at http://michiganmedicalmarijuana.org/topic/40336-michigan-court-of-appeals-rules-in-favor-of-medical-marijuana-patient/.

17. Newbern, Alistair E. (2000). "Good Cop, Bad Cop: Federal Prosecution of State-Legalized Medical Marijuana Use after United States v. Lopez" *California Law Review*, 88 (5): 1575-1634: 1587.

18. Ibid.

19. *People v. Trippet*, Retrieved online at http://www.leagle.com/xmlResult.aspx?xmldoc=1997158856CalApp4th1532_11583.xml.

20. Newbern, Alistair E. (2000). "Good Cop, Bad Cop: Federal Prosecution of State-Legalized Medical Marijuana Use after United States v. Lopez" California Law Review, 88 (5): 1575-1634: 1587.

21. Ibid.

22. Egelko, Bob (February 26, 1998). "Decision barring pot club stands," *Orange County Register, USA Today*, p. 3A.

23. LaGanga, Maria and Mary Curtius (February 27, 1998). "San Francisco Judge Orders Co-Op to Stop Selling Pot," *Los Angeles Times*, p. A3; Chiang, Harriet (February 27, 1998) "Lungren Claims Ruling Closes S.F. Pot Club," *San Francisco Chronicle*, p. A24; "California Supreme Court Refuses Cannabis Club Case; Authorities Expected to Close Marijuana Clubs" Retrieved online at http://ndsn.org/feb98/medmj2.html.

24. Cornerstone Health and Wellness (June 25, 2012). "Cornerstone Health and Wellness: Exempt Medical Marijuana Dispensaries of Long Beach Face Potential Ban; California Supreme Court to Weigh In" Retrived online at http://finance.yahoo.com/news/cornerstone-health-wellness-exempt-medical-162000744.html.

25. California National Organization for the Reform of Marijuana Laws (CalNORML) (May 22, 2008). "Court Strikes Down SB420 Limits," Retrieved at canorml.org.

26. People v. Solis, Retrieved online at http://www.leagle.com/leagle-search/.

27. Elliott, Steve (July 3, 2012). "Medical Marijuana Dispensaries are Legal: California Court" Retrieved online at http://www.tokeofthetown.com/2012/07/medical_marijuana_dispensaries_are_legal_californi.php; Americans for Safe Access (July 3, 2012). "California Court of Appeal Affirms Legality of Medical Marijuana Dispensaries and Rejects Municipal Bans" Retrieved online at http://yubanet.com/california/California-Court-of-Appeal-Affirms-Legality-of-Medical-Marijuana-Dispensaries-and-Rejects-Municipal-Bans.php.

28. Egelko, Bob (March 1, 2012). "Suit over Medical Marijuana Crackdown Thrown out," *San Francisco Chronicle*.

29. *Jenks v. State of Florida* 582 SO.2D 676; Retrieved online at http://www.mpp.org/states/florida/junks-v-stata-of-florida.html.

30. Roberts, Michael (June 1, 2012). "Medical marijuana: CO Supreme Court ruling leaves patient unprotected, plaintiffs say" *Denver Westword Blogs*, Retrieved online at

http://blogs.westword.com/latestword/2012/06/medical_marijuana_supreme_court_rulings_jason_beinor_leonard_watkins.php.

31. Newbern, Alistair E. (2000), "Good Cop, Bad Cop: Federal Prosecution of State-Legalized Medical Marijuana Use after United States v. Lopez" *California Law Review*, 88 (5): 1575-1634: 1595.

Endnotes for Chapter 8

1. Berry, Jeffrey M. (1984). *The Interest Group Society.* Boston: Little, Brown; Hallett, Michael A. and Dennis J. Palumbo (1993). *U.S. Criminal Justice Interest Groups.* Westport, Conn.: Greenwood Press: xiii; Fairchild, Erika S. (1981) "Interest Groups in the Criminal Justice Process," *Journal of Criminal Justice* 9: 181-194: 183; Marion, Nancy E. and Willard M. Oliver (2012). *The Public Policy of Crime and Criminal Justice*, 2nd Ed. Boston: Prentice Hall.

2. Reinarman, Craig (2011). "Cannabis in Cultural and Legal Limbo" in Suzanne Fraser and David Moore, eds. *The Drug Effect* Sydney: Cambridge University Press, pp. 171-188.

3. Smoker, Jay (August 30, 2011). "Alabama Medical Marijuana Coalition Kicks off "Write Your Legislator" Campaign" Retrieved online at http://www.theweedblog.com/alabama-medical-marijuana-coalition-kicks-off-write-your-legislator-campaign/; Alabama Medical Marijuana Coalition, "Alabama Cities censor free speech" Retrieved online at http://www.ammjc.org/; Elliott, Steve (August 5, 2011). "Medical Marijuana Bill Coming to Alabama Legislature," Retrieved online at http://www.tokeofthetown.com/2011/08/medical_marijuana_bill_coming_to_alabama_legislatu.php; http://www.ammjc.org/tag/alabama-medical-marijuana-coalition/page/10/.

4. "Alabama Medical Marijuana Coalition" Retrieved online at http://www.ammjc.org/tag/alabama-medical-marijuana-coalition/page/10/.

5. "Alliance for Cannabis Therapeutics" Retrieved online at http://www.marijuana-as-medicine.org/alliance.htm.

6. American Medical Marijuana Association, Retrieved online at americanmarijuana.org.

7. Reinarman, Craig (2011). "Cannabis in Cultural and Legal Limbo" in Suzanne Fraser and David Moore, eds. *The Drug Effect* Sydney: Cambridge University Press, pp. 171-188.

8. "Americans for Safe Access" retrieved online at http://www.afeaccessnow.org/section.php?id=3.

9. "Arkansans for Compassionate Care" Retrieved online at http://arcompassion.com/.

10. Elliott, Steve (May 23, 2011). "Marijuana Advocates sue Federal Government over rescheduling delay" *Pennsylvanians for Medical Marijuana* Retrieved online at http://pa4mmj.org/.

11. Reuteman, Rob (April 20, 2010). "The Marijuana Lobby: All Grown Up"javascript:void(0); Retrieved online at http://www/cnbc.com/id/36179727.

12. Reinarman, Craig (2011). "Cannabis in Cultural and Legal Limbo" in Suzanne Fraser and David Moore, eds. *The Drug Effect* Sydney: Cambridge University Press, pp. 171-188.

13. Ibid.

14. LEAP: Who We Are" Retrieved online at http://www.leap.cc/about/who-we-are/; "Vision and Mission" Retrieved online at http://www.leap.cc/about/vision-mission/.

15. Reuteman, Rob (April 20, 2010). "The Marijuana Lobby: All Grown Up" Retreived

online at http://www/cnbc.com/id/36179727.

16. Booth, Martin (2003). *Cannabis: A History* New York: St. Martin's Press.

17. Reuteman, Rob. April 20, 2010, "The Marijuana Lobby: All Grown Up" http://www/cnbc.com/id/36179727; Reinarman, Craig (2011). "Cannabis in Cultural and Legal Limbo" in Suzanne Fraser and David Moore, eds. *The Drug Effect* Sydney: Cambridge University Press, pp. 171-188.

18. "NORML: Working to Reform Marijuana Laws, Retrieved online at http://norml.org/marijuana/faq#question8.

19. Kreit, Alex (2003). "The Future of Medical Marijuana: Should the States Grow their Own?" *University of Pennsylvania Law Review* 151 (5): 1787-1826: 1796; Martinez, Martin (2000). *The New Prescription: Marijuana as Medicine*, Oakland: Quick American Archives.

20. "About the Ohio Medical Cannabis Association" Retrieved online at http://www.omca2012.org/aboutus/.

21. "Pennsylvanians for Medical marijuana" Retrieved online at http://www.phillynorml.org/medijuana/pages/news/20110427_Medical_Marijuana_Bill_Re-Introduced_in_Pennsylvania.

22. "People United For Medical Marijuana" Retrieved online at http://www.pufmm.org/.

23. Sensible Colorado, "Making Medical Marijuana Work Since 2004" Retrieved online at http://sensiblecolorado.org/.

24. "Sensible Colorado: Over the Years" Retrieved online at http://sensiblecolorado.org/accomplishments/.

25. Reinarman, Craig (2011). "Cannabis in Cultural and Legal Limbo" in Suzanne Fraser and David Moore, eds. *The Drug Effect* Sydney: Cambridge University Press, pp. 171-188.

26. "Students for Sensible Drug Policy", Retrieved online at http://ssdp.org/about/.

27. Liccardo Pacula, Rosalie, Jamie F. Chriqui, Deborah A. Reichmann, and Yvonne M. Terry-McElrath (2002). "State Medical Marijuana Laws: Understanding the Laws and their Limitations" *The Journal of Public Health Policy*, 23 (4): 413-439: 413.

28. American College of Physicians; "Supporting Research into the Therapeutic role of Marijuana" Retrieved online at http://www.acponline.org/.

Endnotes for Chapter 9

1. Drug Enforcement Administration (2012). "U.S. Drug Enforcement Administration Genealogy." Retrieved online at http://www.justice.gov/dea/agency/genealogy.htm.

2. Drug Enforcement Administration (2012). "U.S. Drug Enforcement Administration Genealogy." Retrieved online at http://www.justice.gov/dea/agency/genealogy.htm.

3. Sloman, Larry (1979). *Reefer Madness: The History of Marijuana in America* Indianapolis: Bobbs-Merrill. Booth, Martin (2003). *Cannabis: A History*. New York: St. Martin's Press.

4. Bonnie, Richard J. and Charles H. Whitebread II (1999). *The Marijuana Conviction: A History of Marijuana Prohibition in the United States* New York: The Lindesmith Center.

5. Bumgarner, Jeffrey B. (2006). *Federal Agents: The Growth of Federal Law Enforcement in America*. Westport, CT: Praeger.

6. Marion, Nancy E. (2011). *Federal Government and Criminal Justice*. New York: Palgrave Macmillan.

7. Drug Enforcement Administration (2003). *Drug Enforcement Administration History*. Retrieved online at http://www.justice.gov/dea/pubs/history/.

8. Ibid.

9. "42.0 Milestones in the History of Marijuana" Retrieved online at http://brainz.org/420-milestones-history-marijuana/.

10. Ibid.

11. Bertham, Eva, Morris Blachman, Kenneth Sharpe, and Peter Andreas (1996) *Drug War Politics*. Berkeley, CA: University of California Press.

12. Drug Enforcement Administration (2003). *Drug Enforcement Administration History. Retrieved online* at http://www.justice.gov/dea/pubs/history/.

13. Ibid.

14. Nixon, Richard. (1973) Executive Order No. 11727, Drug Law Enforcement." *Federal Register*. Available online at http://www.archives.gov/federal-register/codification/executive-order/11727.html.

15. Marion, Nancy E. (2011). *Federal Government and Criminal Justice*. New York: Palgrave Macmillan.

16. Bertham, Eva, Morris Blachman, Kenneth Sharpe, and Peter Andreas (1996). *Drug War Politics*. Berkeley, CA: University of California Press.

17. "DEA Mission Statement" Retrieved online at http://www.justice.gov/dea/agency/mission.htm.

18. "Domestic Cannabis Eradication/Suppression Program" Retrieved online at http://www.justice.gov/dea/progprams/marijuana.htm.

19. "Demand Reduction" Retrieved online at http://www.justice.gov/dea/programs/demand.htm.

20. "About ONDCP" Office of National Drug Control Policy, Retrieved online at http://www.whitehouse.gov/ondcp/about.

21. Office of National Drug Control Policy (April 2012, 2013). "FY 2013 Budget and Performance Summary" Retrieved online at http://www.whitehouse.gov/sites/default/files/ondcp/fy2013_drug_control_budget_and_performance_summary.pdf.

22. Office of National Drug Control Policy, "Drug Endangered Children" Retrieved online at http://www.whitehouse.gov/ondcp/dec-info.

23. Office of National Drug Control Policy, "A Comprehensive Approach to Drug Prevention" Retrieved online at http://www.whitehouse.gov/ondcp/prevention-intro.

24. Office of National Drug Control Policy, "Policy and Research" Retrieved online at http://www.whitehouse.gov/ondcp/policy-and-research.

25. "10 US Surgeons General and their Views on medical Marijuana, 1961-Present" Retrieved online at http://medicalmarijuana.procon.org/view.resource.php?resourceID=004872.

26. "Surgeon General's Advisory on Marijuana (Draft Version): Retrieved online at profiles.nim.nih.gov; 1982.

27. "Myths About Medical Marijuana," (March 26, 2004). *Providence Journal*, Retrieved online at http://www.november.org/stayinfo/breaking2/Elders.html.

28. Letter to the DEA (January 17, 2001), Retrieved online at http://www.justice.gov/dea/index.shtml.

29. Smith, Craig (June 30, 2011). "Ethics and Medical Marijuana—KGUN9 Asks Former Surgeon General," Retrieved online at www.kgun9.com.

30. Solomon, Deborah (January 7, 2011). "Doctor's Orders," Retrieved online at www.nytimes.com.

Endnotes for Chapter 10

1. Kingdon, J.W. (1995). Agendas, Alternatives and Public Policies. New York: Harper Collins College Publishers.

2. Marion, Nancy and Rick Farmer (2004). "A Preliminary Examination of Presidential Anticrime Promises" Criminal Justice Review, 29 (1): 173-194; Polsby, N.W. and A. Wildavsky (1996). Presidential Elections. Chatham, NJ: Chatham House Publishers.

3. Finckenauer, J.O. (1968). "Crime as a national political issue, 1964-76." Crime and Delinquency, 24, 13-27; Packer, H. (1968). The Limits of Criminal Sanction. Stanford, CA: Stanford University Press.

4. Packer, Herbert L. (1968). The Limits of the Criminal Sanction. Stanford: Stanford University Press.; Packer, Herbert L. (1988). "Two Models of the Criminal Process," in George F. Cole, ed., Criminal Justice: Law and Politics. Pacific Grove, CA: Brooks/Cole Publishing Company, pp. 15-31.

5. Caulkins, Jonathan P., Angela Hawken, Beau Kilmer and Mark A. R. Kleiman (2010). Marijuana Legalization: What Everyone Needs to Know. New York: Oxford University Press.

6. Langer, Gary (January 18, 2010). "High Support for Medical Marijuana" ABC News, Retrieved online at http://abcnews.go.com/images/PollingUnit/1100a3MedicalMarijuana.pdf.

7. 60 Minutes/Vanity Fair Poll (January 2011) Retrieved online at http://webapps.ropercenter.uconn.edu/CFIDE/cf/action/ipoll/questionDetail.cfm?keyword=.

8. Backus, Fred (2012). "Marijuana and Medical Marijuana after the 2012 Election" November 16-19, 2012, CBS News Poll, Retrieved online at http://www.cbsnews.com/8301-250_162-57556286/poll-nearly-half-support-legalization-of-marijuana/?pageNum=2.

9. Backus, Fred (2011) "Marijuana and Medical Marijuana after the 2012 Election" November 16-19, 2011, CBS News Poll, Retrieved online at http://www.cbsnews.com/8301-250_162-57556286/poll-nearly-half-support-legalization-of-marijuana/?pageNum=2.

10. Ibid.

11. Ibid.

12. "Majority Now Supports Legalizing Marijuana" April 4, 2013, Pew Research Center for the People and the Press, Retrieved online at http://www.people-press.org/2013/04/04/majority-now-supports-legalizing-marijuana/.

13. Republican Party Platforms: "Republican Party Platform of 2000," July 31, 2000. Online by Gerhard Peters and John T. Woolley, The American Presidency Project. http://www.presidency.ucsb.edu/ws/?pid=25849.

14. Montana Republican Party, Retrieved online at http://www.mtgop.org/index.php/about/party-latform.html.

15. "Grassroots Party" Retrieved online at http://www.grassrootsparty.net/grassroots2012/.

16. "The U.S. Marijuana Party—Mission Statement" Retrieved online at http://usmj-party.org/?showall=&start.

17. "Norml" Retrieved online at http://www.MarijuanaReform.org.

18. Sherer, Step (June 23, 2012). "Wake Up, Obama: Medical Marijuana Patients are Voters" Huff Post Politics, http://www.huffingtonpost.com/steph-sherer/obama-medical-marijuana_b_1695358.html.

19. Kain, Erik (October 7, 2011). "Obama Administration Shatters Campaign promise, escalates Crackdown on Medical Marijuana" Forbes, Retrieved online at

http://www.forbes.com/sites/erikkain/2011/10/07/obama-administration-shatters-campaign-promise-escalates-crackdown-on-medical-marijuana/.

20. Graves, Lucia (July 26, 2012). "Herman Cain says Medical Marijuana Regulation should be Left to the States" Huff Post Politics, Retrieved online at http://www.huffingtonpost.com/2011/11/16/herman-cain-says-medical-marijuana-regulation-should-be-left-to-the-states_n_1097657.html.

21. McCain, John (September 30, 2007). "Should Marijuana be a medical option?" Retrieved online at http://medicalmarijuana.procon.org/view.answers.php?questionID=001325.

22. Graves, Lucia (July 26, 2012). "Herman Cain says Medical Marijuana Regulation should be Left to the States" Huff Post Politics. Retrieved online at http://www.huffingtonpost.com/2011/11/16/herman-cain-says-medical-marijuana-regulation-should-be-left-to-the-states_n_1097657.html.

23. "Romney Position on Marijuana" Retrieved online at http://2012.presidential-candidates.org/Romney/Marijuana.php.

24. "John Kerry on Medical Marijuana" Retrieved online at http://americanmarijuana.org/kerry.html.

25. Graves, Lucia (July 26, 2012). "Herman Cain says Medical Marijuana Regulation should be Left to the States" Huff Post Politics Retrieved online at http://www.huffingtonpost.com/2011/11/16/herman-cain-says-medical-marijuana-regulation-should-be-left-to-the-states_n_1097657.html.

26. Johnson, Kirk (January 26, 2012). "Marijuana Push in Colorado Likens it to Alcohol" The New York Times Retrieved online at http://www.nytimes.com/2012/01/27/us/a-ballot-push-to-legalize-marijuana-with-alcohol-as-the-role-model.html.

27. Clinton, Hillary (October 11, 2007). "Should Marijuana be a medical option?" Retrieved online at http://medicalmarijuana.procon.org/view.answers.php?questionID=001325.

28. Kucinich, Dennis (August 9, 2007). "Should Marijuana be a medical option?" Retrieved online at http://medicalmarijuana.procon.org/view.answers.php?questionID=001325.

29. Giuliani, Rudy (October 3, 2007). "Should Marijuana be a medical option?" Retrieved online at http://medicalmarijuana.procon.org/view.answers.php?questionID=001325.

30. "Jill Stein" (September 20, 2010). Retrieved online at www.web.archive.org.

Gingrich, Newt (October 21, 2011) "Sounding the Alarm Against Medical Marijuana in Florida" Retrieved online at www.youtube.com/watch?v=VDNgFi9aJj0.

31. "Newt Gingrich Letter Supporting Medical Marijuana" Journal of the American Medical Association, March 19, 1982, Retrieved online at http://norml.org/library/medical-marijuana-reports/item/newt-gingrich-s-letter-supporting-medical-marijuana.

Endnotes for Chapter 11

1. "Investor Q&A: Cannabis Market" Retrieved online at http://www.bgmedtech.com/articles/2-cannabis-market.

2. PRNewswire (Dec 23, 2011). "Medical Marijuana Inc., Update" Retrieved online at http://www.prnewswire.com/news-releases/medical-marijuana-inc-update-136136573.html.

3. PRNewswire (November 18, 2011). "Medical Marijuana Inc. to Acquire Biotechnology Company PharmaSphere, LLC from Converted Organics: Executes Option Agreement to acquire a 100% stake in company" Retrieved online at http://www.prnewswire.com/

news-releases/medical-marijuana-inc-to-acquire-biotechnology-company-pharmasphere-llc-from-converted-organics-134128383.html.

4. PRNewswire (February 7, 2012). "Medical Marijuana Inc. (OTC: MJNA) Completes Financing Agreement With CannaBANK Inc For Up To Four Million Dollars To Complete Several Key Acquisitions: Medical Marijuana Inc. (OTC: MJNA) Announces Wellness Managed Services Signs an Additional Management Contract, Increases Annual Revenue by $1,100,000" Retrieved online at http://www.prnewswire.com/news-releases/medical-marijuana-inc-otc-mjna-completes-financing-agreement-with-cannabank-inc-for-up-to-four-million-dollars-to-complete-several-key-acquisitions-140702663.html.

5. PRNewswire (April 24, 2012). "Medical Marijuana Inc (OTC: MJNA) Announces Its Wholly Owned Subsidiary Wellness Managed Services Signs An Additional Management Contract Increasing Annual Revenue By $1,700,000, Quarter Over Quarter Revenue Increase On Pace To Maintain 100% Compounded Quarterly" Retrieved online at http://www.prnewswire.com/news-releases/medical-marijuana-inc-otc-mjna-announces-its-wholly-owned-subsidiary-wellness-managed-services-signs-an-additional-management-contract-increasing-annual-revenue-by-1700000-quarter-over-quarter-revenue-increase-on-pace-to-m-148683255.html.

6. PRNewswire (April 4, 2012). "Medical Marijuana Inc., Corporate Update-Significant Revenue and Net Income Growth 1st Quarter-Division and Corporate Holdings Update" Retrieved online at http://markets.on.nytimes.com/research/stocks/news/press_release.asp?docTag=20130404.

7. PR Newswire (October 16, 2012). "Medical Marijuana, Inc. and CanChew Biotechnologies Have Officially Started Market Trial Sign-Ups for CBD Chewing Gum" Retrieved online at http://www.einpresswire.com/article/119215226/medical-marijuana-inc-and-canchew-biotechnologies-have-officially-started-market-trial-sign-ups-for-cbd-chewing-gum; PRNewswire (November 20, 2012). "Medical Marijuana, Inc. Portfolio Company CanChew BioTechnologies Inc. Updates and Expands Free Product Trial" Retrieved online at http://www.prnewswire.com/news-releases/medical-marijuana-inc-portfolio-company-canchew-biotechnologies-inc-updates-and-expands-free-product-trial-180141391.html.

8. PR Newswire (July 24, 2012). "Medical Marijuana Inc. To Launch Revolutionary CBD Products Into European Market With The Formation of Canipa Holdings." Retrieved online at http://www.equities.com/news/headline-story?dt=2012-07-24&val=300985&cat=material.

9. "KannaLife Sciences Announces $1.5M Series A Financing From Medical Marijuana Inc. (OTC:MJNA) And CannaVest Corp. (OTC:FCLS); KannaLife Sciences, Inc." (March 7, 2013), Retrieved online at http://finance.yahoo.com/news/kannalife-sciences-announces-1-5m-140000539.html.

10. PRNewswire (September 21, 2012). "Can Cannabidiol (CBD) Fight Metastatic Cancer? According to the latest research the answer is yes." Retrieved online at http://www.prnewswire.com/news-releases/can-cannabidiol-cbd-fight-metastatic-cancer-according-to-the-latest-research-the-answer-is-yes-170681736.html.

11. Business Wire (April 17, 2012). "Medical Marijuana, Inc. and Dixie Elixirs Strike Innovative Agreement to Extend Dixie Elixirs Brand to Other MMJ Legal States" Retrieved online at http://www.businesswire.com/news/home/20120417005615/en/Medical-Marijuana-Dixie-Elixirs-Strike-Innovative-Agreement.

12. "Medical Marijuana Inc. Announces Wholesale Distribution Sales Program for Dixie

X CBD Hemp Wellness Product Line" (October 12, 2012). Retrieved online at http://www.macreportmedia.com/ViewSubmission.aspx?submissionRequest=17906.

13. Business Wire (April 17, 2012). "Medical Marijuana, Inc. and Dixie Elixirs Strike Innovative Agreement to Extend Dixie Elixirs Brand to Other MMJ Legal States" Retrieved online at http://www.businesswire.com/news/home/20120417005615/en/Medical-Marijuana-Dixie-Elixirs-Strike-Innovative-Agreement.

14. PRNewswire (August 29, 2012). "Medical Marijuana Inc. Red Dice Holdings Company Announces Dixie X Partnerships in New Mexico and Oregon" Retrieved online at http://www.marketwatch.com/story/medical-marijuana-inc-red-dice-holdings-company-announces-dixie-x-partnerships-in-new-mexico-and-oregon-2012-08-29.

15. PRNewswire (September 13, 2012). "Medical Marijuana Inc. Portfolio Company Red Dice Holdings Achieves Soft Launch of Dixie X With Steady Success" Retrieved online at http://www.prnewswire.com/news-releases/medical-marijuana-inc-portfolio-company-red-dice-holdings-achieves-soft-launch-of-dixie-x-with-steady-success-169608476.html; PRNewswire (September 19, 2012). "Medical Marijuana Inc. Announces Dixie X Compassionate Care Club" Retrieved online at http://www.marketwatch.com/story/medical-marijuana-inc-announces-dixie-x-compassionate-care-club-2012-09-19.

16. PRNewswire (September 19, 2012). "Medical Marijuana Inc. Announces Dixie X Compassionate Care Club" Retrieved online at http://www.marketwatch.com/story/medical-marijuana-inc-announces-dixie-x-compassionate-care-club-2012-09-19.

17. PRNewswire (June 1, 2012). "Medical Marijuana Inc. Portfolio Company, Red Dice Holdings, Sees Continued Brand Recognition With CO-based Dixie Elixirs" Retrieved online at http://www.bizjournals.com/prnewswire/press_releases/2012/06/01/SF17529. "Denver company wants to take medical-pot elixirs national" The Denver Post Retrieved online at http://www.denverpost.com/news/marijuana/ci_20746367/denver-company-wants-take-medical-pot-elixirs-national?source=rss#ixzz1wYtj2lao.

Endnotes for Chapter 12

1. Martinez, Martin (2000). *The New Prescription: Marijuana as Medicine* Oakland: Quick American Archives.

2. Newbern, Alistair E. (2000). "Good Cop, Bad Cop: Federal Prosecution of State-Legalized Medical Marijuana Use after United States v. Lopez" *California Law Review*, 88 (5): 1575-1634: 1625.

3. Ibid., 1628.

4. Ibid.

5. The Economist: April 27, 2006; Retrieved online at http://www.economist.com/science/displaystory.cfm?story_id=6849915.

6. Cohen, Peter J. (May-June 2006). "Medical Marijuana, Compassionate Use, and Public Policy: Expert Opinion or Vox Populi?" The Hastings Center Report, 36 (3): 19-22: 21.

Index